STEP-BY-STEP
ONE-POT
& CASSEROLES
COOKBOOK

STEP-BY-STEP
ONE-POT
& CASSEROLES
COOKBOOK

RECIPES COMPILED BY ANNE McDOWALL

THUNDER BAY
P·R·E·S·S

San Diego, California

Thunder Bay Press
An imprint of the Advantage Publishers Group
THUNDER BAY 5880 Oberlin Drive, San Diego, CA 92121-4794
P · R · E · S · S www.thunderbaybooks.com

Copyright © Salamander Books Ltd, 2003

A member of **Chrysalis** Books plc

All notations of errors or omissions should be addressed to
Thunder Bay Press, Editorial Department, at the above address. All
other correspondence (author inquiries, permissions) concerning the
content of this book should be addressed to Salamander Books Ltd,
8 Blenheim Court, Brewery Road, London, N7 9NY, U.K.

ISBN 1-59223-037-7

Library of Congress Cataloging-in-Publication Data
available on request.

Printed in China

1 2 3 4 5 07 06 05 04 03

CONTENTS

INTRODUCTION

With today's busy pace of life, we all relish food that requires a minimum amount of time spent slaving over a hot burner and washing up, while providing maximum flavor. Many of the recipes in this book can be cooked in a single dish or pan—particularly if you choose cookware that is flameproof as well as ovenproof—and all cook easily in the oven or on the burner, taking from just a few minutes to several hours.

As well as traditional fish, poultry, meat, and vegetable casseroles and stews—including many favorites from the around the world, such as coq au vin, chili con carne, ratatouille, and seafood jambalaya—there are also oven-baked dishes, meals-in-themselves soups, and steamed and baked desserts. In addition, the final two chapters of the book feature recipes specially prepared for cooking in slow cookers and clay pots. Both these chapters also include helpful information on using and caring for this cookware and give advice on how to adapt conventional recipes.

ONE-POT COOKING
The recipes in this book have been chosen to reflect a wide range of cooking styles and use easily available ingredients from all around the world. Many different cooking methods are used, including boiling, roasting, baking, and braising, to show how versatile one-pot cooking can be. In many of the recipes, the meat and vegetables are browned or softened first on top of the cooker before being cooked slowly and gently. Browning meat is not essential, but it does deepen the color of the sauce, while vegetables take on a sweeter flavor if they are sautéed in a little oil or butter first. Long, gentle cooking tenderizes the meat and brings out its flavor to the fullest, while the vegetables and other ingredients add their goodness to the juices.

Marinating is also sometimes used in the recipes. Again, this is not essential but it does add moisture to lean meats, which can be rather dry, and it is also good for tenderizing tougher cuts of meat.

CHOOSING COOKWARE
Investing in good-quality cookware is worthwhile. There are so many different materials and styles available, it can be very difficult to know which one to choose, particularly if you are to rely on only one or two items.

When buying cookware, it is important to be aware of the difference between flameproof and ovenproof items, as some pieces of equipment can be used only with one source of heat. Because of the techniques employed in one-pot cooking, it is best to choose cookware that is suitable for use both on the burner and in the oven. This is more economical, too, as you only need to buy one piece of equipment instead of two. Always buy the best you can afford. Better materials give better cooking results and cheaper items will need to be replaced after only a short time.

FLAMEPROOF COOKWARE

Many recipes require you to start cooking on the burner and then need to be transferred to the oven or placed under the broiler. It is therefore essential that you choose a cooking container for this purpose that is flameproof as well as ovenproof. A dish or casserole that is only ovenproof would buckle or break if used on the burner. A flameproof casserole can receive direct heat through its bottom. For this reason it should have a flat, stable bottom. If it is too thin, the food being cooked in it is apt to burn and the pan may buckle. In addition, the material used to make the pan must be able to conduct the heat evenly from the bottom to the rest of the pan.

The most popular choices for flameproof cookware are made of cast iron or enamel-coated cast iron. These are usually very heavy and fairly deep with straight sides. They conduct heat evenly and gently and are particularly good for dishes that require long, slow cooking. But although they give good cooking results, their weight means they are not an ideal choice for anyone who cannot lift heavy objects. If you are looking for something lighter, then glass ceramic cookware is an excellent choice. It is both flameproof and ovenproof and can also be used under the broiler.

Hard, anodized aluminum dishes and casseroles are also flameproof and ovenproof. They are durable, hard-wearing, and unbreakable. Some have handles that are only suitable for using in the oven at low temperatures, but they are often adequate for casserole cooking. Others have handles made of metal and so will withstand higher temperatures. Many of these pans have a nonstick coating that is extremely easy to clean.

Stainless steel pans with a soundly bonded aluminum bottom are also very good. Some of these have a nonstick coating that is tough enough to allow you to use metal tools and easy to clean. Always check the manufacturer's instructions before buying to ensure that the dish can be used on the burner.

OVENPROOF COOKWARE

When baking or roasting, the heat conductor is the air inside the oven. This means that cookware that is only to be used in the oven does not have to be such a good conductor of heat as it does if it is to go on the burner. A much wider range of materials is therefore suitable. Cast iron, copper, aluminum, glass ceramic, glass, and earthenware are all efficient, but it is worth noting that metal is the best conductor of heat and it may be necessary to increase cooking times given in a recipe if you are using ceramic or glass cookware.

The size of an ovenproof dish is also critical. If it is too large, the juices or liquid in the dish could evaporate too quickly or even burn; if the dish is too small, the food may spill over the sides during cooking. If the dish has a lid, this should fit snugly in order to keep the moisture inside and prevent the food from drying out.

COOKING ON THE BURNER

For best results when cooking on the burner, place the pot over a medium heat to ensure that the outer part does not heat up too quickly and to give good, even cooking without burning. Food could stick to the bottom if too much heat is applied too quickly. Nonstick pans should not be used over high temperatures, as this may reduce the effectiveness of the coating.

Do not allow gas flames to lick up the sides of the pan as this wastes energy—the useful heat is that applied to the bottom. Choose a boiling ring similar in size to the bottom of the pan to make efficient use of the heat.

When cooking casseroles, vegetables, or pasta dishes, half fill the pan with cooking liquid so that it is about three quarters full when all of the ingredients are added. This ensures that there is enough space for the food to move freely around in the liquid and to cook evenly.

Make sure that both the bottom of the pan and the burner are clean and dry before use. This is particularly important when using a glass ceramic or halogen burner. Dampness can cause spitting and affect the efficiency of the burner. Some ceramic burners will switch off if the pan bottom is too damp.

When using a ceramic or halogen burner, avoid dragging the pan over the surface and be careful not to drop it onto the burner as this could damage the burner permanently. Try to avoid dragging a pan over a gas burner, too, as pan supports on some cookers can be a little unstable.

COOKING IN THE OVEN

Ovens give a gentle heat, ideal for braising and casseroles. Preheat the oven ten minutes before use to ensure it has reached the correct temperature and that the temperature is steady. Remember that ovens can vary enormously in the way they work so be prepared to adjust the temperatures given in the recipes to suit your oven.

All cooking temperatures in the recipes are for standard ovens. If you have a convection oven, the temperature and cooking time should be reduced. Consult the manufacturer's instructions for advice on your particular model. In standard ovens the top is always the hottest. Unless otherwise stated in a recipe, the dish should be placed on the middle shelf. In convection ovens the air is constantly circulating so the temperature is even throughout.

COOKING UNDER THE BROILER

The direct heat of a broiler is useful for browning the tops of dishes such as gratins after they have been cooked in the oven. Many cookers have the broiler in the top of the oven so you may have to adjust the position of the top shelf. For best results, preheat the broiler five minutes before using. This enables the surface of the broiler to become evenly heated all over and to reach a steady temperature. Place the dish at least three inches from the surface of the broiler so the heat can distribute itself evenly over the food's surface.

COOKING IN A MICROWAVE

The recipes in this book give instructions for conventional ovens and burners, but many can be adapted for the microwave, or at least partially cooked in it. A microwave can also be used for thawing and reheating frozen dishes.

Never put metallic containers in a microwave. Some glass ceramic dishes can be transferred straight from the freezer, but be sure to check the manufacturer's instructions first. Remember to stir foods frequently during microwaving to ensure they are properly heated throughout, particularly if the food has been frozen. It is vital that food reaches a high enough temperature to kill the bacteria that cause food poisoning.

Cookware that can be taken straight to the table for serving is always useful; choose items that look as good in the dining room as they do in the kitchen.

COOKING FOR THE FREEZER

Most of the recipes in this book are suitable for freezing. If you make larger quantities than you actually need, you can freeze the remainder for another day, saving time and energy. It is a good idea to freeze in small, manageable quantities, such as one or two portions at a time, rather than large blocks. The food is not only easier to thaw this way, it also allows you to be more flexible and cater for any number of people.

Certain flavors intensify when frozen, so if you are cooking for the freezer, you should use smaller amounts of herbs and spices. Frozen dishes containing spices and garlic and salty foods should be eaten within six weeks.

Most foods freeze well, but avoid freezing mayonnaise (unless it is in a mousse), bananas and avocados (they will discolor), whole milk, and cream (although cream will freeze if it is whipped first). Foods with a high water content, such as lettuce and strawberries, become soft when thawed. Raw egg yolks and/or whites will freeze, but hard-boiled eggs will not.

Make sure that you wrap foods well before freezing. Food will dry out in the freezer if the packaging is not airtight. Wrapping materials should be thicker than normal and strong enough not to tear easily. Containers with sealable lids are ideal for freezing, especially square ones, which pack easily. Liquids expand on freezing, so packaging of dishes such as soups and foods with a sauce needs to allow for this. Fill the container to within an inch of the top and do not seal until the food is frozen.

Always label and date the food; it is very easy to forget exactly what you have frozen after a few weeks, and some foods look very similar when in their frozen state. Finally, make sure that all cooked dishes are thoroughly defrosted and reheated before serving.

SOUPS

LENTIL SOUP

2 tablespoons olive oil
1 onion, chopped
2 cloves garlic, chopped
4 oz. thick-cut bacon, diced
1 leek, sliced
2 carrots, diced
1 stalk celery, sliced
¾ cup green or brown lentils
1¾ cups passata or tomato sauce
¼ cup fresh, chopped herbs, e.g., parsley, tarragon,
    thyme, and marjoram
1 bay leaf
salt and freshly ground black pepper
fresh, chopped parsley and croutons, to garnish

BLACK-EYED PEA SOUP

1 cup black-eyed peas
1 large carrot
4 oz. daikon, peeled
1 bunch scallions
4½ cups vegetable stock
2 tablespoons light soy sauce
2 cloves garlic, finely chopped
1 fresh red chili, seeded and finely chopped
salt and freshly ground pepper
carrot and daikon flowers, to garnish (optional)

Heat oil in a saucepan and cook onion, garlic, and bacon, stirring occasionally, for 4 or 5 minutes. Stir in leek, carrots, celery, lentils, passata, chopped herbs, bay leaf, and 3¾ cups water.

Place peas in a saucepan, add enough water to cover, and bring to boil. Cover and simmer 45 minutes or until tender. Drain and rinse. Cut carrot and daikon into thin strips. Cut scallions into fine shreds.

Bring to boil and simmer 25 minutes until vegetables and lentils are tender. Season, garnish with chopped parsley and croutons, and serve.

Makes 4 servings.

Pour stock into a saucepan and stir in soy sauce. Bring to boil and add prepared vegetables, garlic, and chili. Simmer 4 minutes, then add beans. Season with salt and pepper and cook 3 minutes. Skim any scum from the surface. Serve soup garnished with carrot and daikon flowers.

Makes 4 servings.

MINESTRONE

2 tablespoons olive oil
2 oz. lightly smoked bacon, diced
2 large onions, peeled and sliced
2 cloves garlic, crushed
2 medium carrots, peeled and diced
3 stalks celery, trimmed and sliced
1⅓ cups dried kidney beans, soaked
14½ oz. can chopped tomatoes
10 cups beef stock
¾ cup frozen peas
2 medium potatoes, peeled and diced
1½ cups small pasta shapes
½ small green cabbage, shredded
1½ cups topped, tailed, and sliced green beans
3 tablespoons each fresh, chopped parsley and basil
salt and freshly ground pepper

Heat oil in a large saucepan and add bacon, onions, and garlic. Cover and cook gently 5 minutes, stirring occasionally until soft but not colored. Add carrots and celery and cook 2 or 3 minutes until softening. Drain beans and add to the pan with tomatoes and stock. Cover and simmer 1 to 1½ hours, until beans are nearly tender.

Add peas and potatoes and cook an additional 15 minutes, then add pasta, cabbage, green beans, and chopped parsley, and cook an additional 15 minutes. Stir in basil, adjust seasoning, and serve.

Makes 8 servings.

Note: Serve with freshly grated Parmesan cheese.

PASTA & BEAN SOUP

1 cup dried kidney beans, soaked overnight
2 cloves garlic, crushed
7½ cups chicken stock or water
1½ cups pasta shells
4 tomatoes, peeled (see page 174), seeded, and chopped
¼ cup fresh, chopped parsley
salt and freshly ground black pepper

Drain beans and place in a saucepan with garlic and chicken stock or water. Simmer, half covered, 2 to 2½ hours or until tender.

Allow to cool slightly, then transfer beans and cooking liquid to a food processor or blender and purée. Return purée to the pan, add pasta and tomatoes, and simmer gently 15 minutes until tender. (Add a little extra chicken stock or water if soup looks too thick.)

Stir in chopped parsley and season well with salt and pepper. Serve at once.

Makes 6 servings.

HARIRA

¼ cup olive oil
1 large onion, finely chopped
2 cloves garlic, crushed
1 teaspoon turmeric
1 teaspoon ground ginger
1 teaspoon ground cumin
6¾ cups chicken or vegetable stock
1¼ cups green lentils, washed
14½ oz. can chopped tomatoes
15 oz. can chickpeas, drained
3 tablespoons fresh, chopped cilantro
3 tablespoons fresh, chopped parsley
salt and freshly ground black pepper
lemon juice (optional)
olive oil and harissa, to serve

In a large saucepan, heat 2 tablespoons oil. Add onion and cook 10 minutes until soft. Add garlic, turmeric, ginger, and cumin and cook a few more minutes. Stir in stock and add lentils and tomatoes. Bring to boil, cover, and simmer 20 minutes or until lentils are soft. Stir in chickpeas, remaining 2 tablespoons olive oil, cilantro, parsley, salt, pepper, and lemon juice (if using) and simmer 5 more minutes.

To serve, pour some olive oil into a small bowl and spoon some harissa into another small bowl. Ladle the soup into heated bowls and place olive oil and harissa on the table for people to help themselves.

Makes 6 to 8 servings.

Note: Two-thirds cup dried chickpeas may be used in place of canned. They should be soaked overnight and simmered 1 hour or until soft, before adding with lentils.

MUSHROOM & BARLEY BROTH

⅓ cup barley, soaked overnight in cold water to cover
4½ cups vegetable stock
¼ cup dried porcini mushrooms
⅔ cup boiling water
3 tablespoons olive oil
3 shallots, finely chopped
2 teaspoons fresh, chopped thyme
12 oz. mixed fresh mushrooms, sliced
⅔ cup dry cider
1 bay leaf
1 teaspoon Dijon mustard
salt and pepper

Drain barley and place in a large pan with stock. Bring to boil, then reduce heat, cover, and simmer 45 minutes. Soak dried mushrooms in boiling water 20 minutes. Drain, reserving liquid, and chop.

In a large pan, heat oil. Add shallots and thyme and cook 5 minutes. Add dried and fresh mushrooms. Stir-fry over medium heat 5 minutes or until golden. Add cider and boil rapidly until liquid is almost evaporated. Add barley with stock, reserved porcini liquid, bay leaf, and mustard to pan. Simmer, covered, 5 minutes. Season with salt and pepper.

Makes 6 to 8 servings.

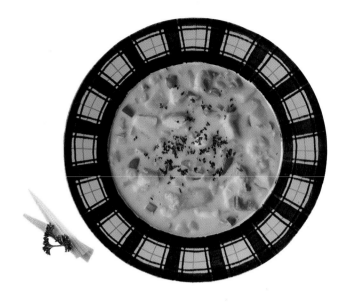

MEDITERRANEAN FISH SOUP

CHOWDER

2½ lb. mixed fish and shellfish, e.g., monkfish, red
   mullet, bass, bream, snapper, shrimp, and mussels,
   cleaned
pinch saffron threads, toasted and crushed
⅓ cup olive oil
2 Spanish onions, sliced
1 stalk celery, sliced
3 cloves garlic, chopped
3 large tomatoes, peeled (see page 174)
bouquet garni of 1 bay leaf, 1 dried thyme sprig,
   1 fennel sprig, 3 parsley sprigs, and 1 strip dried
   orange peel
5½ cups fish stock
salt and pepper
torn basil or fresh, chopped parsley, to garnish
French bread, to serve

½ stick butter
1 large onion, chopped
2 large cloves garlic, chopped
6 stalks celery, chopped
3 medium potatoes, cut into small chunks
large pinch cayenne pepper
2½ cups fish stock
2½ cups milk
bouquet garni
8 oz. smoked haddock fillet
8 oz. fresh haddock fillet
4 oz. cooked, peeled shrimp
½ red bell pepper, seeded and diced
½ cup corn (optional)
salt and pepper
fresh, chopped parsley or dill, to garnish

Skin and fillet fish and cut into fairly large
pieces. Remove shellfish from their shells.
Soak saffron in 2 tablespoons warm water
10 minutes. In a large saucepan, heat oil.
Add onions, celery, and garlic and cook
gently until softened. Chop tomatoes and
add to pan with bouquet garni. Arrange fish
on vegetables, add saffron liquid, then pour
in sufficient stock to cover fish. Simmer,
uncovered, 6 minutes.

In a large saucepan, heat butter, add onion,
garlic, and celery, and cook until beginning
to soften. Stir in potatoes and cayenne
pepper and cook about 2 minutes. Add
stock, milk, and bouquet garni, bring to boil,
then cover pan and simmer about 20
minutes until vegetables are almost tender.

Add shellfish and mussels to pan and cook
an additional 3 or 4 minutes until shellfish
are just tender and mussels open; discard any
mussels that remain closed. Season with salt
and pepper. Serve garnished with basil or
parsley and accompanied by French bread.

Makes 6 servings.

Meanwhile, skin both types of haddock and
cut into bite-sized pieces. Add to pan with
milk and simmer gently 5 to 10 minutes until
fish flakes easily. Stir in shrimp, red bell
pepper, and corn (if using) and heat through.
Season with salt and pepper and serve
sprinkled with parsley.

Makes 4 to 6 servings.

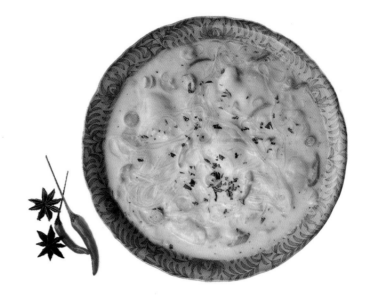

SPINACH & MONKFISH SOUP

6 oz. fresh spinach
1 lb. monkfish, skinned
4½ cups vegetable stock
1 tablespoon light soy sauce
1 teaspoon chili sauce
1 teaspoon brown sugar
salt and freshly ground pepper
2 tablespoons fresh, chopped cilantro
cilantro leaves, to garnish

Remove spinach stems and wash leaves. Cook leaves in a saucepan of boiling water 20 seconds or until just wilted. Drain and rinse in cold water.

Cut monkfish into ¾ in. chunks. Cook in a saucepan of boiling water 2 minutes or until firm and opaque. Drain.

Pour stock into a saucepan. Stir in soy sauce, chili sauce, sugar, salt, and pepper. Bring to boil, add spinach and monkfish, and simmer 5 minutes. Stir in chopped cilantro and cook an additional 2 minutes. Garnish with cilantro and serve.

Makes 4 servings.

THAI SHRIMP & NOODLE SOUP

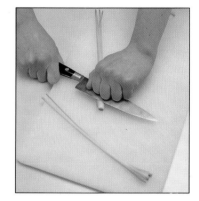

2 cups fish stock
2 stalks lemongrass, crushed and chopped
2 small star anise pods
2 cloves garlic, chopped
2 cups coconut milk
8 large raw peeled shrimp
4 shelled scallops, halved horizontally
3 oz. clear vermicelli, soaked in cold water
  10 minutes, then drained
2 scallions, thinly sliced
2 fresh red chilies, seeded and sliced
juice 1½ limes
1 tablespoon fish sauce
1 tablespoon fresh, chopped cilantro

Bring stock to boil in a saucepan, add lemongrass, star anise, and garlic, then simmer, uncovered, 5 minutes. Cover and let stand 30 minutes.

Add coconut milk to pan and heat to simmering point. Add shrimp and scallops, poach 1 minute, then add vermicelli, scallions, and chilies and cook an additional 1 minute until shrimp are pink. Remove pan from heat and stir in lime juice, fish sauce, and chopped cilantro.

Makes 4 servings.

THREE MUSHROOM SOUP

4 dried Chinese mushrooms, soaked in hot water
  20 minutes
1 oz. oyster mushrooms
2 oz. button mushrooms
4½ cups vegetable stock
½ in. piece fresh ginger, peeled and finely chopped
1 clove garlic, finely chopped
2 tablespoons dry sherry
2 tablespoons dark soy sauce
4 oz. fresh tofu, drained and diced
2 teaspoons cornstarch mixed with 4 teaspoons
  water
2 tablespoons shredded basil leaves

Drain soaked mushrooms and squeeze out excess water. Discard stems and slice caps. Slice oyster mushrooms and cut button mushrooms in half.

Pour stock into a saucepan and add ginger, garlic, sherry, and soy sauce. Bring to boil, reduce heat, and carefully stir in mushrooms and tofu. Simmer 5 minutes, then add cornstarch mixture and cook, stirring, an additional 2 minutes or until thickened. Stir in basil and serve.

Makes 4 servings.

CARIBBEAN FISH SOUP

2 tablespoons oil
1 onion, finely chopped
1 green bell pepper, finely chopped
2 cloves garlic, crushed
10 medium tomatoes, peeled and chopped
2 teaspoons tomato paste
2½ cups fish stock
1¼ cups dry white wine
2 teaspoons arrowroot
1 lb. firm white fish, diced
¼ cup fresh, chopped parsley
4 oz. cooked, peeled shrimp

Heat oil in a large pan. Cook onion, pepper, and garlic 10 minutes.

Add tomatoes, tomato paste, stock, wine, and seasoning. Bring to boil, cover, and simmer 10 minutes. Blend arrowroot with a little water and stir into soup. Add fish and 3 tablespoons parsley and cook gently 5 minutes until fish is just cooked but not breaking up.

Add shrimp and cook an additional 2 minutes until heated through. Serve in warmed soup bowls, garnished with remaining parsley.

Makes 4 to 6 servings.

SEAFOOD & COCONUT SOUP

3 stalks lemongrass, cut into 2 in. lengths
2 in. piece galangal, thinly sliced
1 in. piece fresh ginger, thinly sliced
2 teaspoons finely chopped red chili
4½ cups coconut milk
10 kaffir lime leaves
7 oz. skinless chicken fillet, cut into 1 in. cubes
⅓ cup fish sauce
juice ½ lime
7 oz. large raw shrimp, peeled and deveined
7 oz. firm white fish fillets, cut into 1 in. cubes
small handful each cilantro and Thai basil leaves
cilantro sprigs, to garnish

Put lemongrass, galangal, ginger, and chili in a saucepan and add 1 cup water. Bring to boil, then simmer 5 minutes. Add coconut milk and lime leaves and simmer an additional 10 minutes. Add chicken, fish sauce, and lime juice to pan and poach 5 minutes. Add shrimp and fish. Poach an additional 2 or 3 minutes until shrimp turn pink.

Add cilantro and basil to pan. Stir, then ladle into warmed soup bowls. Remove and discard lemongrass and lime leaves before eating. Garnish with cilantro.

Makes 4 servings.

PENANG HOT-SOUR SOUP

8 oz. whole fish, e.g., trout
5 cups fish or chicken stock
3 to 5 dried red chilies, cored, seeded, and chopped
6 shallots, chopped
1 stalk lemongrass, chopped
3 slices galangal, chopped
1 teaspoon shrimp paste
1 tablespoon paprika
¼ teaspoon ground turmeric
15 fresh mint leaves
1 teaspoon brown sugar
1 teaspoon vegetable oil
3 tablespoons tamarind paste
8 oz. dried rice noodles

Put fish and stock in a saucepan, cover, and simmer 15 minutes. Lift fish from pan. When cool enough to handle, remove flesh from skin and bones. Return bones to pan and simmer gently, uncovered, 15 minutes, then strain. Mash fish. Put chilies and ¼ cup hot water in a blender and let soak 10 minutes. Add shallots, lemongrass, galangal, shrimp paste, paprika, and turmeric. Mix to a smooth paste and add to pan with strained stock.

Add mint, sugar, oil, tamarind, and 1 cup water. Simmer, uncovered, 15 minutes. Add fish and simmer 30 minutes. Meanwhile, soak noodles in hot water 15 minutes until soft, then drain. Cook in boiling salted water 1 minute; drain. Ladle into soup bowls.

Makes 3 or 4 servings.

Note: Serve with mint leaves, shredded lettuce, finely chopped shallots, and strips of fresh pineapple, cucumber, and red chili.

BOUILLABAISSE

2¼ lb. mixed fish fillets and shellfish, e.g., red
   mullet, monkfish, raw shrimp, mussels
3 tablespoons olive oil
1 onion, chopped
1 leek, sliced
1 stalk celery, chopped
2 cloves garlic, crushed
4 ripe tomatoes, peeled (see page 174) and chopped
½ teaspoon dried herbes de Provence
2 strips orange peel
large pinch saffron threads
salt and freshly ground black pepper
⅔ cup dry white wine
2⅓ cups good fish stock
fresh, chopped Italian parsley, to garnish

Cut fish into chunks. Heat oil in a large saucepan. Add onion, leek, celery, and garlic and cook gently 5 minutes until soft. Add chopped tomatoes, herbes de Provence, orange peel, saffron threads, and salt and pepper. Add wine and stock and bring to boil.

Reduce heat, add firmest fish, and simmer 5 minutes. Add more delicate fish and shellfish. Cover and simmer 5 minutes until fish is cooked through but still retains its shape and mussels have opened. Discard any mussels that have not opened. Garnish with chopped parsley and serve.

Makes 6 servings.

Note: Use fish and shellfish trimmings to make stock.

VIETNAMESE FISH SOUP

1 tablespoon vegetable oil
2 cloves garlic, finely chopped
2 shallots or 1 small onion, chopped
1 tablespoon each chili sauce and tomato paste
2 medium tomatoes, diced
3 tablespoons fish sauce
2 tablespoons sugar
3 cups chicken stock
2 tablespoons tamarind water or lime juice
8 oz. firm fish fillet, cut into small slices
4 oz. fresh scallops, sliced
4 oz. raw, peeled shrimp
12 clams or mussels, scrubbed clean
2 or 3 tablespoons dry white wine or sherry
salt and freshly ground black pepper
cilantro, to garnish

Heat oil in a wok or pan and lightly brown garlic and shallots or onion. Add chili sauce, tomato paste, diced tomatoes, fish sauce, and sugar. Blend well, then simmer mixture 2 or 3 minutes. Add stock with tamarind water or lime juice and bring to boil.

Add seafood and wine or sherry to broth, and bring back to boil. Cover and simmer 3 or 4 minutes until clam or mussel shells have opened; discard any that remain closed after cooking. Taste soup and adjust seasoning. Serve hot, garnished with cilantro.

Makes 4 to 6 servings.

Note: Take care not to overcook seafood. If using shelled clams or mussels, reduce cooking time by half.

COCK-A-LEEKIE SOUP

CHICKEN & ASPARAGUS SOUP

6 skinless chicken thighs
4½ cups chicken stock
3 leeks

Place chicken thighs in a large pan with chicken stock and simmer gently 35 to 40 minutes.

8 to 10 fresh asparagus spears
4½ cups chicken stock
2 tablespoons light soy sauce
2 tablespoons dry sherry
2 teaspoons brown sugar
2 oz. vermicelli rice noodles
½ in. piece fresh ginger, peeled and chopped
12 oz. lean, cooked chicken, finely shredded
salt and ground white pepper
2 scallions, finely chopped, to garnish

Meanwhile, trim leeks and slice into rings. Remove cooked chicken from stock with a slotted spoon. Remove meat from bones and cut into bite-sized pieces. Set aside.

Trim ends from asparagus spears and slice spears into 1½ in. pieces. Pour stock into a large saucepan along with soy sauce and sherry. Stir in brown sugar, bring to boil, and add asparagus and noodles. Simmer, covered, 5 or 6 minutes.

Increase the heat and bring stock to a fast simmer. Add prepared leeks and cook 3 or 4 minutes until leeks are just tender. Add chicken to the pan and simmer 2 or 3 minutes. Serve hot with warm rolls.

Makes 4 servings.

Variation: Add 12 pitted and quartered prunes with chicken in step 3.

Stir in chopped ginger and shredded chicken and season with salt and pepper. Simmer 3 or 4 minutes to heat through. Garnish with chopped scallions and serve.

Makes 4 servings.

CHICKEN PASTA SOUP

1 lb. 2 oz. skinless, boneless chicken thighs
1 onion, chopped
1 clove garlic, chopped
2 stalks celery, chopped
2 carrots, thinly sliced
salt and freshly ground black pepper
2 leeks, washed and thinly sliced
1 cup quick-cook dried macaroni
¼ cup thick sour cream (optional)
2 tablespoons fresh, chopped parsley
parsley sprigs, to garnish

Put chicken, onion, garlic, celery, carrots, and salt and pepper in a large saucepan and add 5 cups water.

Bring to boil and remove and discard any scum that rises to the surface. Reduce heat, cover, and simmer 45 minutes. Lift out chicken with a slotted spoon and break into smaller pieces, then return chicken to soup.

Stir in leeks and pasta and return to boil. Cover and simmer an additional 10 to 15 minutes, stirring occasionally, until pasta is cooked. Stir in thick sour cream (if using) and chopped parsley, then ladle into warmed soup bowls. Garnish with parsley sprigs and serve.

Makes 4 to 6 servings.

Variation: Use fresh, chopped cilantro instead of parsley.

HOT & SOUR TURKEY SOUP

4 oz. (½ cup) lean ground turkey
1 oz. dried Chinese mushrooms, soaked in hot water 20 minutes
4 oz. assorted vegetables, shredded
4½ cups chicken stock
2 teaspoons brown sugar
2 tablespoons red rice vinegar
large pinch ground white pepper
1 tablespoon dark soy sauce
2 teaspoons cornstarch blended with 4 teaspoons water
2 scallions, finely chopped
2 tablespoons fresh, chopped cilantro

Cook turkey in a saucepan of boiling water 3 minutes. Drain and set aside. Drain mushrooms and squeeze out excess water. Discard stems and slice caps.

Place turkey, sliced mushrooms, vegetables, chicken stock, sugar, vinegar, pepper, and soy sauce in a saucepan. Bring to boil and simmer 3 minutes. Add cornstarch mixture and cook, stirring, until thickened. Add chopped scallions and cilantro and serve.

Makes 4 servings.

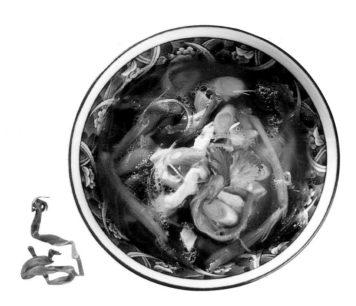

VIETNAMESE CHICKEN SOUP

1 tablespoon vegetable oil
½ teaspoon minced garlic
2 shallots or 1 small onion, thinly sliced
3 cups chicken stock
8 oz. cooked chicken meat, thinly shredded
1 oz. bean thread vermicelli, soaked and cut into
    short lengths
1 tablespoon black fungus, soaked and cut into small
    pieces
12 to 16 lily buds, soaked and trimmed
2 tablespoons fish sauce
salt and freshly ground black pepper
2 or 3 scallions, sliced
cilantro, to garnish

Heat oil in a wok or pan over medium heat and stir-fry garlic and shallots or onion until aromatic; do not brown. Add chicken stock and bring to boil. Add chicken, vermicelli, fungus, lily buds, and fish sauce, bring back to boil, reduce heat, and simmer about 3 minutes.

Taste and adjust seasoning, then add scallions. Serve soup hot, garnished with cilantro.

Makes 4 to 6 servings.

Note: If cooked chicken is not available, raw chicken fillet may be used instead, but increase cooking time by at least 2 minutes or until chicken is cooked.

CHICKEN & NOODLE SOUP

6 oz. thin rice noodles
8 oz. chicken fillet
2½ cups chicken stock
2½ cups coconut milk
½ oz. tamarind paste
½ oz. fresh ginger, grated
1 stalk lemongrass, very finely chopped
3 tablespoons shrimp paste, toasted (see Note)
7 oz. raw peeled shrimp
¾ cup bean sprouts
¾ cup peeled, seeded, and chopped cucumber

Cook noodles in boiling water 3 or 4 minutes. Drain and rinse under cold running water. Drain very well and set aside.

Put chicken and stock in a saucepan, bring to a simmer, and poach 8 minutes. Lift chicken from stock, reserving stock. When cool enough to handle, shred and set aside. Add coconut milk to pan with tamarind, ginger, lemongrass, and shrimp paste. Bring to boil, then simmer 5 minutes.

Add shrimp and simmer 3 or 4 minutes, then add bean sprouts and cucumber. Heat through 1 or 2 minutes.

Makes 4 to 6 servings.

Note: To toast shrimp paste, hold it in tongs over an open flame or wrap it in aluminum foil and cook it in a skillet until it is crumbly and smells fragrant.

BEAN & BACON SOUP

¾ cup white kidney beans, soaked overnight
4½ cups chicken stock
4 slices smoked bacon, chopped
1 head romaine, shredded
2 egg yolks
⅔ cup sour cream
1 tablespoon white wine vinegar
salt and freshly ground black pepper
fresh, chopped cilantro, to garnish

Drain beans. Rinse and drain again. Put into a large, flameproof casserole and cover with cold water. Bring to boil, skimming the scum from the surface. Drain.

Return beans to casserole, add stock, and bring to boil. Add bacon and simmer 1½ hours, until beans are tender, topping up with water if necessary. Remove about half of the beans with a slotted spoon and roughly mash. Return to soup and stir well. Add shredded romaine and simmer 15 minutes.

In a bowl, mix together egg yolks, thick sour cream, and vinegar. Add to soup and heat gently, stirring, until warmed through. Season with salt and pepper. Garnish with chopped cilantro and serve.

Makes 6 to 8 servings.

BEEF & WATER CHESTNUT SOUP

12 oz. lean beef round or sirloin steak
4½ cups beef stock
1 whole cinnamon stick, broken
2 star anise
2 tablespoons dark soy sauce
2 tablespoons dry sherry
3 tablespoons tomato paste
1 to 2 tablespoons chili sauce
4 oz. can water chestnuts, rinsed and sliced
2 scallions, chopped, to garnish

Trim away any fat from beef and cut into thin strips.

Place beef, stock, cinnamon stick, star anise, soy sauce, sherry, tomato paste, chili sauce, and water chestnuts in a large saucepan. Bring to boil, skimming away surface scum. Cover and simmer 20 minutes or until beef is tender.

Skim soup again and discard cinnamon stick and star anise. Blot surface with absorbent paper towels to remove fat. Garnish with scallions and serve.

Makes 4 servings.

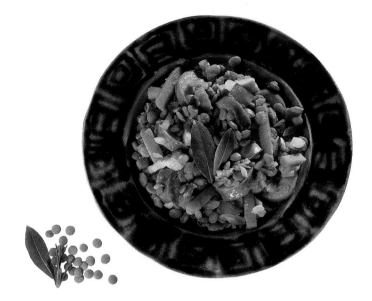

LENTIL CHORIZO POTAGE

2½ cups green or brown lentils
1 Spanish onion, chopped
2 carrots, chopped
6 cloves garlic
6 to 8 oz. cooking chorizo
4 oz. piece side of pork, rind removed
1 bay leaf
2 beefsteak tomatoes, peeled (see page 174), seeded, and chopped
1 red bell pepper, seeded and chopped
1½ tablespoons olive oil
1 Spanish onion, finely chopped
salt and freshly ground black pepper

Put lentils, chopped onion, carrots, garlic, chorizo, pork, bay leaf, tomatoes, and bell pepper into a flameproof casserole or a saucepan. Just cover with water and bring to a boil. Cover and simmer gently about 30 minutes until lentils are tender, pork is cooked, and there is sufficient liquid left to make a thick soup.

Meanwhile, heat oil in a heavy-bottomed casserole, add finely chopped onion, and cook very gently about 15 minutes, stirring occasionally, until soft and lightly caramelized. Stir into lentils and season with salt and pepper. Discard bay leaf. Slice chorizo and pork and return to lentils and heat through.

Makes 4 or 5 servings.

SPICY CHICKPEA POTAGE

1⅓ cups chickpeas, soaked overnight, then drained
¼ cup olive oil
1 slice bread, crust removed
1 Spanish onion, finely chopped
8 oz. cooking chorizo, thickly sliced
3 beefsteak tomatoes, peeled (see page 174), seeded, and chopped
1 tablespoon paprika
¼ or ½ teaspoon cumin seeds, finely crushed
1 lb. spinach, trimmed and chopped
3 cloves garlic

Cook chickpeas in 2 cups boiling water 1½ to 2 hours until tender.

Meanwhile, heat 2 tablespoons oil in a small skillet, add bread, and fry until golden on both sides. Remove and drain on absorbent paper towels. Add onion to pan and cook slowly, stirring occasionally, 5 minutes. Add chorizo and cook an additional 5 to 10 minutes until onion has softened but not colored. Stir tomatoes into onion and cook, stirring occasionally, about 10 minutes.

Heat remaining oil in a saucepan, stir in paprika and cumin, then add spinach. Cook until spinach has wilted. Using a mortar and pestle, pound garlic with a pinch of salt. Add fried bread and pound again. Drain chickpeas, reserving liquid. Stir chickpeas into spinach with tomato and garlic mixtures and ¾ cup chickpea liquid. Cover pan and simmer about 30 minutes; add more liquid if mixture becomes too dry.

Makes 4 servings.

FRANKFURTER SOUP

1 tablespoon olive oil
1 onion, chopped
2 slices bacon, chopped
1 small white cabbage, shredded
3 medium carrots, sliced
3 medium potatoes, diced
4½ cups vegetable stock
6 frankfurters, each cut into 4 pieces
large pinch freshly grated nutmeg
salt and freshly ground black pepper
3 tablespoons sour cream

Heat oil in a large, flameproof casserole. Add onion and bacon and cook gently, stirring occasionally, 5 minutes.

Add cabbage, carrots, potatoes, and vegetable stock. Bring to boil and simmer gently 15 minutes.

Add frankfurters and simmer gently 10 minutes. Season with nutmeg and salt and pepper. Stir in sour cream and heat gently to warm through.

Makes 6 servings.

PAPAYA & PORK SOUP

4½ cups chicken stock or water
4 pork chops, each weighing about 3 oz.
1 small, unripe green papaya, peeled and cut into small cubes
2 tablespoons fish sauce
salt and freshly ground black pepper
1 tablespoon chopped scallions
cilantro, to garnish

Bring stock or water to boil in a pan over high heat and add pork. Bring back to boil and skim off the scum. Reduce heat, cover, and simmer 25 to 30 minutes.

Add papaya cubes and fish sauce, bring back to boil, and cook soup 5 minutes.

To serve, place salt, pepper, and chopped scallions in a tureen. Pour boiling soup over, garnish with cilantro, and serve at once. Pork should be so tender that one can easily tear it apart into small pieces for eating.

Makes 4 servings.

PORK & PEANUT SOUP

BEEF & KIDNEY BEAN SOUP

4 cilantro roots, chopped
2 cloves garlic, chopped
1 teaspoon black peppercorns, cracked
1 tablespoon vegetable oil
8 oz. lean pork, finely chopped
4 scallions, chopped
3 cups veal stock
⅓ cup peanuts
6 pieces dried Chinese black mushrooms, soaked
  20 minutes, drained and chopped
4 oz. bamboo shoots, roughly chopped
1 tablespoon fish sauce

Using a mortar and pestle, pound cilantro, garlic, and peppercorns to a paste.

In a wok or pan, heat oil, add peppercorn paste, and cook 2 or 3 minutes, stirring occasionally. Add pork and scallions and stir 1½ minutes.

Stir stock, peanuts, and mushrooms into pan, then cook at just below boiling point 7 minutes. Add bamboo shoots and fish sauce and continue to cook gently 3 or 4 minutes.

Makes 3 or 4 servings.

1 tablespoon olive oil
3 onions, chopped
1 lb. (2 cups) lean ground beef
3 cloves garlic, crushed
1 teaspoon dried thyme
1 teaspoon paprika
2 teaspoons tomato paste
15 oz. can red kidney beans, drained
3¾ cups beef stock
1¼ cups tomato juice
1 teaspoon cayenne pepper
2 tablespoons fresh, chopped parsley

Heat oil in a large, flameproof casserole. Add onions and ground beef.

Cook gently, stirring and breaking up ground beef, until onions are soft and beef is browned all over. Add garlic, thyme, paprika, and tomato paste. Cook gently 5 minutes, stirring constantly. Stir in beans, stock, and tomato juice.

Bring to boil, cover, and simmer gently 10 minutes. Add cayenne pepper and half the parsley and season with salt. Garnish with remaining parsley and serve.

Makes 6 to 8 servings.

FISH & SEAFOOD

COD WITH SPINACH

1 tablespoon light olive oil
1 small onion, finely chopped
6 oz. button mushrooms, sliced
2¼ lb. spinach, stalks removed
2 tablespoons butter
pinch freshly grated nutmeg
4 cod fillets, skinned and halved lengthwise
2 tablespoons finely grated Parmesan cheese
salt and pepper
dill sprigs and Parmesan cheese shavings, to serve

Preheat oven to 350°F. Butter a shallow baking dish. In nonstick pan, heat oil, add onion, and cook fairly slowly until softened but not browned.

Increase heat, add mushrooms, and cook 2 or 3 minutes. Add spinach to pan and heat, stirring frequently, until no surplus liquid is visible. Add butter and season with nutmeg, salt, and pepper.

Spread spinach mixture in baking dish. Season cod, roll up with skinned side in, and secure with wooden toothpicks. Arrange cod on top of spinach mixture. Sprinkle with Parmesan cheese, cover, and bake in the oven about 20 to 25 minutes. Serve garnished with dill sprigs and Parmesan cheese shavings.

Makes 4 servings.

CHUNKY FISH CASSEROLE

1½ cups pasta shells
3 tablespoons olive oil
2 cloves garlic, finely crushed
3 baby onions, halved
4 oz. button mushrooms, halved
1 lb. firm white fish, such as cod or monkfish
8 oz. trout fillets
3 tablespoons seasoned flour
8 oz. fava beans
½ cup dry white wine
1¼ cups fish stock
large bouquet garni
grated zest and juice 1 lemon
5 oz. cooked, peeled shrimp or cooked, shelled mussels or clams
fresh, chopped herbs, to garnish

Preheat oven to 350°F. Cook pasta in plenty of boiling salted water about 10 minutes. Drain and rinse under cold running water; set aside. In a large skillet, heat half the oil, add garlic, onions, and mushrooms, and cook 3 or 4 minutes. Using a slotted spoon, transfer to a large, deep baking dish. Meanwhile, skin fish and cut into 1 in. chunks, then toss in seasoned flour.

Add remaining oil to pan, heat, and then add fish, in batches if necessary. Fry 2 or 3 minutes, turning pieces carefully. Transfer to dish and add pasta and beans. Stir wine, stock, bouquet garni, and lemon zest and juice into pan and bring to boil. Simmer a few minutes, then pour into dish. Cover and cook in the oven about 30 minutes. Add shrimp, mussels, or clams, cover again, and cook about 5 minutes. Garnish with plenty of chopped herbs.

Makes 4 servings.

MONKFISH ON RATATOUILLE

2 eggplants, halved lengthwise
3 zucchini, sliced
salt and pepper
2 monkfish tails, total weight about 2½ lb.
6 cloves garlic
⅓ cup olive oil
1 Spanish onion, very thinly sliced
2 large red bell peppers, thinly sliced
4 large tomatoes, peeled (see page 174), seeded, and
  chopped
leaves from a few thyme, marjoram, and oregano
  sprigs
about 2 tablespoons chopped parsley
about 2 tablespoons torn basil

In a heavy, flameproof casserole, heat 2 tablespoons oil, add eggplant slices, and sauté a few minutes. Add another tablespoon oil and the onion and garlic, and sauté a few minutes. Add bell peppers and cook 1 minute, stirring occasionally.

Cut eggplant into 1 in. slices. Put into a colander with zucchini slices, sprinkle with salt, and leave 1 hour. Rinse well, then dry thoroughly with absorbent paper towels.

Add 2 more tablespoons oil and the zucchini. Stir occasionally a few minutes, then add tomatoes, snip in thyme, marjoram, and oregano leaves and season lightly. Cover and cook very gently 30 to 40 minutes, stirring occasionally, until fairly dry.

Meanwhile, remove fine skin from monkfish and cut slits in flesh. Cut 3 garlic cloves into thin slivers and insert in slits. Season with salt and pepper and set aside. Chop remaining garlic.

Preheat oven to 400°F. Stir parsley into ratatouille and tip into a baking dish. Lay monkfish on top and cook 30 to 40 minutes, turning fish occasionally. Sprinkle with basil just before end of cooking.

Makes 4 to 6 servings.

COD BAKED WITH POTATOES

COD IN WHITE WINE

5 or 6 medium yellow potatoes, very thinly sliced, rinsed, and dried
1 red bell pepper, cored and seeded
1 onion, thinly sliced
1 large tomato, chopped
3 cloves garlic, slivered
¼ cup fresh, chopped parsley
salt and pepper
1 cup fish stock or water
1½ lb. cod cutlets with skin, 1 in. thick
1 bay leaf
3 thyme sprigs
4 thin slices lemon
1 tablespoon olive oil
¼ cup dry sherry
oregano sprigs, to garnish

3 tablespoons butter
2 zucchini, diagonally sliced
3 shallots, thinly sliced
⅓ cup all-purpose flour
¾ cup fish stock
1¾ cup dry white wine
2 tablespoons fresh, chopped, mixed herbs
salt and freshly ground black pepper
1 lb. cod fillet, skinned and diced
fresh parsley, to garnish

Preheat the oven to 375°F. In a large saucepan, melt butter over low heat. Add zucchini and shallots and cook 3 minutes.

Preheat oven to 375°F. Place half the potato slices in a large, lightly oiled baking dish. Chop bell pepper, then sprinkle it over potatoes with onion, tomato, garlic, and parsley. Season with salt and pepper and cover with remaining potato slices. Pour over stock or water, cover dish, and bake in the oven 1 hour. Increase oven temperature to 425°F, uncover dish, and bake about 7 minutes.

Stir in flour and cook 1 minute, stirring. Remove the pan from heat and gradually stir in stock and wine. Bring slowly to boil, stirring, and continue to cook, stirring, until mixture thickens.

Season fish. Place bay leaf and 3 thyme sprigs on potatoes, then place fish on top and nestle it into potatoes. Lay lemon slices on fish, sprinkle with oil, and return to the oven 8 minutes until potatoes are crisp and browned. Pour sherry over fish and return to oven an additional 2 minutes. Serve garnished with oregano sprigs.

Makes 4 servings.

Add herbs, salt and pepper, and fish and mix gently but thoroughly. Transfer to an ovenproof dish. Cover and cook in the oven 20 to 25 minutes, stirring once. Garnish with parsley and serve with freshly cooked spaghetti or linguine.

Makes 4 servings.

COD WITH GARLIC & ROSEMARY

2 tablespoons butter
3 shallots, finely chopped
3 cloves garlic, crushed
1 green bell pepper, sliced
¼ cup all-purpose flour
1¼ cups fish stock
⅔ cup dry white wine
2 tablespoons lemon juice
2 teaspoons dried rosemary
1 lb. cod steaks, skinned and diced
6 oz. frozen fava beans
salt and freshly ground black pepper

Preheat oven to 350°F. In a large saucepan, melt butter over low heat.

Add shallots, garlic, and pepper and cook gently 3 minutes, stirring. Add flour and cook 1 minute, stirring. Remove pan from heat and gradually stir in stock, wine, and lemon juice. Bring slowly to boil, stirring, and continue to cook, stirring, until mixture thickens.

Add rosemary, cod, fava beans, and salt and pepper to the saucepan and mix well. Transfer cod mixture to an ovenproof dish, cover, and cook in the oven 25 minutes, stirring once. Garnish with rosemary sprigs and serve with freshly cooked tagliatelle.

Makes 6 servings.

SWORDFISH WITH TOMATOES

3 tablespoons olive oil
4 swordfish steaks
1 small onion, finely chopped
2 cloves garlic, crushed
6 medium tomatoes, peeled, seeded, and chopped
2 halves sun-dried tomatoes, finely chopped
2 tablespoons fresh, chopped parsley
1 bay leaf, torn
8 oil-cured black olives, halved and pitted
rice and zucchini, cut into matchstick strips, to serve (optional)
basil sprigs, to garnish (optional)

In a skillet, heat half the oil. Add fish and cook quickly to brown on both sides.

Transfer fish to a plate. Heat remaining oil in pan, add onion and garlic, and cook until softened but not colored. Stir in chopped tomatoes, sun-dried tomatoes, chopped parsley, and bay leaf, stir about 1 minute, then boil until thickened.

Season tomato mixture with pepper, add fish, and baste with sauce. Cook gently, turning fish once, 10 to 15 minutes until fish is cooked through. Just before the end of cooking time, sprinkle with olives. Serve with rice and zucchini, garnished with basil sprigs.

Makes 4 servings.

SPICY RICE WITH MONKFISH

2 teaspoons sunflower oil
1 teaspoon chili oil
1 clove garlic, finely chopped
1 whole cinnamon stick, broken
2 star anise
1¼ cups long-grain white rice, rinsed
3½ cups vegetable stock
salt and freshly ground pepper
1 lb. monkfish tails, skinned and cut into chunks
8 oz. cooked, shelled mussels
6 scallions, chopped
grazed zest 1 lime
strips lime peel, to garnish

Heat sunflower and chili oils in a nonstick or well-seasoned wok or pan. Gently stir-fry garlic, cinnamon, star anise, and rice 3 minutes until rice is opaque but not browned. Add stock, bring to boil, and reduce to a simmer. Cook 15 minutes.

Season with salt and pepper and stir in monkfish. Simmer 10 minutes or until most of the liquid has been absorbed. Gently stir in cooked shelled mussels, scallions, and lime zest and heat through 3 or 4 minutes. Discard cinnamon stick and star anise. Garnish with strips of lime peel to serve.

Makes 4 servings.

ISHIKARI STEW

4 salmon steaks, scaled
1 onion
2 potatoes
1 or 2 carrots
4 to 8 shiitake or button mushrooms
2 cups cilantro or watercress
9 oz. (1 cake) firm tofu
10 oz. (1 cake) konnyaku (optional)
2 tablespoons butter
4 in. piece dried konbu (kelp) (optional)
3 to 5 tablespoons miso
2 scallions, finely chopped

Leaving skin on, cut salmon steaks into chunks. Cut onion in half and slice.

Slice potatoes and carrots into ½ in. thick disks (if large, cut into half-moons) and parboil separately. Drain and set aside. Slice shiitake mushrooms diagonally into 4 slices. Chop cilantro or watercress into 2½ in. lengths. Cut tofu and konnyaku (if using) in half lengthwise, then cut tofu into ½ in. squares and konnyaku into ¼ in. slices. Melt butter in a large, flameproof pot and stir-fry onion slices 1 or 2 minutes. Add konbu and enough water to half fill pot.

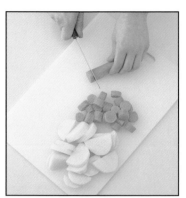

Bring to boil over medium heat, discard konbu, and lower heat. Dissolve miso in a bowl with some of the soup, then stir back into pan. Add potatoes, carrots, salmon, mushrooms, and konnyaku, then cover and cook over low heat 5 minutes. Add cilantro or watercress and tofu; simmer 3 or 4 minutes. Serve sprinkled with chopped scallion.

Makes 4 to 6 servings.

Note: Ishikari is a river on the northern island of Japan that is famous for salmon.

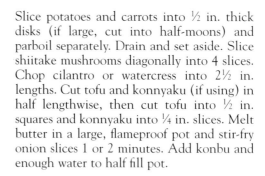

CARIBBEAN SWORDFISH STEAKS

3 tablespoons oil
6 shallots, finely chopped
1 clove garlic, crushed
1 fresh green chili, seeded and finely chopped
14½ oz. can chopped tomatoes
2 bay leaves
¼ teaspoon cayenne pepper
1 teaspoon crushed allspice berries
juice 2 limes
4 swordfish steaks
1 teaspoon brown sugar
2 teaspoons Angostura bitters

Heat oil in a pan. Add shallots and cook 10 minutes until soft.

Add crushed garlic and chili and cook 2 minutes, then stir in tomatoes, bay leaves, cayenne pepper, allspice, lime juice, and salt. Cook gently 15 minutes.

Add swordfish steaks to pan and baste with tomato sauce. Cover and cook 10 minutes until steaks are cooked. Transfer swordfish steaks to a warmed dish and keep hot. Stir sugar and Angostura bitters into sauce. Simmer 2 minutes, remove bay leaves, then serve sauce with fish.

Makes 4 servings.

CREAMY SAFFRON FISH CURRY

1½ lb. white fish fillets, e.g., sole, flounder, or cod
pinch saffron threads
2 tablespoons boiling water
3 tablespoons vegetable oil
2 onions, chopped
3 cloves garlic, crushed
1 in. piece fresh ginger, grated
1 teaspoon turmeric
1 tablespoon ground coriander
2 teaspoons garam masala
salt and cayenne pepper
2 teaspoons chickpea flour
1 cup plain yogurt
¼ cup heavy cream
strips lemon peel and red bell pepper, to garnish

Wash fish, remove any skin and bones, and pat dry with absorbent paper towels. Cut into large chunks and set aside. Put saffron in a small bowl with boiling water and let soak about 5 minutes. Heat oil in a large, shallow pan, add onions, and cook, stirring, about 5 minutes until soft but not colored.

Add garlic, ginger, turmeric, coriander, garam masala, and salt and pepper and fry an additional 1 minute. Stir in flour and cook 1 minute, then remove from heat. Stir in yogurt and cream, then return to heat and slowly bring to boil. Add fish, saffron, and soaking water and simmer gently, covered, 10 to 15 minutes until fish is tender and flakes easily. Serve fish hot, garnished with strips of lemon peel and red bell pepper.

Makes 4 servings.

SEA BASS WITH FENNEL

¼ cup olive oil
2 onions, thinly sliced
2 fennel bulbs, thinly sliced
1 fresh bay leaf
1 sea bass, weighing about 2¾ lb., cleaned and scaled
1 lemon, thinly sliced
salt and freshly ground black pepper
⅓ cup dry white wine
fennel leaves, to garnish

Preheat the oven to 350°F. Heat 2 tablespoons oil in a large skillet. Add onions and fennel and cook gently 3 minutes until beginning to soften.

Transfer to a baking pan. Put bay leaf inside fish and season with salt and pepper. Put fish on top of vegetables and cover it with lemon slices.

Pour over wine. Cover dish with aluminum foil and bake 30 minutes or until fish flakes easily when tested with a knife. Remove lemon slices and sprinkle fish with remaining oil. Cut fish into 4 fillets, garnish with fennel leaves, and serve with vegetables and cooking juices.

Makes 4 servings.

MONKFISH & ALMOND SAUCE

⅓ cup olive oil
½ Spanish onion, finely chopped
2¼ lb. monkfish tail, skinned and cut into 8 slices
salt and freshly ground black pepper
2 cloves garlic, crushed
12 blanched almonds, toasted and finely ground
1 tablespoon fresh, chopped parsley
pinch saffron threads, finely crushed
2 tablespoons dry white wine, fish stock, or water
1½ cups shelled fresh or frozen peas
strips lemon peel and herbs, to garnish

Heat 2 tablespoons oil in a flameproof casserole, add onion, and cook 2 or 3 minutes. Season monkfish and place on onion, sprinkle with remaining oil, and cook 5 minutes.

Meanwhile, using a mortar and pestle, pound garlic, almonds, parsley, and saffron together to make a smooth paste. Stir in wine, stock, or water. Spoon over monkfish, add fresh peas to casserole, and cook 7 to 10 minutes until fish flakes when pierced with a knife and peas are tender. If using frozen peas, add them about 3 minutes before end of cooking time. Serve garnished with strips of lemon peel and herbs.

Makes 4 servings.

FISH WITH COUSBAREIA SAUCE

4 tomatoes
2 tablespoons olive oil
1 onion, chopped
1 clove garlic, crushed
¾ cup hazelnuts, finely chopped
½ cup pine nuts
3 tablespoons fresh, chopped parsley
salt and freshly ground black pepper
fillets from 4 red mullet, skinned
parsley sprigs, to garnish

Place tomatoes in a bowl and cover with boiling water. Let stand 1 minute, then drain and cover with cold water.

Let stand 1 minute, then peel skins off tomatoes. Remove seeds and dice flesh. Add onion and garlic and cook 10 to 15 minutes until soft. Add hazelnuts and pine nuts and fry 2 more minutes. Stir in tomatoes and cook 3 or 4 minutes until soft. Add ⅔ cup water to cover, parsley, salt, and pepper and simmer 5 minutes.

Place red mullet fillets in the pan and spoon some of sauce over. Cover and simmer 10 to 15 minutes until fish flakes easily when tested with a knife. Serve fish fillets on heated plates with sauce poured around. Garnish with parsley sprigs and serve with lettuce leaves.

Makes 4 servings.

FISH TAGINE WITH TOMATOES

8 plum tomatoes, cut in half lengthwise
2 teaspoons superfine sugar
⅓ cup olive oil
1 bream, weighing about 3 lb., cleaned
1 carrot, cut into matchsticks
2 stalks celery, cut into matchsticks
peel ½ preserved lemon, cut into strips
fresh parsley, to garnish
CHERMOULA:
4 cloves garlic, crushed with 1 teaspoon salt
juice 2 lemons
1 tablespoon ground cumin
2 teaspoons paprika
1 fresh red chili, cored, seeded, and roughly chopped
⅓ cup fresh, chopped cilantro
⅓ cup fresh, chopped parsley

Preheat the oven to 475°F. To make chermoula, blend all ingredients in a food processor, then gradually add about ¼ cup olive oil to make a coarse purée. Place tomatoes in an ovenproof dish, cut-side up. Sprinkle with sugar, salt and pepper, and remaining olive oil and roast in the oven 30 to 40 minutes until soft and slightly charred. Remove from dish and set aside. Rub fish inside and out with chermoula. Arrange carrot and celery in the bottom of the dish and place fish on top.

Add remaining chermoula and arrange tomatoes and lemon peel around the sides. Reduce the oven temperature to 400°F. Cover the dish with a lid or aluminum foil and bake in the oven 30 minutes. Remove the foil and spoon any juices over fish. Return to the oven, uncovered, and cook an additional 10 minutes or until fish flakes easily when tested with a knife and most of the liquid has evaporated. Garnish with parsley.

Makes 4 servings.

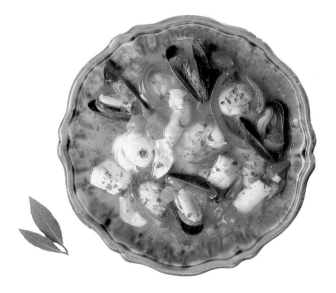

CIOPPINO

2 tablespoons light olive oil
1 large onion, chopped
3 cloves garlic, chopped
1 small red chili, seeded and thinly sliced
1 red bell pepper, seeded and sliced
6 medium tomatoes
2 cups fish stock
½ cup dry white wine
1 teaspoon dried oregano
1½ teaspoons each fresh, chopped thyme and marjoram
1 bay leaf
8 oz. haddock, cod, or halibut fillet, skinned
8 oz. large raw shrimp
16 mussels, cleaned
4 large scallops, shelled
2½ tablespoons fresh, chopped parsley

In a large, heavy-bottomed saucepan, heat oil, add onion, garlic, chili, and red bell pepper, and cook gently until onion begins to color. Meanwhile, peel, seed, and chop tomatoes (see page 174) and add to pan with stock, wine, oregano, thyme, marjoram, and bay leaf. Cover and simmer 45 minutes.

Dice fish and peel shrimp. Add mussels to pan, simmer 1 minute, then add haddock, shrimp, and scallops. Cook over low heat 3 to 5 minutes until mussels have opened; discard any that remain closed. Sprinkle with parsley and serve at once.

Makes 4 servings.

Note: Garnish with eight large, cooked, unpeeled shrimp.

TUNA PEPERONATA

6 slices tuna, each about 1 in. thick
4 cloves garlic
⅓ cup olive oil
1 large onion, finely chopped
1 large red bell pepper, seeded, cored, and thinly sliced
1 green bell pepper, seeded, cored, and thinly sliced
4 medium tomatoes, peeled (see page 174), seeded, and diced
1 tablespoon sun-dried tomato paste
3 thyme sprigs
1 bay leaf
salt and pepper
parsley sprigs, to garnish

Cut slits in tuna. Cut 2 cloves of garlic into slivers and insert in slits in tuna. In a large skillet, heat half the oil, add tuna, and cook until lightly browned on both sides. Remove tuna from pan and set aside. Add remaining oil to pan, add onion and bell peppers, and cook over moderate heat, stirring frequently, about 10 minutes until soft.

Chop remaining garlic, add to pan, cook 1 minute, then add tomatoes, sun-dried tomato paste, thyme, and bay leaf. Simmer, uncovered, 15 to 20 minutes, stirring occasionally. Return tuna to pan, season with salt and pepper, then cover with buttered waxed paper and cook gently 15 minutes. Serve garnished with parsley sprigs.

Makes 6 servings.

MIXED FISH STEW

1 red mullet, red snapper, bream, or trout, weighing
   about 12 oz.
6 oz. piece sea bass
12 oz. monkfish fillet
½ bay leaf
1½ tablespoons olive oil
1 small fennel bulb
3 small carrots
1 medium onion, thinly sliced
1 small clove garlic, finely crushed
pinch saffron threads, toasted and crushed
⅔ cup dry white wine
⅓ cup light cream
salt and pepper
½ bunch scallions, cut diagonally into thin strips
dill sprigs, to garnish

In a flameproof casserole, heat oil. Cut
fennel and carrots into thin strips and add to
casserole with onion, garlic, and saffron.
Cook 3 or 4 minutes. Add ¼ cup wine and
boil until most of the liquid has evaporated.
Add remaining wine and boil until reduced
by half.

Thickly slice mullet, snapper, bream, or trout
and place head and tail in a small saucepan.
Remove skin and bones from bass and add
them to pan.

Stir in reserved stock, 2½ tablespoons cream,
and monkfish and season with salt and
pepper. Cover and cook very gently
10 minutes.

Trim fine skin from monkfish and add skin to
pan with bay leaf and ⅔ cup water. Simmer
20 minutes, then strain and reserve stock.
Thickly slice raw bass and monkfish.

Add mullet and bass, cover, and cook an
additional 10 minutes or until fish is just
cooked. Gently stir in remaining cream and
sprinkle with scallions. Serve garnished with
dill sprigs.

Makes 4 servings.

CRISPY FISH STEW

2 medium zucchini, thinly sliced
2 red dessert apples, cored and thinly sliced
1 large onion, sliced
1½ cups topped, tailed, and sliced green beans
1 teaspoon dried sage
1¼ cups fish stock
1½ lb. cod fillet, skinned and diced
salt and freshly ground black pepper
2 or 3 medium potatoes, unpeeled and thinly sliced
¾ cup shredded cheddar cheese

Preheat oven to 375°F. Arrange layers of zucchini, apples, onion, and beans in an ovenproof casserole.

Sprinkle with sage and pour in stock. Cover and cook in the oven 30 minutes. Remove from the oven, arrange fish on top, and season with salt and pepper.

Arrange sliced potatoes on top, sprinkle with cheese, and bake 35 to 40 minutes until potatoes are tender and cheese is melted and golden.

Makes 4 to 6 servings.

Variation: Any firm white fish fillets can be used in this recipe.

CHEESY COD BAKE

1½ lb. cod fillets, skinned and diced
salt and freshly ground black pepper
4 basil leaves, torn
grated zest and juice 1 lemon
8 oz. frozen puff pastry
1¼ cups plain yogurt
7 oz. can corn kernels, drained
1 cup shredded Emmental cheese
basil sprigs, to garnish

Preheat oven to 425°F. Put cod in a shallow, flameproof dish. Season with salt and pepper, add basil, and sprinkle with lemon juice.

Cover with a lid or piece of aluminum foil and cook 10 to 15 minutes. Meanwhile, allow pastry to thaw 10 minutes. Add lemon zest, plain yogurt, corn, and cheese to fish mixture and stir well. Grate pastry evenly over the top.

Bake 30 to 40 minutes until topping is crisp and golden brown. Garnish with basil sprigs and serve.

Makes 4 to 6 servings.

SEAFOOD LASAGNA

KEDGEREE

2 tablespoons olive oil
1 leek, thinly sliced
8 oz. mushrooms, thinly sliced
8 oz. haddock fillet, skinned and diced
4 oz. cooked, peeled shrimp
10 oz. cod fillet, skinned and diced
2 tablespoons lemon juice
4 eggs, beaten
⅔ cup finely grated Parmesan cheese
2¼ cups plain yogurt
6 sheets fresh lasagna
8 oz. mozzarella cheese, sliced

1 lb. smoked haddock
2 tablespoons olive oil
1 onion, chopped
1¾ cups white rice
4 hard-boiled eggs, shelled
2 tablespoons sour cream
2 tablespoons butter
3 tablespoons fresh, chopped parsley

Heat oil in a large, flameproof dish and add leek and mushrooms.

Put haddock in a flameproof casserole with 3¾ cups water. Bring to boil and simmer 10 minutes until fish is tender. Remove with a slotted spoon and keep warm.

Cook gently 10 minutes, stirring occasionally, until soft. Add haddock, shrimp, cod, lemon juice, and salt and pepper and cook, stirring, 5 minutes. Preheat oven to 350°F. Mix together eggs, Parmesan cheese, and yogurt. Stir into fish mixture. Remove two thirds of the fish mixture from the dish.

Pour cooking liquid from the casserole and set aside. Heat oil in casserole, add chopped onion, and cook, stirring occasionally, 5 minutes until soft. Add rice and cook, stirring, 1 minute. Pour reserved cooking liquid over rice, bring to boil, cover, and simmer 15 to 20 minutes until liquid has been absorbed and rice is tender. Remove from the heat.

Cover fish mixture in the dish with 2 sheets of lasagna. Cover with half the remaining mixture then 2 more sheets of lasagna. Reserve a ladleful of the liquid from the fish mixture and spread remaining mixture over lasagna. Cover with 2 sheets of lasagna and pour reserved liquid over the top. Cover with cheese and bake 40 to 50 minutes until topping is golden and pasta is tender.

Makes 6 to 8 servings.

Cut hard-boiled eggs into wedges. Flake haddock and gently mix into rice with eggs, sour cream, butter, and parsley. Season with salt and pepper. Return to the heat and cook gently 2 or 3 minutes to warm through.

Makes 4 servings.

FISH PLAKI

2½ lb. fish such as bream, bass, grey mullet, red
    snapper, or pompano, scaled
juice ½ lemon
2 tablespoons olive oil
1 onion, chopped
1 carrot, finely chopped
1 stalk celery, chopped
2 cloves garlic, chopped
1 teaspoon coriander, crushed
5 medium tomatoes, peeled (see page 174), seeded,
    and chopped
3 halves sun-dried tomato, finely chopped
⅓ cup dry white wine
leaves from bunch parsley, finely chopped
salt and pepper
parsley sprigs, to garnish

Preheat oven to 375°F. Put fish into a baking
dish and sprinkle with lemon juice. Heat oil
in a saucepan, add onion, carrot, and celery,
and cook, stirring occasionally, until onion
has softened but not colored. Stir in garlic
and cook about 3 minutes. Stir coriander
seeds, tomatoes, sun-dried tomatoes, wine,
and parsley into pan, season with salt
and pepper, and simmer a few minutes until
well blended.

Using a fish slice, lift fish and pour about one
quarter of tomato mixture underneath. Lay
fish down again and pour over remaining
tomato mixture. Cover dish and bake in the
oven about 40 minutes. Serve garnished
with parsley sprigs.

Makes 4 servings.

HADDOCK & SALMON PIE

½ stick butter
½ cup all-purpose flour
1¼ cups milk
1¼ cups fish stock
12 shallots
3 medium potatoes, diced
2 cloves garlic, crushed
2 tablespoons olive oil
1 tablespoon thick cream
salt and freshly ground black pepper
2 tablespoons whole-grain mustard
¼ cup fresh, chopped parsley
1 lb. salmon fillet, skinned and diced
8 oz. smoked haddock, skinned and diced
12 small button mushrooms
1 egg, beaten

Melt butter in a flameproof casserole, add
flour, and cook over gentle heat, stirring,
2 minutes. Gradually stir in milk and fish
stock, then add shallots. Bring to boil and
simmer 30 minutes. Meanwhile, cook
potatoes and garlic in boiling salted water
20 minutes until potatoes are tender. Drain.
Mash potatoes and garlic and stir in olive oil,
cream, and salt and pepper. Set aside.
Preheat oven to 400°F.

Season shallot sauce with salt and pepper
and add mustard and parsley. Add salmon,
haddock, and button mushrooms and
simmer gently 10 minutes. Pipe or spoon
potato on top of fish mixture and bake
10 minutes. Take out of the oven and brush
with a little beaten egg. Return to the oven
and bake 20 minutes until potato is golden.

Makes 4 to 6 servings.

TUNA-STUFFED BELL PEPPERS

4 large green bell peppers
1 cup long-grain rice, cooked
6 oz. can tuna in water, drained and flaked
1 small onion, shredded
7 oz. can corn kernels, drained
2 oz. mushrooms, finely chopped
1 teaspoon paprika
salt and freshly ground black pepper
½ cup shredded cheddar cheese
4 slices tomato

Trim the bottom of each pepper so it will stand and scoop out seeds and pith. Combine rice, tuna, onion, corn, mushrooms, paprika, and salt and pepper. Pack into peppers.

Preheat the oven to 350°F. Place bell peppers in a shallow, ovenproof dish. Pour 3¾ cups water into the dish and bake 30 minutes.

Remove from the oven and increase the temperature to 400°F. Sprinkle peppers with cheese. Top each one with a slice of tomato and return to oven for 10 minutes.

Makes 4 servings.

PASTA WITH TUNA SAUCE

3 cups pasta twists
6 oz. can tuna in water, drained
7 oz. can corn kernels, drained
1 green bell pepper, diced
4 scallions, cut into 1 in. lengths
10 oz. can condensed cream of mushroom soup
   mixed with ½ can water
salt and freshly ground black pepper
Italian parsley sprigs, to garnish

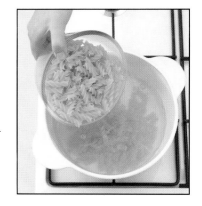

Add pasta twists to a large, flameproof casserole of boiling salted water and cook about 10 minutes, or according to package directions, until just tender.

Drain pasta and return to the casserole. Add tuna, corn, bell pepper, and scallions and stir to combine.

Stir soup into the casserole. Cook gently, stirring occasionally, 20 minutes. Season with salt and pepper. Garnish with Italian parsley and serve.

Makes 4 servings.

YUCATAN-STYLE COD

4 fresh cod cutlets, each weighing 4 to 6 oz.
2 tablespoons fresh lime juice
salt and pepper
1 tablespoon olive oil
1 small onion, finely chopped
1 small green bell pepper, seeded and chopped
⅓ cup pumpkin seeds
2 tablespoons finely chopped cilantro
¼ cup orange juice
2 hard-boiled eggs, quartered, and lime wedges to
   garnish

Wipe fish with absorbent paper towels. Rub lime juice into fish. Place cutlets in a shallow, ovenproof dish and season lightly.

Preheat oven to 350°F. Heat oil in a medium saucepan. Add onion, bell pepper, pumpkin seeds, and half the cilantro. Fry gently 5 to 10 minutes until onion is soft but not browned.

Place vegetable mixture in cavities in cutlets and spread remainder over the top. Pour over orange juice. Cover and bake 15 to 20 minutes or until fish flakes easily when tested with the back of a knife. Garnish with egg quarters and lime wedges.

Makes 4 servings.

CHILI FISH

2 tablespoons butter
1 teaspoon hot chili powder
2 medium onions, finely chopped
1 clove garlic crushed with ¼ teaspoon salt
2½ cups chicken stock
2 tablespoons tomato paste
juice 1 lemon
2 teaspoons honey
1 lb. cod or haddock fillet, cut into 1 in. pieces
salt and pepper

Melt butter in a saucepan. Add chili powder and cook over low heat 1 minute. Add onions and garlic and fry 3 minutes. Stir in stock, tomato paste, lemon juice, and honey. Cover and simmer 30 minutes until quite thick. Add fish and simmer an additional 10 minutes. Season with salt and pepper to taste.

Makes 4 servings.

Variation: Substitute 8 oz. cooked, peeled shrimp for 8 oz. fish. Add halfway through cooking.

VERACRUZ-STYLE RED SNAPPER

2 tablespoons olive oil
1 medium onion, chopped
3 cloves garlic, peeled and very finely chopped
5 medium tomatoes, peeled (see page 174) and
  chopped
10 green olives, pitted and chopped
2 tablespoons capers
3 bay leaves
6 black peppercorns
salt
2¼ lb. red snapper or other white fish fillets

MEXICAN TUNA CASSEROLE

1 tablespoon oil
1 medium onion, chopped
1 clove garlic, crushed with ½ teaspoon salt
5 medium tomatoes, blanched, peeled (see page 174),
  and chopped
1 tablespoon tomato paste
8 black olives, pitted and sliced
1 green chili, seeded and chopped
½ green bell pepper, seeded and chopped
1 teaspoon ground cumin
6 oz. can tuna, drained
¾ cup cottage cheese
1 egg
1½ cups shredded cheddar cheese
4 corn or flour tortillas, cut into strips

Heat oil in a large saucepan. Add onion and garlic and fry gently 5 to 10 minutes until soft but not browned. Add tomatoes, olives, capers, bay leaves, peppercorns, and salt. Bring to boil, then reduce the heat and simmer, uncovered, 10 minutes. Place fish in a large skillet and sprinkle with salt.

Preheat the oven to 350°F. Heat oil in a medium saucepan, add garlic and onion, and fry gently until soft but not browned. Add tomatoes, tomato paste, olives, chili, bell pepper, and cumin. Bring to boil, cover, then simmer 15 minutes until fairly thick; remove the lid if necessary. Add tuna and carefully stir well.

Pour tomato mixture over fish. Bring slowly to boil, reduce the heat, cover, and simmer about 7 minutes until fish flakes easily when tested with the back of a knife.

Makes 6 servings.

Mix cottage cheese with egg. Place half the tomato and tuna mixture in a shallow, ovenproof dish. Cover with half the shredded cheese. Spread cottage cheese mixture over the top, then cover with tortilla strips. Spoon over remaining tomato and tuna mixture. Sprinkle with remaining shredded cheese. Bake 30 minutes until bubbling and golden brown on top.

Makes 4 servings.

SEAFOOD RISOTTO

1 tablespoon olive oil
6 scallions, chopped
1 clove garlic, crushed
1¼ cups risotto rice
½ teaspoon turmeric
¼ cup dry white wine
4 tomatoes, chopped
2¼ cups fish stock
1 lb. mixed, cooked seafood
12 jumbo shrimp
1¼ cups frozen peas
salt and freshly ground black pepper
¼ cup fresh, chopped parsley

Heat oil in a large, flameproof casserole. Add scallions and garlic and cook, stirring, 3 minutes until soft. Cover and cook over gentle heat 2 minutes. Add rice and turmeric and cook, stirring, 1 minute. Add wine, tomatoes, and half the stock to the casserole. Bring to boil, cover, and simmer 10 minutes.

Add remaining stock, bring back to boil, cover, and cook 15 minutes until rice has absorbed most of the liquid. Stir in seafood, shrimp, and peas and season with salt and pepper. Cook gently, stirring occasionally, 10 minutes. Stir in parsley and serve.

Makes 4 servings.

MACKEREL WITH SOUR CREAM

4 mackerel fillets, each weighing 4 oz., skinned
1 leek, thinly sliced
1 cup canned chopped tomatoes
1 tablespoon fresh, chopped dill
½ teaspoon mild paprika
juice ½ lemon
salt
⅔ cup sour cream
dill sprigs, to garnish

Preheat oven to 400°F. Place mackerel fillets in a shallow, ovenproof dish.

In a large bowl, mix together leek, tomatoes, dill, paprika, and lemon juice and pour over mackerel. Season with salt.

Cover with a lid or piece of aluminum foil and cook in the oven 50 minutes until fish is cooked through. Drizzle with sour cream, garnish with dill sprigs, and serve.

Makes 4 servings.

BAKED SALMON

½ stick butter, softened
1 clove garlic, crushed
juice ½ lemon
2 tablespoons fresh, chopped parsley
1½ lb. salmon, filleted
1 tablespoon olive oil, plus extra for greasing
6 shallots, chopped
⅔ cup fish stock
¾ cup red wine
1 cup veal stock
salt and freshly ground black pepper

In a small bowl, mix butter with garlic, lemon juice, and 1 tablespoon chopped parsley.

Spread one of the halves of salmon with butter mixture and sandwich pieces back together. Wrap tightly in plastic wrap and put in the freezer about 1 hour to set. Do not freeze. Preheat oven to 400°F. Lightly oil a large piece of aluminum foil. Take salmon out of plastic wrap and wrap tightly in aluminum foil. Place in a shallow, ovenproof dish and cook in the oven 30 to 35 minutes. Remove from the dish and keep warm.

Heat oil in the dish, add shallots, and cook gently, stirring, 3 minutes until soft. Add fish stock and red wine and boil until reduced and syrupy. Add veal stock and boil to reduce slightly. Add remaining parsley and season with salt and pepper. Divide sauce among warmed serving plates. Slice salmon, place on top of sauce, and serve.

Makes 4 servings.

TROUT WITH VEGETABLES

2 × 14½ oz. cans chopped tomatoes
1 leek, finely sliced
12 basil leaves, torn
2 teaspoons fresh, chopped oregano
3 stalks celery, diced
2 zucchini, diced
¾ cup red wine
2 tablespoons red wine vinegar
4 trout, cleaned
4 basil sprigs
8 oregano sprigs

Put tomatoes, leek, torn basil, chopped oregano, celery, zucchini, wine, and vinegar in a shallow, flameproof dish.

Bring to boil, cover with a lid or piece of aluminum foil, and simmer 10 minutes. Season with salt and pepper. Stuff trout cavities with basil sprigs and half the oregano sprigs.

Place trout on top of vegetable mixture. Cover again and simmer gently 20 to 25 minutes until trout is cooked through. Garnish with remaining oregano sprigs and serve.

Makes 4 servings.

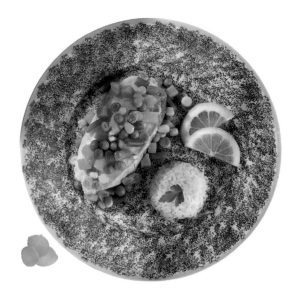

COD & VEGETABLE PACKAGES

PASTA WITH SALMON TROUT

vegetable oil for greasing
4 cod steaks, each weighing about 6 oz.
1½ cups frozen mixed vegetables
6 scallions, sliced
2 tablespoons ginger wine
2 teaspoons soy sauce
½ in. piece fresh ginger, peeled and thinly sliced
lemon slices, to serve

Preheat oven to 400°F. Lightly oil four large squares of aluminum foil. Place a cod steak on each one. Arrange frozen vegetables and scallions on top.

1 tablespoon olive oil
8 oz. salmon trout fillets, skinned and diced
1 cup small broccoli florets
10 oz. tagliatelle
⅔ cup light cream
1 tablespoon fresh, chopped dill
salt and freshly ground black pepper
¼ cup slivered almonds, toasted

Heat oil in a flameproof casserole. Add salmon and broccoli and cook, stirring occasionally, 10 to 15 minutes until fish is just cooked and broccoli is tender.

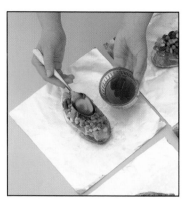

Mix together ginger wine and soy sauce and spoon over cod steaks. Sprinkle with sliced ginger.

Meanwhile, cook tagliatelle in boiling salted water 8 to 10 minutes, or according to package directions, until just tender. Drain and stir into the casserole.

Bring the foil up over steaks and fold edges together to seal. Put packages in an ovenproof dish and bake 20 to 25 minutes. Remove fish and vegetables from packages and serve with lemon slices.

Makes 4 servings.

Stir in cream and dill and season with salt and pepper. Sprinkle with toasted slivered almonds and serve.

Makes 4 servings.

TUNA, TOMATO, & PENNE

2 tablespoons olive oil
1 onion, chopped
2 cloves garlic, finely chopped
2 × 14½ oz. cans peeled tomatoes
1 tablespoon tomato paste
1 tablespoon fresh, chopped or 1 teaspoon dried
   oregano
½ cup sun-dried tomatoes in oil, drained and
   chopped
salt and freshly ground black pepper
4 cups penne or rigatoni
½ cup black olives, coarsely chopped
2 tablespoons capers, drained
6 oz. can light tuna, drained
2 tablespoons fresh, chopped parsley
fresh Parmesan cheese, to serve

Heat a wok or pan until hot. Add oil and swirl to coat. Add onion and garlic and stir-fry 1 or 2 minutes until beginning to soften. Add tomatoes, stirring to break up large pieces. Stir in tomato paste, oregano, and sun-dried tomatoes. Bring to boil and simmer 10 to 12 minutes until sauce is slightly thickened. Season with salt and pepper. Meanwhile, in a large saucepan of boiling water, cook penne according to package directions.

Stir black olives, capers, and tuna into sauce. Drain pasta and add to sauce, stirring gently to mix well. Stir in chopped parsley and serve immediately. Using a swivel-bladed vegetable peeler, shave flakes of Parmesan over each serving.

Makes 4 servings.

TUNA & CORN BAKE

1 tablespoon olive oil
1 onion, finely chopped
1 yellow bell pepper, seeded and diced
2 stalks celery, finely chopped
2 zucchini, finely diced
14½ oz. can chopped tomatoes
⅔ cup dry white wine
2 teaspoons dried Italian herb seasoning
salt and freshly ground black pepper
10 oz. dried penne rigate
15¼ oz. can corn kernels, drained
12 oz. can tuna in water, drained and flaked
⅔ cup finely grated Parmesan cheese
herb sprigs, to garnish (optional)

Preheat oven to 375°F. Heat oil in a saucepan, add onion, bell pepper, and celery, and cook 5 minutes, stirring occasionally. Stir in zucchini, tomatoes, wine, dried herbs, and salt and pepper. Bring to boil, then reduce heat, cover, and simmer 10 minutes, stirring occasionally. Uncover, increase heat slightly, and cook an additional 5 minutes or until sauce has reduced and thickened slightly. Meanwhile, cook pasta in a large saucepan of lightly salted boiling water 10 minutes or until just cooked or al dente. Drain and return to rinsed-out pan.

Add tomato sauce, corn, and tuna and toss well to mix. Transfer to an ovenproof dish and sprinkle with Parmesan cheese. Bake 20 to 25 minutes or until bubbling and golden. Garnish with herb sprigs.

Makes 4 to 6 servings.

Variations: Use canned salmon or cooked smoked cod or haddock instead of tuna. Use cheddar or Gruyère cheese instead of Parmesan.

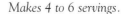

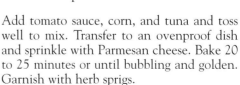

FISH IN CURRY SAUCE

1 lb. fish fillet or steak, e.g., halibut, cod, or
  monkfish, cut into bite-sized pieces
freshly ground black pepper
2 tablespoons fish sauce
1 tablespoon sugar
1 tablespoon vegetable oil
1 clove garlic, finely chopped
2 or 3 shallots, finely chopped
2 or 3 tablespoons mild curry powder
1 cup Vietnamese hot sauce
1½ cups chicken stock or water
9 oz. (1 cake) firm tofu, cut into small cubes
½ teaspoon salt
2 or 3 scallions, cut into short lengths, to garnish
1 or 2 small red chilies, seeded and chopped
  (optional)

In a dish, marinate fish pieces with pepper,
fish sauce, and sugar 15 to 20 minutes. Heat
oil in a saucepan and stir-fry garlic and
shallots about 1 minute. Add curry powder
and hot sauce and cook 1 minute, stirring
constantly. Add stock or water, blend well,
and bring to boil.

Add fish, tofu pieces, and salt and stir very
gently. Reduce heat, cover, and simmer 10
minutes. Serve hot, garnished with scallions
and chilies.

Makes 4 servings.

SMOKED MACKEREL GRATIN

1 lb. peppered, smoked mackerel, skinned and flaked
¼ cup fresh, chopped parsley
2¼ cups sour cream
2 tablespoons horseradish sauce
6 to 8 drops Tabasco sauce
1 red onion, finely chopped
2 tablespoons finely grated Parmesan cheese
3 cups fresh whole-wheat bread crumbs
3 tablespoons sunflower seeds

Preheat oven to 400°F. Mix together
mackerel, parsley, sour cream, horseradish
sauce, Tabasco sauce, and onion.

Spread mackerel mixture into a shallow,
ovenproof dish. Mix together Parmesan
cheese, bread crumbs, and sunflower seeds.

Sprinkle over mackerel mixture and bake 20
minutes until golden.

Makes 4 to 6 servings.

GRAY MULLET TAGINE

⅔ cup raisins
4 grey mullet fillets
2 tablespoons olive oil
1 onion, finely chopped
¼ teaspoon coarsely crushed black peppercorns
¼ teaspoon ground cinnamon
¼ cup white wine vinegar
¼ cup honey
salt
2 tablespoons fresh, chopped parsley
Italian parsley sprigs and lemon slices, to garnish
MARINADE:
¼ cup olive oil
½ teaspoon ground cinnamon
¼ teaspoon chili powder
½ teaspoon allspice

Put raisins in a bowl and cover with boiling water. Set aside. Put mullet in a shallow dish. To make marinade, mix together olive oil, 2 tablespoons water, cinnamon, chili powder, and allspice. Pour over fish and leave in a cool place 2 hours. Heat olive oil in a skillet. Add onion and cook 5 minutes until soft. Stir in peppercorns, cinnamon, vinegar, honey, and salt.

Drain raisins and add to the pan. Remove fish from marinade with a slotted spoon and set aside. Add marinade to the pan. Bring to boil and simmer gently 15 minutes. Add chopped parsley and fish, spoon over sauce, and simmer gently 10 minutes or until flesh flakes easily when tested with a knife. Garnish with parsley sprigs and lemon slices and serve.

Makes 4 servings.

STEAMED FISH & VEGETABLES

4 whole red mullet, red snapper, or sea bream, each
   weighing about 8 oz., cleaned
4 teaspoons garam masala
½ teaspoon turmeric
2 tablespoons fresh, chopped cilantro
1 tablespoon fresh, chopped parsley
1 in. piece fresh ginger, grated
4 lemon slices
2 tablespoons vegetable oil
8 new potatoes, sliced
3 carrots, sliced
4 zucchini, sliced
salt and pepper
cilantro, to garnish

Wash fish and pat dry with absorbent paper towels, then slash three times on each side. Mix garam masala, turmeric, cilantro, parsley, and ginger together and rub into flesh and skin of fish. Tuck a slice of lemon inside each fish and set aside. Heat oil in a skillet, add potatoes and carrots, and fry, stirring frequently, 5 or 6 minutes until slightly softened and beginning to brown.

Add zucchini to pan and fry an additional 1 minute. Season with salt and pepper. Using a slotted spoon, transfer vegetables to a steamer. Lay fish on top, cover, and steam 20 to 25 minutes or until fish flakes easily and vegetables are tender. Serve at once, garnished with cilantro.

Makes 4 servings.

COD & EGGPLANT

1 eggplant, diced
salt and freshly ground black pepper
1½ lb. thick cod fillet, cut into 4 equal pieces
5 oz. cured chorizo, skinned and thinly sliced
¼ cup olive oil
1 Spanish onion, finely chopped
2 cloves garlic, very finely chopped
1 red bell pepper, peeled, seeded, and cut into strips
2 or 3 beefsteak tomatoes, peeled (see page 174),
    seeded, and chopped
½ cup dry white wine
fresh, chopped parsley, to garnish

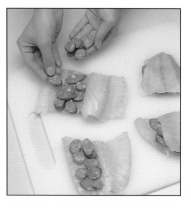

Place eggplant in a colander, sprinkle with salt, and leave 30 minutes. Rinse well and dry with absorbent paper towels. Halve each piece of cod horizontally without cutting completely in half. Open out like a book. Lay one quarter of the chorizo on one "page" of each "book," then cover with other "page." Heat oil in a flameproof casserole, add fish, and cook until evenly browned. Using a fish slice, remove fish from casserole and set aside.

Add onion to casserole and cook slowly, about 7 minutes, stirring occasionally, until soft but not colored. Stir in garlic, eggplant, and bell pepper. Cook about 4 minutes, then add tomatoes and wine and simmer about 20 minutes until vegetables are tender. Season tomato mixture and return fish to casserole. Cook an additional 10 minutes. Garnish with parsley to serve.

Makes 4 servings.

COCONUT CURRIED FISH

6 cloves garlic, chopped
1 in. piece fresh ginger, chopped
1 large fresh red chili, cored, seeded, and chopped
¼ cup vegetable oil
1 large onion, quartered and sliced
2 teaspoons ground cumin
½ teaspoon ground turmeric
1¾ cups coconut milk
salt
1 lb. firm white fish fillet, such as cod or halibut, cut
    into 2 in. pieces
cilantro sprigs and lime wedges, to garnish

Put garlic, ginger, chili, and ⅔ cup water in a blender and mix until smooth.

In a wok or sauté pan over medium heat, heat oil. Add onion and fry 5 to 7 minutes until beginning to color. Add cumin and turmeric and stir 30 seconds. Stir in garlic mixture. Cook, stirring, about 2 minutes until liquid has evaporated.

Pour coconut milk into pan. Bring to boil and bubble until sauce is reduced by half. Add salt to taste. Add fish and spoon sauce over so it is covered. Heat to a simmer and cook gently 4 to 6 minutes until fish just flakes when tested with the point of a sharp knife. Garnish with cilantro sprigs and lime wedges. Serve with rice.

Makes 3 or 4 servings.

FISH COUSCOUS

1 tablespoon vegetable oil
2 onions, chopped
8 oz. baby carrots, trimmed
8 oz. baby turnips, quartered
2 stalks celery, cut into chunks
2½ cups fish stock
salt and freshly ground black pepper
½ teaspoon saffron threads
1½ teaspoons tabil (see Note)
8 oz. baby zucchini, trimmed
1 bunch scallions
2 or 3 medium tomatoes, peeled and quartered
¾ cup shelled fresh peas
2¼ lb. skinless cod fillet, cut into large pieces
2½ cups couscous
harissa, to serve

In a large saucepan, heat oil. Add onions and cook gently 10 minutes until soft. Add carrots, turnips, celery, and stock. Season generously with salt and pepper and add saffron and tabil. Bring to boil, cover, and simmer 10 minutes. Add zucchini and simmer 10 minutes, then add scallions, tomatoes, and peas.

Place fish on top of vegetables, cover, and simmer 10 minutes. Meanwhile, prepare couscous as directed on the package. To serve, pile couscous in a large serving dish and arrange vegetables and fish on top. Stir harissa into broth and pour some over couscous. Serve with extra broth and harissa.

Makes 6 servings.

Note: Tabil is a Tunisian spice mix of coriander, caraway seeds, garlic, and dried crushed chilies.

SEAFOOD GUMBO

2 tablespoons olive oil
2 onions, chopped
2 cloves garlic, crushed
1 green bell pepper, seeded and chopped
1 stalk celery, chopped
2 tablespoons seasoned flour
3 cups fish stock
14½ oz. can chopped tomatoes
½ cup diced cooked ham
bouquet garni
8 oz. fresh okra, sliced
8 oz. white crabmeat, chopped
8 oz. cooked, peeled shrimp
14 oz. firm white fish fillets, cut into chunks
lemon juice and Tabasco sauce, to taste
fresh, chopped parsley, to garnish (optional)

In a heavy, flameproof casserole, heat oil. Add onions and cook until softened. Add garlic, bell pepper, and celery and cook, stirring frequently, 5 minutes. Sprinkle with seasoned flour and stir 1 minute. Stir stock, tomatoes, ham, and bouquet garni into casserole, partially cover, and simmer 30 minutes. Add okra and simmer, covered, 30 minutes.

Add chopped fish fillets to casserole and cook about 7 minutes. Add crabmeat and shrimp and cook about 2½ minutes until shrimp are hot. Add lemon juice and Tabasco sauce to taste. Sprinkle with fresh, chopped parsley. Serve with rice.

Makes 4 to 6 servings.

MONKFISH & ARTICHOKES

¼ cup white wine vinegar
4 globe artichokes
2 tablespoons olive oil
1¼ lb. monkfish fillets, cut into 1½ in. slices
salt and freshly ground black pepper
1 small Spanish onion, finely chopped
4 cloves garlic, chopped
1 cup full-bodied, dry white wine
12 medium tomatoes
8 oil-cured black olives, pitted and halved
2 teaspoons capers
1 bay leaf
1 tablespoon fresh, chopped parsley

Heat oil in a skillet over high heat, add fish, and sear on each side 1 minute. Transfer to a plate and season. Add onion to pan, lower heat to moderate, and cook onion about 4 minutes, stirring occasionally, until softened but not colored. Stir in garlic, cook 1 minute, then add wine and boil until almost evaporated.

Pour water into a saucepan to a depth of about 2 in. and add vinegar. Break or cut off stalk of one artichoke. Snap off and discard outer leaves, starting at bottom and continuing until pale yellow leaves are reached. Cut top two thirds off artichoke. Using a small, sharp knife, pare off any dark green leaves that remain on the artichoke bottom. Cut the bottom into quarters; trim away any purple leaves and remove hairy choke. Cut each quarter into four pieces. Drop into pan.

Stir in tomatoes, olives, capers, bay leaf, and parsley. Boil about 10 minutes until reduced by half.

Repeat with remaining artichokes, then simmer about 15 minutes until tender. Drain and set aside.

Add artichokes and place monkfish on top. Reduce heat to moderate, cover pan, and cook until fish flakes easily, about 10 minutes. Transfer fish to a warmed plate. Boil sauce to thicken slightly, adjust seasoning, and pour over fish.

Makes 4 servings.

SEAFOOD JAMBALAYA

2 tablespoons vegetable oil
1 lb. medium raw shrimp, peeled and deveined
8 oz. sea scallops
8 oz. pork sausage meat
1 tablespoon flour
1 large onion, chopped
3 cloves garlic, chopped
2 stalks celery, thinly sliced
1 green and 1 red bell pepper, diced
1 tablespoon Cajun seasoning mix or chili powder
1¾ cups long-grain rice
14½ oz. can chopped tomatoes
2 cups chicken stock
salt and freshly ground black pepper
1 lb. cooked crayfish tails or meat from 1 crab
fresh, chopped parsley, to garnish

Heat wok until hot, add oil, and swirl to coat wok. Add shrimp and stir-fry 2 or 3 minutes until they turn pink. Remove to a bowl. Add scallops to wok and stir-fry 2 or 3 minutes until opaque and firm. Remove scallops to bowl. Stir sausage meat into wok and stir-fry 4 or 5 minutes until well browned. Stir flour into sausage meat until completely blended, then add onion, garlic, celery, bell peppers, and Cajun seasoning mix or chili powder. Stir-fry 4 or 5 minutes until vegetables begin to soften, then stir in rice.

Add chopped tomatoes with their liquid and chicken stock, stir well, and season with salt and freshly ground black pepper. Bring to simmering point and cook, covered, 20 minutes until rice is tender and liquid is absorbed. Stir in reserved shrimp, scallops, and cooked crayfish tails or crab pieces and cook, covered, an additional 5 minutes until seafood is heated through. Garnish with fresh parsley and serve with rice.

Makes 6 servings.

SEAFOOD & RICE

2 tablespoons olive oil
1 onion, finely chopped
1 clove garlic, crushed
2 tomatoes, peeled (see page 174) and chopped
generous pinch saffron threads
1¾ cups long-grain rice
2½ cups chicken stock
1 teaspoon hot pepper sauce
salt and freshly ground black pepper
1 tablespoon fresh, chopped parsley
1 tablespoon chopped cilantro
1½ cups frozen peas
14 oz. package frozen seafood mixture, thawed
shrimp in shells and cilantro sprigs, to garnish

In a large pan, heat oil. Add onion and garlic and cook 10 minutes until soft. Add tomatoes, saffron, and rice and cook 5 minutes, stirring. Stir in stock, hot pepper sauce, and seasoning and bring to boil. Lower the heat, cover, and simmer 15 minutes.

Carefully stir in parsley, cilantro, peas, and seafood. Cook, covered, 10 minutes until peas and seafood have heated through, rice is tender, and liquid has been absorbed. Add a little water if rice is too dry, or cook a little longer if all the stock has not been absorbed. Garnish with shrimp and cilantro sprigs.

Makes 4 servings.

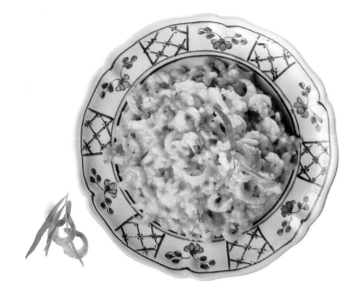

SHRIMP RISOTTO

1¼ lb. small, unpeeled shrimp
bouquet garni
5 black peppercorns
1 clove garlic, crushed
½ onion stuck with 1 clove
1¼ cups medium-bodied, dry white wine
2 shallots, finely chopped
5 tablespoons unsalted butter
pinch saffron threads, toasted and crushed
1½ cups arborio (Italian risotto) rice
2 tablespoons fresh, chopped tarragon
salt and pepper

Peel shrimp and set aside.

Put shrimp shells, bouquet garni, peppercorns, garlic, onion, wine, and 4½ cups water in a saucepan, bring to boil, and simmer 20 minutes. Strain through a strainer, pressing hard on shells. Measure stock up to 5 cups with water if necessary. Bring to boil.

In a thick-bottomed saucepan, cook shallots in half the butter until translucent. Stir in saffron and rice, using a wooden spoon, and cook, stirring, 1 or 2 minutes until rice is well coated and has absorbed butter.

Over moderate heat, stir in about ⅔ cup boiling stock and continue to cook at a steady, but not too violent, boil, stirring constantly, until there is no liquid and rice is creamy. Stir in an additional ⅔ cup boiling stock.

Continue to cook risotto, gradually adding smaller amounts of stock until rice is soft outside but is firm within, creamy, and bound together, neither moist nor dry; about 15 to 20 minutes altogether. Add shrimp toward end of cooking time.

Remove pan from heat, dice remaining butter, and stir in with tarragon. Cover and leave 1 minute for butter to be absorbed. Stir, taste, and add salt, if necessary, then serve immediately.

Makes 4 servings.

Note: Garnish with tarragon sprigs.

BABY CLAM RICE

3 cups Japanese rice
2 tablespoons sake or white wine
2 tablespoons shoyu
1 teaspoon sugar
9 oz. canned baby clams, drained
⅔ teaspoon salt
2 scallions, finely shredded

Put rice in a deep, flameproof casserole and wash well, changing water several times until water becomes clear. Leave to soak in just enough water to cover rice 1 hour.

Meanwhile, in a saucepan, mix sake, shoyu, and sugar over high heat and quickly toss in clams. Skim surface and remove from heat. Pour juice from pan into a measuring cup and keep clams warm in the pan.

Drain rice. Add enough water to cap to make pan juices up to 1 cup and dissolve salt in it. Pour mixture over rice, cover, and place on high heat. Bring to boil and cook 7 or 8 minutes until it sizzles, then lower heat and simmer 10 minutes. Place clams and scallions on top. Cover and cook over high heat 2 seconds. Remove from heat and let stand 10 to 15 minutes. Gently mix clams and scallions into rice. Serve in rice bowls.

Makes 4 to 6 servings.

SPICED MUSSEL LINGUINE

1 tablespoon olive oil
1 red onion, finely chopped
1 red bell pepper, seeded and finely diced
2 cloves garlic, crushed
2 small fresh chilies, seeded and finely chopped
2 teaspoons ground coriander
2 teaspoons ground cumin
14½ oz. can and 8 oz. can chopped tomatoes
⅔ cup dry white wine
2 tablespoons tomato paste
salt and freshly ground black pepper
12 oz. cooked shelled mussels
1 lb. 2 oz. fresh linguine
8 fresh, cooked mussels in their shells
herb sprigs, to garnish

Heat oil in a saucepan, add onion, red bell pepper, garlic, and chilies, and cook 5 minutes, stirring. Add ground coriander and cumin and cook 1 minute, stirring. Stir in chopped tomatoes, wine, tomato paste, and salt and pepper. Bring to boil, then cook, uncovered, over moderate heat about 15 minutes, stirring occasionally, until sauce has thickened slightly. Stir in shelled mussels and cook about 5 minutes, stirring occasionally, until piping hot.

Meanwhile, cook pasta in a large saucepan of lightly salted boiling water 3 minutes or until just cooked or al dente. Drain thoroughly and serve on warmed plates. Spoon mussel sauce over pasta and garnish with fresh mussels in their shells and herb sprigs. Alternatively, toss mussel sauce and cooked pasta together before serving.

Makes 4 servings.

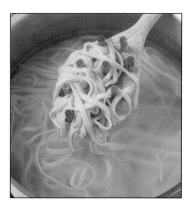

CLAMS WITH ZUCCHINI

2 teaspoons sunflower oil
1 bunch scallions, cut into ½ in. lengths
1 green bell pepper, sliced
4 oz. mushrooms, sliced
2 zucchini, sliced
5 medium tomatoes, peeled and finely chopped
¼ cup dry sherry
1 lb. venus clams, scrubbed
juice 1 lime
1 tablespoon fresh, chopped, mixed herbs
1 tablespoon cornstarch
cooked spaghetti, to serve (optional)

In a large skillet or wok, heat oil and cook scallions and bell pepper 5 minutes.

Add mushrooms, zucchini, tomatoes, and sherry and mix well. Bring gently to boil, cover, and simmer 15 minutes, stirring occasionally. Add clams, lime juice, herbs, and salt and pepper and mix well. Cover and cook 5 minutes, stirring occasionally. In a small bowl, blend cornstarch with 2 tablespoons water and add to the pan.

Cook, stirring, until mixture has thickened, then simmer 3 minutes. Serve with freshly cooked spaghetti.

Makes 6 servings.

Note: Before cooking, discard any cracked or open clams. Once clams have been cooked, discard any unopened ones.

SQUID IN TOMATO SAUCE

1½ lb. squid
2 tablespoons olive oil
1 onion, chopped
1 clove garlic, chopped
14½ oz. can chopped tomatoes
½ cup dry white wine
1 tablespoon tomato paste
2 teaspoons fresh, chopped oregano
GREMOLATA:
2 tablespoons fresh, chopped parsley
grated zest 1 lemon
1 clove garlic, finely chopped

To make gremolata, mix together parsley, lemon zest, and garlic. Set aside.

To clean squid, pull head and tentacles away from body sac, bringing innards with it. Cut off tentacles and reserve. Remove ink sac. Pull transparent "quill" from body. Rinse body and tentacles and dry well. Cut body into rings and cut tentacles in half.

Heat oil in a saucepan. Add onion and garlic and cook 5 minutes until soft. Stir in tomatoes, wine, tomato paste, and oregano and season with salt and pepper. Add squid and bring to boil. Cover and simmer 30 to 40 minutes until squid is tender. Sprinkle with gremolata and serve.

Makes 4 servings.

GREEK SEAFOOD CASSEROLE

1 tablespoon olive oil
1 onion, chopped
1 clove garlic, crushed
1 stalk celery, chopped
grated zest and juice ½ lemon
4 large, ripe tomatoes, peeled (see page 174) and
 chopped
2 tablespoons fresh, chopped parsley
1 fresh bay leaf
1 teaspoon dried oregano
salt and freshly ground black pepper
12 oz. monkfish fillet, skinned and diced
8 oz. squid, cleaned and cut into rings (see opposite)
1 lb. mussels, cleaned
chopped green olives, to garnish

Heat olive oil in a flameproof casserole. Add onion, garlic, and celery and cook 5 minutes until soft. Add lemon zest and juice, tomatoes, parsley, bay leaf, oregano, and salt and pepper. Bring to boil, cover, and simmer 20 minutes. Add monkfish to the casserole, adding a little water if necessary. Return to boil, cover, and cook 3 minutes.

Stir in squid and place mussels on top. Return to boil, cover tightly, and cook 5 minutes until fish is tender and mussels have opened. Discard any mussels that remain closed. Garnish with chopped olives and serve.

Makes 4 servings.

SQUID WITH RED WINE

1½ lb. squid
½ cup olive oil
1 large onion, chopped
2 cloves garlic, crushed
5 medium tomatoes, peeled (see page 174) and
 roughly chopped
⅔ cup red wine
salt and pepper
½ teaspoon sugar
1 in. cinnamon stick
1 tablespoon fresh, chopped parsley
6 slices bread, crusts removed

Clean squid and cut into rings (see opposite). Dry thoroughly with absorbent paper towels. In a large saucepan, heat ¼ cup olive oil. Add onion and garlic and cook until soft. Add squid and fry until lightly browned. Add tomatoes, wine, salt, pepper, sugar, and cinnamon stick. Simmer, uncovered, 30 minutes or until squid is tender. Stir in parsley.

Sauce should be thick and rich. If not, transfer squid to a hot dish and boil sauce to reduce. Cut bread into triangles. In a skillet, heat 3 tablespoons olive oil and fry bread until golden on both sides. Serve squid in individual dishes, with fried bread tucked around the sides.

Makes 6 servings.

SCALLOPS WITH LEMON

4 saffron threads
juice 1 lemon
1 tablespoon olive oil
8 scallops, sliced
1 bunch scallions, sliced
1 clove garlic, crushed
salt and freshly ground black pepper
2 teaspoons sour cream
lemon twists, to garnish

In a bowl, soak saffron in lemon juice 1 hour. Heat oil in a flameproof casserole. Add scallops and cook, stirring, 2 or 3 minutes.

Remove with a slotted spoon and keep warm. Add scallions and garlic to the pan and cook gently, stirring occasionally, 3 minutes until soft. Strain lemon juice, discarding saffron stands. Add lemon juice to the casserole and stir well to incorporate all the juices.

Season with salt and pepper. Remove from the heat and stir in sour cream. Arrange scallops on individual serving plates and spoon over sauce. Garnish with twists of lemon and serve.

Makes 4 servings.

Note: If scallops still have their roe attached when you buy them, you can use that in the dish, too.

SEAFOOD PAELLA

3 tablespoons olive oil
9 oz. monkfish fillet, skinned and diced
1 Spanish onion, chopped
2 cloves garlic, finely chopped
1 green bell pepper, diced
1⅓ cups arborio (Italian risotto) rice
3 cups fish stock
⅔ cup dry white wine
3 ripe tomatoes, peeled (see page 174) and chopped
1 teaspoon saffron threads
14 oz. mixed, cooked shellfish
¾ cup shelled fresh peas

Heat olive oil in a large skillet. Add monkfish and cook 5 minutes.

Remove with a slotted spoon and set aside. Add onion and garlic to the pan and cook 5 minutes until soft. Add pepper and cook 2 minutes. Add rice and stir to coat with oil. Pour in stock and wine and add tomatoes and saffron. Bring to boil and simmer, uncovered, 20 minutes.

Add monkfish and cook 5 to 10 minutes until most of the stock has been absorbed and rice is tender. Reserve some shellfish for garnish and add remainder to the pan with peas. Cook 5 minutes until heated through. Add a little more stock if necessary. Season with salt and pepper, garnish with reserved shellfish, and serve.

Makes 4 servings.

CHICKEN & TURKEY

CHICKEN VEGETABLE STEW

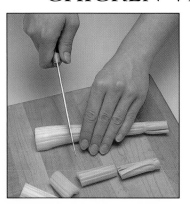

½ stick butter
4 slices smoked bacon, chopped
2 large chicken quarters, halved
2 carrots, peeled and sliced
1 onion, sliced
2 stalks celery, cut into 2 in. lengths
2 leeks, trimmed and sliced
2 tablespoons all-purpose flour
6 medium potatoes, peeled
2 tablespoons fresh, chopped thyme
2 tablespoons fresh, chopped parsley
salt and pepper
2 cups chicken stock

Preheat oven to 300°F. Heat half the butter in a skillet, add bacon and chicken, and fry until golden. Remove from the pan and drain on absorbent paper towels to remove excess fat. Add carrots, onion, celery, and leeks to the pan and fry 2 or 3 minutes until vegetables are turning golden. Sprinkle with flour and mix well.

Slice potatoes into ¼ in. thick slices. Arrange half the slices in the bottom of a casserole, add chicken and bacon, cover with vegetables and chopped thyme and parsley, and season well with salt and pepper. Cover with remaining sliced potato, dot with remaining butter, and pour over stock. Cover and bake 1 hour, then uncover and continue cooking an additional 25 to 30 minutes until chicken is tender and cooked and potatoes are crisp and browned.

Makes 4 servings.

LENTIL-BAKED CHICKEN

1¼ cups green lentils
2 tablespoons butter
1 tablespoon olive oil
3½ lb. chicken
6 slices smoked bacon
12 shallots, halved
4 cloves garlic, thickly sliced
⅔ cup dry white wine
1¼ cups chicken stock
1 bouquet garni
fresh, chopped parsley, to garnish

Preheat oven to 400°F. Place lentils in a pan of salted water, bring to boil, and simmer 15 minutes.

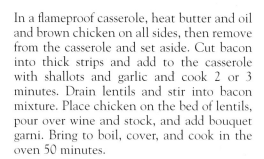

In a flameproof casserole, heat butter and oil and brown chicken on all sides, then remove from the casserole and set aside. Cut bacon into thick strips and add to the casserole with shallots and garlic and cook 2 or 3 minutes. Drain lentils and stir into bacon mixture. Place chicken on the bed of lentils, pour over wine and stock, and add bouquet garni. Bring to boil, cover, and cook in the oven 50 minutes.

Remove the lid of the casserole, add a little water if lentil mixture is looking too dry, and return to the oven, uncovered, an additional 35 to 40 minutes until juices of the chicken run clear when pierced. Remove bouquet garni and garnish with fresh, chopped parsley.

Makes 4 to 6 servings.

CHICKEN & VEGETABLES

1 tablespoon oil
4 slices smoked bacon, chopped
2 cloves garlic, peeled
12 shallots, peeled
1 stalk celery, cut into 1 in. lengths
2 small turnips, peeled and quartered
2 carrots, peeled and cut into matchstick strips
8 oz. button mushrooms
⅔ cup dry white wine
⅔ cup chicken stock
3 lb. chicken, without giblets
¼ cup heavy cream
juice ½ lemon
salt and pepper

COQ AU VIN

2½ cups red wine
3 cloves garlic, sliced
1 small onion, chopped
2 tablespoons olive oil
1 teaspoon brown sugar
1 teaspoon mixed peppercorns, crushed
1 teaspoon coriander, crushed
1 bouquet garni
3½ lb. chicken, cut into 8 pieces
3 tablespoons seasoned flour
4 oz. piece smoked bacon, diced
6 baby onions, peeled
6 oz. button mushrooms
2 cups chicken stock
2 tablespoons chopped parsley
croutons, to garnish

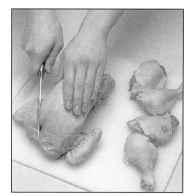

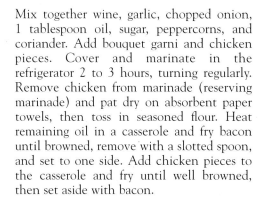

Preheat oven to 400°F. In a flameproof casserole, heat oil. Add bacon, garlic, and shallots and fry 2 or 3 minutes. Add celery, turnips, carrots, and mushrooms and fry an additional 2 or 3 minutes until bacon is starting to turn golden brown. Pour wine over vegetables and boil rapidly to reduce liquid by half. Add chicken stock. Remove the casserole from the heat and add chicken. Cover and cook in the oven 45 to 55 minutes.

Mix together wine, garlic, chopped onion, 1 tablespoon oil, sugar, peppercorns, and coriander. Add bouquet garni and chicken pieces. Cover and marinate in the refrigerator 2 to 3 hours, turning regularly. Remove chicken from marinade (reserving marinade) and pat dry on absorbent paper towels, then toss in seasoned flour. Heat remaining oil in a casserole and fry bacon until browned, remove with a slotted spoon, and set to one side. Add chicken pieces to the casserole and fry until well browned, then set aside with bacon.

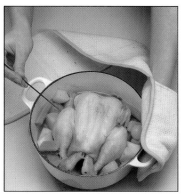

To check if chicken is done, test with a meat thermometer. When cooked, remove chicken and vegetables to a serving dish. Cover and keep warm. Return the casserole to the heat, skim off any fat, and boil vigorously to reduce to just over ⅔ cup. Add cream and simmer 2 minutes; add lemon juice and salt and pepper. Serve hot with chicken.

Makes 4 servings.

Add baby onions and cook until browned. Add mushrooms and any remaining flour. Cook 1 minute. Add stock and marinade, stirring until thick. Return chicken and bacon, cover, and simmer 40 minutes. Remove chicken and vegetables to a serving dish with a slotted spoon; keep warm. Bring sauce to boil and cook 3 or 4 minutes until thick. Check seasoning and stir in parsley. Spoon sauce over chicken and garnish with croutons.

Makes 4 servings.

BRAISED CHICKEN WITH SPICES

4 cloves garlic, chopped
2 shallots, chopped
2 in. piece fresh ginger, chopped
1¾ cups coconut milk
2 teaspoons ground coriander
2 teaspoons ground cumin
¼ teaspoon ground turmeric
2 tablespoons vegetable oil
6 green cardamom pods
6 star anise
6 dried red chilies
1 cinnamon stick
4 cloves
20 fresh curry leaves
4 each chicken thighs and drumsticks, total weight
   about 2¼ lb., skinless

Put garlic, shallots, ginger, coconut milk, coriander, cumin, and turmeric into a small blender. Mix to a fine purée. In a heavy-bottomed saucepan, large enough to hold chicken in a single layer, heat oil over medium heat. Add cardamom, star anise, chilies, cinnamon stick, cloves, and curry leaves. Fry, stirring, 2 or 3 minutes. Add one third of the coconut milk mixture. Bring to boil, then add chicken pieces. Turn to coat, then cook 5 minutes.

Add remaining coconut milk mixture. Bring to a simmer, then lower heat and cook gently, uncovered, 50 minutes, stirring frequently. Cook an additional 10 minutes, stirring every minute. The chicken should be golden brown and most of the milk evaporated. Pour away oily residue. Increase heat to high. Add 3 or 4 tablespoons water and stir to deglaze pan. Serve chicken with Thai rice and sauce.

Makes 4 servings.

CHICKEN IN SPICED SAUCE

2 tablespoons vegetable oil
6 each chicken thighs and drumsticks
2 lemongrass stalks, chopped
4 shallots, chopped
4 cloves garlic, chopped
2½ in. piece fresh ginger, chopped
3 tablespoons ground coriander
2 teaspoons ground turmeric
4 fresh bay leaves
1½ cups coconut milk
¼ cup Chinese chili sauce
about 2 tablespoons brown sugar, or to taste
⅓ cup roasted cashews, finely chopped
salt

In a large skillet over medium heat, heat oil. Add chicken and brown evenly. Transfer to absorbent paper towels to drain. Pour all but 1½ tablespoons fat from the pan. Put lemongrass, shallots, garlic, and ginger in a blender and mix to a paste. Gently heat pan of fat, add spice paste, and stir 2 minutes. Stir in coriander, turmeric, and bay leaves and cook 1 minute. Stir in coconut milk, chili sauce, sugar, nuts, and salt and cook an additional 1 minute.

Return chicken to pan and turn in sauce. Cover and cook gently 20 minutes, stirring and turning chicken frequently, until chicken juices run clear. Discard bay leaves before serving.

Makes 6 servings.

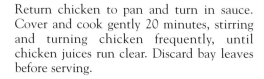

DEVIL'S CURRY

⅓ cup vegetable oil
6 shallots, thinly sliced
3 cloves garlic, thinly sliced
1 teaspoon black mustard seeds, lightly crushed
3½ lb. chicken, jointed, or small chicken portions
6 small potatoes, halved
2 teaspoons mustard powder
2 tablespoons rice vinegar
1 tablespoon dark soy sauce
SPICE PASTE
10 fresh red chilies, cored, seeded, and chopped
2 in. piece fresh ginger, chopped
6 shallots, chopped
3 cloves garlic, chopped
1 tablespoon ground coriander
½ teaspoon ground turmeric
8 cashews

To make spice paste, put chilies, ginger, chopped shallots and garlic, coriander, turmeric, and cashews in a blender and mix to a paste. In a large wok or sauté pan, heat oil over medium-high heat. Add sliced shallots and garlic and fry until lightly browned. Stir in spice paste and cook about 5 minutes, stirring. Add mustard seeds, stir once or twice, then add chicken. Cook, stirring frequently, until chicken pieces turn white.

Add potatoes and 2½ cups water. Bring to boil, cover, then simmer 15 minutes. Stir together mustard powder, rice vinegar, and soy sauce. Stir into pan, cover, and cook an additional 15 to 20 minutes until chicken is tender, stirring occasionally.

Makes 4 to 6 servings.

AROMATIC CHICKEN

2 teaspoons tamarind paste
salt
3½ lb. chicken, cut into 10 pieces, or chicken portions, chopped
12 fresh green chilies, cored, seeded, and chopped
2 small onions, chopped
5 cloves garlic, crushed
1 ripe tomato, chopped
⅓ cup vegetable oil
4 kaffir lime leaves
1 stalk lemongrass, crushed

Blend tamarind paste with 1 teaspoon salt and 2 tablespoons hot water. Pour mixture over chicken and rub in. Let stand 1 hour.

Put chilies, onions, garlic, and tomato in a blender. Mix to a paste. In a wok or large, heavy sauté pan, heat oil. Add chicken and marinade. Turn to brown on both sides, then remove with a slotted spoon.

Add spice paste, lime leaves, and lemongrass to pan. Cook, stirring, 6 or 7 minutes until paste is browned. Return chicken to pan, add 1¼ cups water, and bring to a simmer. Cover and simmer gently 30 minutes until chicken juices run clear, turning chicken occasionally.

Makes 4 servings.

JAMBALAYA

1 tablespoon olive oil
1 tablespoon butter
12 oz. boneless, skinless chicken
6 oz. chorizo sausage
1 onion, thinly sliced
2 cloves garlic, sliced
1 red bell pepper, sliced
1 yellow bell pepper, sliced
1 green bell pepper, sliced
4 oz. mushrooms, sliced
¾ cup long-grain rice
½ teaspoon ground allspice
1¼ cups chicken stock
⅔ cup white wine
4 oz. large, cooked, peeled shrimp
lime wedges and whole shrimp, to garnish

In a large skillet or paella pan, heat oil and butter. Cut chicken into thick strips and fry until well browned, then remove from the pan and set aside. Cut chorizo into chunks and fry 1 minute, stirring well, then with a slotted spoon, remove from the pan and add to chicken. Fry onion and garlic until slightly softened, add bell peppers, mushrooms, rice, and allspice, and cook an additional 1 minute.

Pour in stock and wine and bring to boil. Return chicken and chorizo to pan and simmer, uncovered, 15 to 20 minutes until liquid is absorbed and rice tender. Stir in shrimp, cook an additional 5 minutes, then season to taste. Serve garnished with wedges of lime and whole shrimp.

Makes 4 servings.

CHICKEN CHILI TACOS

2 tablespoons oil
1 lb. chicken fillet, diced
8 scallions, chopped into 1 in. pieces
1 green bell pepper, chopped
1 clove garlic, crushed
2 fresh green chilies, seeded and finely chopped
1 teaspoon each fresh basil and oregano
14½ oz. can chopped tomatoes
2 teaspoons chili sauce
2 teaspoons tomato paste
1 teaspoon sugar
7 oz. can red kidney beans, drained
salt and pepper
8 taco shells
1 head iceberg lettuce, shredded
⅔ cup sour cream

In a large pan, heat oil and fry chicken 2 or 3 minutes. Add scallions, bell pepper, garlic, chilies, basil, and oregano and cook an additional 2 minutes. Add chopped tomatoes, chili sauce, tomato paste, sugar, kidney beans, and salt and pepper and simmer 20 to 25 minutes or until sauce starts to thicken.

Spoon some shredded lettuce into each taco shell, top with chili chicken, and spoon over a little sour cream.

Makes 4 servings.

Variation: Use a mixture of shredded cheese, chopped sun-dried tomatoes, and chopped olives as a topping for tacos.

LEMON CHICKEN WITH BASIL

CHICKEN & ZUCCHINI PASTA

finely grated zest 1 lemon
juice 2 lemons
2 cloves garlic, crushed
1 tablespoon olive oil
¼ cup fresh, chopped basil
salt and freshly ground black pepper
1 lb. chicken fillets, diced
1 onion, sliced
3 stalks celery, thinly sliced
6 oz. button mushrooms, halved
2 tablespoons all-purpose flour
⅔ cup chicken stock
⅔ cup dry white wine
lemon zest, lemon twists, and basil sprigs, to garnish
freshly cooked linguine, to serve (optional)

½ stick butter
6 shallots, thinly sliced
3 zucchini, cut into matchstick strips
1 cup dry white wine
12 oz. dried fusilli lunghi (long fusilli pasta)
salt and freshly ground black pepper
12 oz. cooked chicken fillet, cut into strips
1 tablespoon fresh, chopped tarragon
1¼ cups sour cream
1 cup finely grated Parmesan cheese
tarragon sprigs, to garnish

Melt butter in a saucepan, add shallots and zucchini, and cook gently 10 minutes, stirring occasionally, until softened.

In a bowl, mix together lemon zest and juice, garlic, 2 teaspoons oil, 2 tablespoons basil, and salt and pepper. Add chicken and mix well. Cover and chill 1 hour. Heat remaining 1 teaspoon oil in a large skillet or wok and cook onion 3 minutes. Remove chicken from marinade with a slotted spoon, reserving marinade, and add chicken to the pan. Cook until chicken is lightly browned. Add celery and mushrooms and cook 2 minutes.

Add wine and cook over moderate heat until reduced by half. Meanwhile, cook pasta in a large pan of lightly salted boiling water 10 to 12 minutes until al dente. Add chicken, chopped tarragon, and salt and pepper to shallot mixture, reduce heat, and cook 2 minutes, stirring.

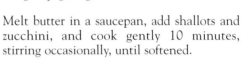

Add flour and cook 1 minute, stirring. Remove pan from heat and gradually add stock, wine, and marinade. Bring to boil and cook, stirring, until mixture thickens. Cover and simmer gently 15 minutes, stirring occasionally. Stir in remaining basil. Garnish and serve with freshly cooked linguine.

Makes 4 servings.

Stir in sour cream and heat gently until hot and bubbling. Stir in Parmesan. Drain pasta thoroughly and return to the rinsed-out pan. Add chicken sauce and toss well to mix. Serve on warmed plates and garnish with tarragon sprigs.

Makes 4 servings.

Variation: Use cooked turkey breast or cooked flaked salmon instead of chicken.

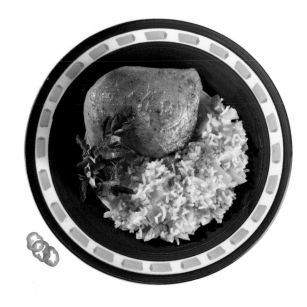

SPICY CHICKEN

CHILI CHICKEN WITH RICE

2 cloves garlic, crushed
½ in. piece fresh ginger, peeled and very thinly sliced
1 tablespoon soy sauce
½ teaspoon five-spice powder
3 lb. chicken, cut into 8 pieces
2 tablespoons olive oil
2 onions, thinly sliced
1 red bell pepper, thinly sliced
8 plum tomatoes, peeled, quartered, and seeded
2 tablespoons chopped cilantro

In a large bowl, mix together garlic, ginger, soy sauce, and five-spice powder. Add chicken and turn to coat. Cover and let marinate 2 hours. Preheat oven to 350°F.

Heat oil in a large, flameproof casserole. Add onions and bell pepper, cover, and cook gently 10 to 15 minutes until soft but not colored. Add tomatoes.

Add chicken and marinade, cover, and cook in the oven 25 to 30 minutes until chicken is cooked through. Sprinkle with cilantro and serve.

Makes 4 servings.

4 chicken portions
salt and freshly ground black pepper
⅔ cup chicken stock
⅔ cup dry white wine
1 teaspoon chili sauce
1¼ cups basmati rice
1 onion, chopped
1 yellow bell pepper, chopped
1 fresh green chili, cored, seeded, and chopped
14½ oz. can chopped tomatoes
Italian parsley sprigs, to garnish

Preheat oven to 425°F. Place chicken portions in a large, flameproof casserole. Season with salt and pepper.

Cook in the oven 20 minutes. Remove chicken from the casserole and keep warm. Lower oven temperature to 375°F. Add stock, white wine, chili sauce, and ½ cup boiling water to the casserole. Add rice, onion, and bell pepper. Stir in chopped green chili and tomatoes.

Place chicken on top of rice mixture. Cover and bake 45 minutes until rice is tender and liquid has been absorbed. Garnish with Italian parsley and serve.

Makes 4 servings.

CHICKEN BLANQUETTE

4 slices thick-cut bacon, diced
1 tablespoon butter
1 small onion, chopped
4 chicken fillets
1 lb. celery, chopped
1 bay leaf
1 cup dry white wine or chicken stock
⅔ cup sour cream
salt and freshly ground black pepper

Heat a flameproof casserole, add bacon, and dry-fry until fat runs. Remove with a slotted spoon and set aside.

Heat butter in casserole, add onion, and cook, stirring occasionally, 2 or 3 minutes. Add chicken and celery and cook, stirring occasionally and turning chicken once or twice, 5 minutes. Add bacon, bay leaf, wine or stock, and enough water to cover. Bring to boil, cover, and simmer gently 30 minutes until chicken is tender.

Remove chicken, bacon, and vegetables with a slotted spoon, transfer to a warmed plate, and keep warm. Boil cooking liquid to thicken slightly. Discard bay leaf, stir in cream, return to boil, and simmer 3 to 4 minutes. Return chicken, bacon, and vegetables to casserole, season with salt and pepper, and heat gently to warm through.

Makes 4 servings.

FLEMISH BRAISED CHICKEN

½ stick butter
4 lb. chicken
1 lb. leeks, sliced
2 or 3 carrots, sliced
½ head celery, chopped
4 oz. button mushrooms, halved
2½ cups chicken stock
2 bay leaves
12 small new potatoes
1 cup dry white wine
⅓ cup heavy cream
2 egg yolks

Melt butter in a flameproof casserole. Add chicken and brown all over.

Remove from the casserole. Preheat oven to 400°F. Add leeks, carrots, celery, and mushrooms to the casserole and stir well. Cover and cook 5 to 10 minutes until soft. Add stock and bay leaves. Bring to boil and add chicken. Cover and cook in the oven 30 minutes. Add potatoes and cook 30 minutes. Lift out chicken and remove vegetables with a slotted spoon. Keep warm.

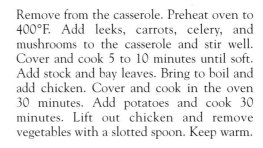

Add wine to the casserole and bring to boil. Reduce to a simmer. In a large bowl, mix together cream and egg yolks. Pour simmering stock onto cream mixture, stirring constantly. Return to the casserole and heat gently. Do not boil. Return vegetables to the casserole. Carve chicken, garnish with parsley, and serve with vegetables and sauce.

Makes 6 servings.

CHICKEN WITH OLIVES

3 cloves garlic, crushed, or 1 tablespoon garlic paste
1 teaspoon paprika
1 teaspoon ground ginger
½ teaspoon ground cumin
¼ cup olive oil
4 skinless chicken fillets
1 large onion, finely chopped
¼ cup fresh, chopped parsley
pinch saffron threads
⅔ cup chicken stock
12 green olives
finely grated zest and juice ½ lemon

Mix garlic, paprika, ginger, and cumin with 3 tablespoons olive oil.

Place chicken portions in a shallow dish, sprinkle with spice mix, and let marinate 3 to 4 hours. Heat remaining oil in a pan, add onion, and cook gently 2 or 3 minutes. Add chicken pieces and marinade to pan and brown chicken slightly. Add parsley, saffron, and chicken stock, cover, and simmer 30 minutes or until chicken is cooked.

Remove chicken from the pan and keep warm. Add olives and lemon zest and juice, and season with a little salt and pepper. Bring to boil and boil rapidly until reduced to approximately ⅔ cup. Pour over chicken and serve immediately.

Makes 4 servings.

BOURRIDE OF CHICKEN

2 tablespoons olive oil
3 lb. chicken, cut into 8 pieces
4 shallots, chopped
1 leek, chopped
⅔ cup dry white wine
½ teaspoon saffron threads
cooked baby leeks, to serve
GARLIC SAUCE:
8 cloves garlic
⅔ cup mayonnaise

Heat olive oil in a flameproof casserole. Add chicken pieces and cook until browned all over. Remove with a slotted spoon and set aside.

Add shallots and leek to the casserole and cook 3 minutes until soft. Return chicken to the casserole and add wine and saffron. Bring to boil, cover, and simmer 30 to 40 minutes until chicken is cooked through. Meanwhile, make garlic sauce. Put unpeeled garlic cloves in a small saucepan and cover with water. Bring to boil and simmer 15 minutes until soft. Drain and let cool.

Put mayonnaise in a food processor or blender. Squeeze softened garlic out of skins into the food processor or blender. Remove chicken from the casserole and place on a warmed serving dish. Add cooking juices to the food processor or blender and quickly process. Pour over chicken. Serve with baby leeks.

Makes 4 servings.

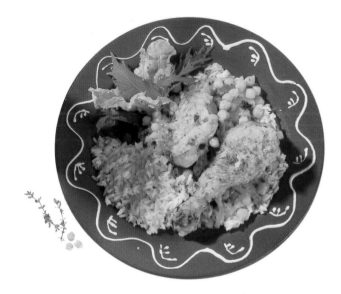

SAFFRON CHICKEN CASSEROLE

⅔ cup dried chickpeas
½ teaspoon paprika
½ teaspoon each ground cumin and ground coriander
4½ lb. chicken, cut into pieces
½ stick butter
1 tablespoon vegetable oil
2 large mild onions, thinly sliced
½ teaspoon saffron threads
about 4 cups chicken stock
1 thyme sprig
¼ cup fresh, chopped parsley
1¼ cups long-grain rice, to serve

Place chickpeas in a bowl. Cover with cold water and leave overnight to soak.

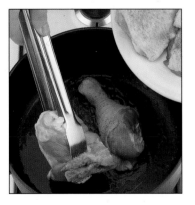

Drain chickpeas and place in a saucepan, cover with water, and bring to boil. Boil 1 hour. In a bowl, mix together paprika, cumin, and coriander and add salt and pepper. Toss chicken pieces in the mixture. Heat butter and oil in a large, flameproof casserole. Add chicken pieces and sauté until browned. Transfer to a plate. Add onions to the casserole and cook 10 minutes until soft. Return chicken pieces to the casserole and add chickpeas.

Add saffron threads to stock and pour over chicken to cover. Bring to boil and add thyme. Cover and simmer gently about 1 hour or until chicken is tender. Stir in chopped parsley and check seasoning. Meanwhile, cook rice in boiling salted water about 12 minutes. To serve, drain rice and arrange half of it in a heated serving dish. Place chicken and onions on top and pour over as much saffron sauce as desired. Add remaining rice and serve with salad.

Makes 6 servings.

CHICKEN TAGINE

2 lemons
2 tablespoons vegetable oil, plus oil for frying
1 onion, chopped
3½ lb. chicken, cut into pieces
1 teaspoon ground cumin
1 teaspoon ground paprika
1 teaspoon ground ginger
large pinch saffron threads, crushed
1 cinnamon stick
salt and freshly ground black pepper
½ cup pitted green olives
peel from 1 preserved lemon, cut into strips
2 tablespoons chopped cilantro
1 tablespoon fresh, chopped parsley
harissa, to serve

With a zester, remove zest from lemons and place in a bowl. Sprinkle with juice and set aside. In a heavy-bottomed casserole, heat oil. Add onion and cook 10 minutes until soft. Remove onion and add chicken pieces. Cook until browned all over. Stir in cumin, paprika, ginger, saffron, and cinnamon stick. Cook 1 minute, then return onions to the casserole. Pour in 1 cup water. Season with salt and pepper and bring to boil. Cover and simmer gently 45 minutes.

Stir in olives, preserved lemon peel, cilantro, and parsley and cook an additional 10 to 15 minutes until chicken is cooked. Meanwhile, drain lemon zest and pat dry with absorbent paper towels. In a small saucepan, heat ½ in. oil. Add zest, which will crisp almost immediately. Quickly drain off oil through a strainer. Serve chicken and sauce sprinkled with fried lemon zest. Serve with bread and harissa.

Makes 6 servings.

CHICKEN & WILD MUSHROOMS

LEMON & CHILI CHICKEN

¼ cup olive oil
2 cloves garlic, crushed
4 chicken fillets
⅔ cup dry white vermouth
salt and pepper
1 lb. mixed wild mushrooms or a mixture of
   cultivated mushrooms, e.g., brown cap, shiitake,
   and oyster
2 tablespoons fresh, chopped oregano
oregano sprigs, to garnish

Heat half the olive oil in a sauté pan. Add
garlic and cook 2 minutes until golden. Add
chicken fillets, skin-side down, and brown
well on all sides.

Pour in vermouth and season well with salt
and pepper. Bring to boil, cover, and simmer
20 to 30 minutes until tender.

Meanwhile, halve or slice mushrooms, if
large. Heat remaining oil, add mushrooms,
and sauté 3 to 5 minutes until browned and
tender, but still firm. Gently stir mushrooms
and any cooking juices into chicken with
chopped oregano. Garnish with oregano
sprigs and serve at once, with rice.

Makes 4 servings.

3½ lb. chicken, cut into 8 pieces
4 ripe, juicy lemons
8 cloves garlic
1 small red chili, seeded and chopped
1 tablespoon honey
¼ cup fresh, chopped parsley
salt and freshly ground black pepper

Place chicken portions in a shallow,
ovenproof baking dish. Squeeze juice from
lemons and pour into a small bowl. Reserve
lemon halves.

Peel and crush 2 garlic cloves and add to
lemon juice with chili and honey. Stir well
and pour mixture over chicken, tucking
lemon halves around portions. Cover and let
marinate for at least 2 hours, turning once or
twice. Preheat oven to 400°F.

Turn chicken skin-side up and place lemon
halves cut-side down around portions
with remaining whole garlic. Roast in oven
45 minutes or until golden brown and
tender. Stir in parsley, taste, and season.
Garnish with roasted lemon halves and serve
with mashed potatoes.

Makes 4 servings.

GARLIC ROASTED CHICKEN

2 tablespoons olive oil
6 cloves garlic, thinly sliced
8 chicken thighs
4 oz. fennel, cut into wide strips
1 carrot, cut into wide strips
1 parsnip, cut into wide strips
1 large potato, diced
1 red bell pepper, diced
1 green bell pepper, diced

CHICKEN CRUMBLE

1 tablespoon olive oil
1 lb. skinless chicken fillet, diced
1 leek, sliced
8 oz. mushrooms, thinly sliced
¾ cup frozen peas
2 cups plain yogurt
2 teaspoons whole-grain mustard
salt and freshly ground black pepper
⅔ cup rolled oats
½ cup whole-wheat flour
½ stick butter
1 cup fresh whole-wheat bread crumbs
1 tablespoon finely grated Parmesan cheese
2 teaspoons dried thyme
1 tablespoon sesame seeds
thyme sprigs, to garnish

Preheat oven to 425°F. Heat oil in a shallow, flameproof dish. Add garlic and cook 2 or 3 minutes. Add chicken, fennel, carrot, parsnip, potato, and bell peppers and turn to coat.

Heat oil in a large, flameproof casserole. Add diced chicken and cook, stirring, until golden on all sides. Add leek and cook, stirring occasionally, 10 minutes until leek is soft. Preheat oven to 400°F. Add mushrooms and peas to casserole and cook 3 to 5 minutes until peas have thawed. Remove from the heat and stir in yogurt, mustard, and salt and pepper.

Roast 55 to 60 minutes until chicken is cooked through and golden.

Makes 4 servings.

Put oats and flour in a bowl and cut in butter until mixture resembles bread crumbs. Stir in whole-wheat bread crumbs, Parmesan cheese, thyme, and sesame seeds. Sprinkle mixture evenly over the top of chicken and bake 40 to 45 minutes until topping is golden brown. Garnish with thyme sprigs and serve.

Makes 4 servings.

POULET PROVENÇAL

10 cloves garlic
1 tablespoon fresh, finely chopped thyme
1 tablespoon fresh, finely chopped marjoram
salt and freshly ground black pepper
3½ lb. chicken, cut into 8 pieces
2 tablespoons lemon juice
¼ cup olive oil
1 small rosemary sprig
1 thyme sprig
6 basil leaves, shredded
8 anchovy fillets, drained and chopped
4 beefsteak tomatoes, peeled (see page 174), seeded, and chopped
⅔ cup dry white wine
24 Niçoise olives
fresh, chopped herbs and basil sprigs, to garnish

Crush two garlic cloves and mix with fresh, chopped thyme and marjoram and a small pinch of salt. Cut small incisions in chicken pieces and insert a little herb mixture into each incision. Rub chicken with lemon juice and pepper and let stand in a cool place 2 hours. Preheat oven to 325°F. Heat half the oil in a saucepan. Finely chop remaining garlic and add to pan with rosemary, thyme, and basil. Cook, stirring occasionally, 5 minutes. Stir in anchovy fillets, tomatoes, wine, and bell pepper. Bring to boil and simmer 15 minutes.

Heat remaining oil in a heavy, flameproof casserole, add chicken, and cook until browned all over. Pour over sauce, cover, and cook in the oven 45 minutes, turning chicken once or twice. Add olives and cook an additional 15 minutes. Garnish with mixed fresh herbs and basil sprigs and serve.

Makes 4 servings.

Note: Niçoise olives have a special flavor, as they are marinated in oil and herbs. If they are not available, use plain black olives.

CIDER APPLE CHICKEN

pared peel from 1 lemon plus 1 teaspoon juice
½ cinnamon stick
1 onion, quartered
3½ lb. chicken
salt and pepper
¾ stick butter
1 tablespoon oil
3 tablespoons brandy
4 dessert apples, peeled and cored
⅔ cup cider
1¼ cups sour cream
1 tablespoon each fresh, chopped chives and parsley

Place lemon peel, cinnamon stick, and onion inside chicken. Season well.

Preheat oven to 350°F. In a flameproof casserole, heat ½ stick butter and oil and brown chicken on all sides. Sprinkle with brandy and ignite. Thinly slice one of the apples and add to the casserole once the flames have died down. Add cider to the casserole, bring to boil, cover, and cook in the oven 1¼ hours.

Melt remaining butter in a pan, cut remaining apples into thick slices, and sauté until just cooked. Remove chicken from the casserole, place on a warmed serving platter, and surround with sautéed apples. Add sour cream and lemon juice to the casserole, stir well, and boil to reduce slightly. Season well and pour over chicken. Sprinkle with chopped chives and parsley and serve.

Makes 4 to 6 servings.

CHICKEN PUTTANESCA

¼ cup olive oil
1 red onion, chopped
2 cloves garlic, crushed
2 oz. can anchovies in olive oil, drained
9 black olives, pitted
¼ cup sun-dried tomatoes
14½ oz. can chopped tomatoes
½ teaspoon crushed, dried chilies
2 teaspoons fresh, chopped oregano
1 tablespoon balsamic vinegar
8 skinless, boneless chicken thighs
oregano sprigs, to garnish

Heat half the oil in a large saucepan. Add onion and garlic and cook 5 minutes.

Chop anchovies, olives, and sun-dried tomatoes. Add to the pan with tomatoes, chilies, oregano, balsamic vinegar, and salt and pepper. Bring to boil. Heat remaining oil in a large skillet. Add chicken and cook until browned all over.

Remove with a slotted spoon and add to the saucepan. Turn to coat with sauce. Cover and simmer 30 minutes or until chicken is cooked through. Garnish with oregano sprigs and serve.

Makes 4 servings.

BURGUNDY CHICKEN

2 tablespoons butter
4 chicken legs
1 shallot, finely chopped
2 tablespoons Marc de Bourgogne or brandy
1 cup white Burgundy or other Chardonnay wine
2 thyme sprigs
salt and freshly ground black pepper
1 cup seedless green grapes, halved
¼ cup heavy cream
Italian parsley and thyme sprigs, to garnish

Heat butter in a heavy, flameproof casserole, add chicken, and cook until browned all over. Remove and drain on absorbent paper towels.

Add shallot to casserole and cook, stirring occasionally, 2 or 3 minutes until soft. Return chicken to casserole. Sprinkle with Marc de Bourgogne or brandy and ignite. When flames have died down, add wine, thyme, and salt and pepper.

Bring to boil, cover, and simmer very gently, turning chicken 2 or 3 times, 50 to 60 minutes. Transfer chicken to warmed serving plates and keep warm. Add grapes to casserole and boil until sauce is thickened slightly. Stir in cream and simmer to thicken slightly. Pour over chicken, garnish with Italian parsley and thyme, and serve.

Makes 4 servings.

COUNTRY-STYLE CHICKEN

CHICKEN ITALIENNE

2 teaspoons olive oil
1 onion, sliced
2 cloves garlic, crushed
1 green bell pepper, sliced
2 carrots, sliced
1 lb. chicken fillets, cut into thin strips
2 slices lean smoked bacon, diced
6 oz. button mushrooms
2 cups chicken stock
3 tablespoons tomato paste
1 teaspoon dried, mixed herbs
salt and freshly ground black pepper
1 tablespoon cornstarch
marjoram sprigs, to garnish

1 lb. chicken fillets, diced
2 tablespoons seasoned flour
2 teaspoons olive oil
12 baby onions, halved
1 clove garlic, crushed
1 cup chicken stock
¾ cup dry white wine
8 oz. can chopped tomatoes
1 tablespoon tomato paste
1 tablespoon fresh, chopped, mixed herbs
salt and freshly ground black pepper
Italian parsley, to garnish

Toss chicken in seasoned flour.

In a large skillet or wok, heat oil, add onion, garlic, bell pepper, and carrots, and cook 5 minutes. Add chicken and bacon and cook until chicken is lightly browned all over, stirring occasionally. Stir in mushrooms, stock, tomato paste, mixed herbs, and salt and pepper, mixing well. Bring slowly to boil, cover, and simmer gently 15 minutes until chicken is cooked and tender, stirring occasionally.

In a large saucepan, heat oil and cook onions and garlic 5 minutes. Add chicken and cook until lightly browned all over. Gradually stir in stock and wine, then add tomatoes, tomato paste, herbs, and salt and pepper, mixing well.

In a small bowl, blend cornstarch with 2 tablespoons water and add to the pan. Bring back to boil and continue to cook, stirring continuously, until mixture thickens. Simmer 2 or 3 minutes. Garnish with marjoram sprigs and serve with freshly cooked pasta.

Makes 6 servings.

Bring slowly to boil, cover, and simmer 25 minutes, stirring occasionally, until chicken is cooked and tender. Garnish with Italian parsley and serve with freshly cooked linguine or fettucine.

Makes 6 servings.

THAI RED CURRY CHICKEN

2 teaspoons olive oil
1 fresh red chili, cored, seeded, and finely chopped
1 in. fresh ginger, peeled and grated
1 teaspoon lemongrass paste
8 oz. chanterelle mushrooms
1 or 2 teaspoons Thai red curry paste
1 cup coconut milk
1 tablespoon light soy sauce
12 oz. skinless chicken fillet, diced
cilantro sprigs and chopped cilantro, to garnish

Heat oil in a flameproof casserole. Add chili, ginger, lemongrass paste, and mushrooms and stir-fry 2 or 3 minutes.

Add curry paste and stir-fry 1 minute. Add coconut milk and soy sauce and bring to boil.

Add chicken and simmer 10 minutes until chicken is tender and cooked through. Garnish with cilantro sprigs and chopped cilantro to serve.

Makes 4 servings.

Note: If lemongrass paste is not available, replace it with 1 teaspoon fresh, chopped lemongrass, or ½ teaspoon dried.

CHICKEN WITH PEANUT SAUCE

1 in. piece galangal, chopped
2 cloves garlic, chopped
1½ tablespoons Thai fragrant curry paste
¼ cup coconut cream
1 lb. skinless chicken fillet, cut into large pieces
3 shallots, chopped
¼ cup dry-roasted peanuts, chopped
1 cup coconut milk
½ teaspoon finely chopped, dried red chili
2 teaspoons fish sauce
freshly cooked broccoli, to serve

Using a mortar and pestle or small blender, pound or mix together galangal, garlic, and curry paste. Mix in coconut cream. Place chicken in a bowl and stir in spice mixture; set aside 1 hour.

Heat a wok or pan, add shallots and coated chicken, and stir-fry 3 or 4 minutes. In a blender, mix peanuts with coconut milk, then stir into chicken with chili and fish sauce. Cook gently about 30 minutes until chicken is tender and sauce thickens. Transfer to the center of a warmed serving plate and arrange cooked broccoli around.

Makes 4 servings.

SUGARED CHICKEN CASSEROLE

CHICKEN WITH MUSHROOMS

8 chicken thighs
3 tablespoons oil
2 teaspoons sugar
1 onion, finely chopped
2 stalks celery, chopped
½ cup chicken stock
2 large plum tomatoes, peeled, seeded, and chopped
8 oz. okra
MARINADE:
1 red onion, roughly chopped
2 cloves garlic, roughly chopped
1 in. piece fresh ginger, chopped
1 red chili, seeded and roughly chopped
2 tablespoons chopped cilantro
1 tablespoon olive oil
juice ½ lime

1 tablespoon olive oil
1 tablespoon unsalted butter, diced
4 chicken quarters
12 oz. chestnut, oyster, shiitake, or chanterelle
  mushrooms, or a mixture
1 onion, finely chopped
¾ cup medium-dry white wine
2 tablespoons fresh, chopped tarragon leaves
½ cup plain yogurt
salt and freshly ground black pepper
tarragon sprigs, to garnish

Heat oil and butter in a heavy, flameproof casserole, add chicken, and cook until browned. Remove with a slotted spoon.

To make marinade, put onion, garlic, ginger, chili, cilantro, olive oil, lime juice, and seasoning in a blender or food processor and process to a paste. Rub over chicken thighs and place in a dish. Cover and refrigerate overnight. Scrape marinade off chicken and reserve. Dry chicken thighs on absorbent paper towels. In a skillet, heat oil. Add sugar and cook gently until sugar dissolves. Add chicken and cook, turning frequently, until well browned. Transfer to a casserole.

Preheat oven to 325°F. Cut large mushrooms into quarters and oyster mushrooms into 1 in. strips. Add to casserole with onion and cook, stirring occasionally, 5 minutes until soft. Stir in wine and bring to boil. Return chicken to casserole and sprinkle with tarragon. Cover tightly and cook in the oven 1 hour.

Add onion and celery to oil in skillet and cook 10 minutes until soft. Stir chicken stock into pan, scraping up any brown bits, then pour over chicken. Bring to boil, then cover and simmer gently 20 minutes. Add tomatoes and okra and cook an additional 15 minutes. Add 2 or 3 tablespoons reserved marinade, according to taste. Season and serve.

Makes 4 servings.

Using a slotted spoon, transfer chicken and vegetables to a warmed plate and keep warm. Boil cooking liquid to thicken slightly. Stir in yogurt and reheat gently without boiling. Season with salt and pepper. Return chicken and vegetables to casserole, turn in sauce, and heat gently to warm through. Garnish with tarragon sprigs and serve.

Makes 4 servings.

CHICKEN PILAF

1 onion, roughly chopped
2 cloves garlic
2 stalks celery, roughly chopped
2 tablespoons fresh, chopped chives
1 tablespoon fresh thyme leaves
liquid from 1 fresh coconut
flesh from ½ fresh coconut, chopped
1 Scotch bonnet chili
2 tablespoons oil
3¾ lb. chicken, cut into 2 in. pieces
15 oz. can gungo peas, drained
1¼ cups long-grain rice, washed
1⅓ cups chicken stock
salt and freshly ground black pepper
12 pimiento-stuffed olives, halved, to garnish

Place onion, garlic, celery, chives, and thyme in a blender or food processor with ¼ cup water and process to a paste. Transfer to a saucepan. Put coconut liquid and coconut flesh in the blender or food processor and blend until it will coat the back of a spoon. Add water if too thick. Stir into onion mixture with chili and cook gently 15 minutes.

Put oil and sugar in a wide-bottomed, flameproof casserole. Heat gently until sugar begins to caramelize. Add chicken pieces and cook 20 minutes, turning frequently, until well browned. Stir in coconut mixture, gungo peas, rice, and stock. Season and bring to boil; cover and simmer 20 minutes until chicken is tender, rice is cooked, and liquid has been absorbed. Remove and discard chili. Garnish with halved pimiento-stuffed olives and serve.

Makes 6 servings.

MEXICALI CHICKEN

2 tablespoons sunflower oil
1 medium onion, chopped
1 small fresh green chili, seeded and chopped
1 clove garlic, finely chopped
2 tablespoons tomato paste
1 teaspoon ground cumin
1 tablespoon finely chopped cilantro
1 cup cooked red kidney beans
5 medium tomatoes, peeled (see page 174) and chopped
3 cups cooked, diced chicken
salt and pepper

Heat oil in a heavy-bottomed saucepan and fry onion, chili, and garlic over medium heat 4 or 5 minutes until onion is soft but not browned.

Stir in tomato paste, cumin, cilantro, kidney beans, tomatoes, and chicken; season with salt and pepper. Cover and simmer 20 minutes until thick; if necessary, uncover and simmer an additional 10 minutes. Serve with rice or tortillas and a salad.

Makes 4 servings.

CHICKEN CHASSEUR

1 tablespoon olive oil
3 tablespoons butter
4 chicken quarters
3 shallots, finely chopped
1 clove garlic, finely chopped
1 tablespoon all-purpose flour
5 oz. brown cap or shiitake mushrooms, sliced
1 cup dry white wine
2 beefsteak tomatoes, peeled, seeded, and chopped
several tarragon and parsley sprigs
tarragon sprigs, to garnish

Heat oil and 2 tablespoons butter in a heavy, flameproof casserole, add chicken, and cook until browned all over.

Remove chicken and set aside. Add shallots and garlic to casserole and cook, stirring occasionally, 5 minutes until soft. Add flour and mushrooms and cook, stirring until flour has browned lightly. Stir in wine and tomatoes. Bring to boil, stirring.

Return chicken to casserole and add tarragon, parsley, salt, and pepper. Cover tightly and cook gently 50 to 60 minutes. Remove chicken with a slotted spoon, transfer to warmed serving plates, and keep warm. Remove herbs from sauce and discard. Boil sauce to thicken slightly. Lower heat and stir in remaining butter. Pour sauce over chicken, garnish with tarragon sprigs, and serve.

Makes 4 servings.

POULET BASQUAISE

3 red bell peppers
3 lb. chicken, cut into 8 pieces
salt and freshly ground black pepper
3 tablespoons olive oil
2 onions, thinly sliced
3 cloves garlic, chopped
½ fresh red chili, cored, seeded, and chopped
4 ripe tomatoes, peeled, seeded, and chopped
bouquet garni
4 oz. Bayonne or Parma ham, diced
½ cup dry white wine
fresh, chopped parsley, to garnish

Preheat broiler. Broil bell peppers until charred and blistered all over.

Leave peppers until cool enough to handle, then peel. Halve, remove cores and seeds, and cut flesh into strips. Season chicken with salt and pepper. Heat oil in a heavy, flameproof casserole, add chicken, and cook until browned all over. Remove with a slotted spoon, transfer to a large plate, and set aside.

Add onions and garlic to casserole and cook, stirring occasionally, 5 minutes until soft. Stir in chili, tomatoes, and bouquet garni and simmer 15 minutes. Stir in ham, wine, and bell peppers. Bring to boil, add chicken and any juices on plate, and season with pepper. Cover tightly and simmer gently 50 to 60 minutes. Transfer chicken to warmed serving plates. Boil sauce to thicken, pour over chicken, garnish with chopped parsley, and serve.

Makes 4 servings.

LEMON CHICKEN

½ stick butter
3½ lb. chicken quarters
16 baby onions
1 cup chicken stock
1 cup dry white wine
bouquet garni
salt and freshly ground black pepper
12 button mushrooms, quartered
2 large egg yolks, lightly beaten
juice ½ lemon
fresh, chopped parsley, to garnish

Heat butter in a heavy, flameproof casserole, add chicken pieces and onions, and cook 10 minutes until chicken is browned.

Remove onions with a slotted spoon and set aside. Add stock, wine, bouquet garni, and salt and pepper. Bring to boil, cover, and simmer 20 minutes. Return onions to casserole and cook 20 minutes. Add mushrooms and cook 10 minutes.

Using a slotted spoon, transfer chicken and vegetables to a warmed plate, cover, and keep warm. Boil cooking liquid until reduced by one third. Remove a ladleful of cooking liquid, allow to cool slightly, then stir into egg yolks. Reduce heat, stir egg yolk mixture into casserole, and heat very gently, stirring, until slightly thickened. Do not boil. Stir in lemon juice. Return chicken and vegetables to casserole and turn in sauce. Garnish with parsley and serve.

Makes 4 servings.

BRAISED CHICKEN

3½ lb. chicken
1 onion, halved
2 cloves
4 slices bacon, chopped (optional)
about 4 cups stock or water
bouquet garni
salt and freshly ground black pepper
4 stalks celery, quartered
4 carrots, quartered
4 small turnips, quartered
12 small leeks, halved
bay leaves, to garnish

Put chicken into a large, heavy, flameproof casserole. Stud each onion half with 1 clove.

Add onion halves to casserole with bacon, if using. Add enough stock or water to cover and bring to boil. Add bouquet garni and salt and pepper. Skim scum from surface, cover, and simmer very gently 1 hour.

Add celery, carrots, and turnips, cover, and cook 30 minutes. Add leeks and cook 15 minutes until chicken and vegetables are tender. Transfer chicken and vegetables to a warmed serving plate and keep warm. Boil sauce to thicken slightly. Carve chicken and serve with vegetables and sauce, garnished with bay leaves.

Makes 4 servings.

SPANISH-STYLE RICE & CHICKEN

3 tablespoons olive oil
3 lb. chicken, cut into 8 pieces, or 4 large chicken
   pieces, halved
1 Spanish onion, finely chopped
2 cloves garlic, chopped
1 large red bell pepper, cut into strips
1 tablespoon paprika
1 large beefsteak tomato, peeled (see page 174),
   seeded, and chopped
1¾ cups arborio (Italian risotto) rice
¼ teaspoon saffron threads, finely crushed
3¾ cups boiling chicken stock or water
1 cup small shelled fresh or frozen peas
2 tablespoons fresh, chopped parsley
lime wedges, to garnish

Heat oil in a paella pan or large skillet. Add chicken and cook 10 minutes until a light golden color all over. Remove and set aside. Add onion, garlic, and red bell pepper to pan and cook gently 8 to 10 minutes until vegetables are soft. Stir in paprika, heat about 30 to 60 seconds, then add tomatoes and cook about 10 minutes until mixture is thick.

Add rice, stir 2 minutes, then add saffron and stock or water and quickly bring to boil. Return chicken to pan and simmer 15 minutes. Add peas, if using fresh ones, and continue to simmer about 10 minutes until chicken and rice are tender and most of liquid has been absorbed. Add frozen peas, if using. Remove from heat, cover pan, and leave 5 to 10 minutes. Sprinkle with parsley. Serve from pan if a paella pan has been used.

Makes 4 servings.

CHICKEN WITH LENTILS

8 oz. chicken fillets
1¼ cups red split lentils
½ teaspoon turmeric
¼ cup vegetable oil
6 green cardamom pods, bruised
1 onion, finely sliced
½ in. piece fresh ginger, grated
salt and cayenne pepper
2 tablespoons lemon juice
1 teaspoon cumin seeds
2 cloves garlic, finely sliced

Wash chicken, pat dry, and cut into cubes. Set aside.

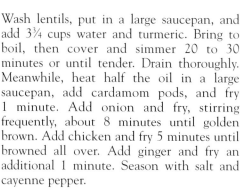

Wash lentils, put in a large saucepan, and add 3¾ cups water and turmeric. Bring to boil, then cover and simmer 20 to 30 minutes or until tender. Drain thoroughly. Meanwhile, heat half the oil in a large saucepan, add cardamom pods, and fry 1 minute. Add onion and fry, stirring frequently, about 8 minutes until golden brown. Add chicken and fry 5 minutes until browned all over. Add ginger and fry an additional 1 minute. Season with salt and cayenne pepper.

Stir in lemon juice and ⅔ cup water and cover. Simmer 25 to 30 minutes or until chicken is tender. Stir in lentil mixture and cook, stirring, 5 minutes. Meanwhile, heat remaining oil, add cumin seeds and garlic, and fry, stirring, for 1 or 2 minutes until garlic is golden. Transfer chicken and lentils to serving dish and sprinkle with garlic mixture. Serve hot.

Makes 4 servings.

VIETNAMESE CHICKEN STEW

LAKSA LEMAK

1 lb. skinless boneless chicken thighs, cut into bite-sized pieces
salt and freshly ground pepper
2 teaspoons sugar
1 tablespoon each lime juice and fish sauce
1 tablespoon vegetable oil
2 cloves garlic, sliced, and 2 shallots, chopped
1 tablespoon dried small red chilies
2 tablespoons crushed yellow bean sauce
about 2 cups chicken stock
2 scallions, cut into short sections
cilantro, to garnish

Marinate chicken with salt, pepper, sugar, lime juice, and fish sauce 1 to 2 hours.

Heat oil in a flameproof casserole over high heat and stir-fry garlic, shallots, and chilies about 1 minute, then add yellow bean sauce and stir until smooth.

Add chicken pieces and stir-fry 1 or 2 minutes. Add chicken stock, blend well, and bring to boil, then reduce heat, cover, and simmer 15 to 20 minutes. Uncover and stir in scallions. Garnish with cilantro sprigs and serve straight from the pot. Serve with rice.

Makes 4 servings.

3 dried red chilies, cored, seeded, and chopped
3 cloves garlic, crushed
6 shallots, chopped
2 in. piece fresh ginger, chopped
1 tablespoon ground coriander
1½ teaspoons ground turmeric
4 oz. thin rice noodles
2 tablespoons vegetable oil
1½ lb. skinless chicken fillet, diced
2 cups chicken stock
1 lb. medium, raw, unpeeled shrimp
8 oz. bean curd, cut into 1 in. cubes
2 cups bean sprouts
2 cups coconut milk
small bunch scallions

Soak chilies in 3 tablespoons hot water in a blender 10 minutes. Add garlic, shallots, ginger, coriander, and turmeric and grind to a paste. Soak noodles in hot water 3 to 5 minutes, stirring occasionally. Drain. In a wok or saucepan over medium heat, heat oil. Stir in spice paste and cook 3 or 4 minutes. Add chicken and cook, stirring, 3 or 4 minutes. Add stock; simmer gently 20 to 25 minutes.

Add shrimp and simmer 3 or 4 minutes until they turn pink. Add bean curd, bean sprouts, noodles, and coconut milk. Stir and simmer 5 minutes. Thickly slice scallions on diagonal, including some green. Add half to pan. Serve garnished with remaining scallions.

Makes 6 servings.

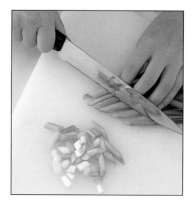

LEMON & CILANTRO CHICKEN

4 chicken thighs, skinless
4 chicken drumsticks, skinless
¼ cup vegetable oil
2 in. piece fresh ginger, grated
4 cloves garlic, crushed
1 fresh green chili, seeded and finely chopped
½ teaspoon turmeric
1 teaspoon ground cumin
1 teaspoon ground coriander
salt and cayenne pepper
grated zest and juice 1 lemon
3 cups chopped cilantro
cilantro and lemon slices, to garnish

Wash chicken portions and pat dry with absorbent paper towels. Heat oil in a large skillet, add chicken, and fry, stirring frequently, until browned all over. Remove from pan with a slotted spoon and set aside. Add ginger and garlic to pan and fry 1 minute. Stir in chili, turmeric, cumin, and ground coriander and season with salt and cayenne pepper, then cook 1 minute.

Return chicken to pan and add ½ cup water and lemon zest and juice. Bring to boil, then cover and cook over medium heat 25 to 30 minutes or until chicken is tender. Stir in chopped cilantro, then serve hot, garnished with cilantro and lemon slices.

Makes 4 servings.

Variation: Use fresh parsley, or parsley and mint, instead of cilantro.

CHICKEN GUMBO

2 tablespoons butter
1 tablespoon oil
3½ lb. chicken, cut into 8 pieces
¼ cup seasoned flour
1 large onion, sliced
2 cloves garlic, sliced
2 teaspoons chili powder
14½ oz. can chopped tomatoes
2 tablespoons tomato paste
1¼ cups chicken stock
½ cup red wine
1 red bell pepper, seeded and sliced
1 green bell pepper, seeded and sliced
12 oz. small okra, trimmed
2 teaspoons lemon juice
pinch sugar

Preheat oven to 350°F. Heat butter and oil in a flameproof casserole. Toss chicken pieces in seasoned flour, then fry in the hot fats until golden. Remove from the pan and set aside. Cook onion and garlic in the casserole until slightly softened, stir in chili powder and any remaining flour, then add tomatoes, tomato paste, stock, and wine and bring to boil.

Stir in bell peppers, okra, lemon juice, and sugar and return chicken to the casserole. Cover and cook in the oven 50 to 60 minutes. Serve with rice.

Makes 4 servings.

CHICKEN BIRYANI

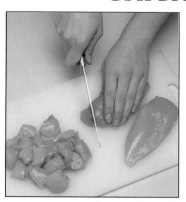

½ cup vegetable oil
1 stick cinnamon
8 cloves
6 cardamom pods, bruised
1 in. piece fresh ginger, finely chopped
1½ lb. skinless, boneless chicken, diced
2 cloves garlic, crushed
1 teaspoon chili powder
1¼ cups plain yogurt
⅔ cup chicken stock
pinch saffron threads
¼ cup boiling water
1¾ cups basmati rice
¼ cup golden raisins
¼ cup slivered almonds
1 onion, sliced

Preheat oven to 375°F. In a flameproof casserole, heat ¼ cup oil. Add cinnamon stick, cloves, cardamom, and ginger and fry 15 seconds. Add chicken, garlic, and chili and fry 4 minutes. Add yogurt, 1 tablespoon at a time, stirring between each addition until yogurt is absorbed by spices. Add stock and simmer 20 to 25 minutes. Transfer to a bowl. Soak saffron in boiling water and set aside. Wash rice under cold running water until water runs clear, then cook in boiling, salted water 3 minutes and drain.

Put 2 tablespoons oil in the casserole, spoon in a layer of rice, sprinkle with a little of the saffron water, and cover with a layer of chicken. Repeat, ending with a layer of rice. Add any cooking juices left from chicken, cover tightly, and cook in the oven 25 to 30 minutes. In a pan, heat remaining oil and fry golden raisins and almonds until golden; remove. Fry onions until crisp and golden. Sprinkle biryani with almonds, onions, and golden raisins.

Makes 4 servings.

APRICOT & CHICKEN CURRY

2½ lb. chicken portions, skinless
½ teaspoon chili powder
1 tablespoon garam masala
1 in. piece fresh ginger, grated
2 cloves garlic, crushed
1 cup dried apricots
2 tablespoons vegetable oil
2 onions, finely sliced
14½ oz. can chopped tomatoes
1 tablespoon sugar
2 tablespoons white wine vinegar
salt

Wash chicken and pat dry with absorbent paper towels. Cut each portion into 4 pieces and put in a large bowl. Add chili powder, garam masala, ginger, and garlic and toss well to coat chicken pieces. Cover and leave in a cool place 2 to 3 hours to allow chicken to absorb flavors. Put apricots and ⅔ cup water in a separate bowl and let soak 2 to 3 hours.

Heat oil in a large, heavy-bottomed pan and add chicken. Fry over high heat 5 minutes or until browned all over. Remove from pan and set aside. Add onions to pan and cook, stirring, about 5 minutes until soft. Return chicken to pan with tomatoes and cook, covered, over low heat 20 minutes. Drain apricots and add to pan with sugar and vinegar. Season with salt. Simmer, covered, 10 to 15 minutes. Serve hot.

Makes 4 servings.

SPICY SPANISH CHICKEN

CHICKEN WITH SHERRY

¼ cup olive oil
4 slices dried French bread
8 cloves garlic
3½ lb. chicken, skinless and cut into small pieces
1¼ cups medium-bodied dry white wine
large pinch saffron threads, finely crushed
3 tablespoons fresh, chopped parsley
3 cloves
freshly grated nutmeg
salt and freshly ground black pepper

Heat oil in a flameproof casserole, add bread and 5 garlic cloves, and fry until browned.

¼ cup raisins
1 cup oloroso sherry
3 tablespoons olive oil
3½ lb. chicken, cut into 8 pieces
1 Spanish onion, finely chopped
1 clove garlic, finely chopped
1 cup chicken stock
salt and freshly ground black pepper
¼ cup pine nuts

In a small bowl, soak raisins in sherry 30 minutes.

Transfer to a mortar and crush with a pestle, then transfer to a bowl. Crush remaining garlic and add to casserole with chicken. Cook until chicken changes color. Pour in wine and just enough water to cover chicken. Cover casserole and simmer gently about 30 minutes until chicken juices run clear when thickest part is pierced with a sharp knife.

In a flameproof casserole, heat 2 tablespoons oil, add chicken, and cook gently until lightly and evenly browned, about 10 minutes. Transfer to absorbent paper towels to drain. Add onion and garlic to casserole and cook gently, stirring occasionally, until softened and lightly colored, about 7 minutes. Strain raisins and set aside.

Meanwhile, in a bowl, dissolve saffron in 2 tablespoons of the chicken cooking liquid. Put parsley, cloves, and nutmeg in the mortar and pound to a paste. Stir in saffron. Mix with crushed bread, then stir mixture into the casserole and cook 10 minutes. Season to taste and serve.

Makes 4 servings.

Stir sherry into casserole. Simmer until reduced by half. Add stock, chicken, and seasoning, bring to boil, then simmer gently about 35 minutes until chicken is cooked. In a small pan, fry pine nuts in remaining oil until lightly colored. Drain on absorbent paper towels, then stir into casserole with raisins. Transfer chicken to a warmed serving dish. Boil liquid in casserole to concentrate slightly. Pour over chicken.

Makes 4 servings.

CHICKEN IN VINEGAR SAUCE

4 chicken fillets
salt and freshly ground black pepper
⅓ cup olive oil
12 cloves garlic
1 small onion, finely chopped
about 3 tablespoons sherry vinegar
1 tablespoon paprika
1½ tablespoons fresh, chopped oregano
2 tablespoons fresh bread crumbs
1¼ cups chicken stock
fresh herbs, to garnish

Season chicken with salt and pepper. Heat oil in a heavy, flameproof casserole, add chicken, and cook 10 minutes.

Meanwhile, slice four of the garlic cloves. Add sliced garlic to casserole with onion and cook until chicken is lightly browned all over, about an additional 5 minutes.

Remove chicken from casserole, stir in vinegar, and boil 2 or 3 minutes. Pound remaining garlic with a little salt, paprika, and oregano, then stir in bread crumbs and one quarter of the stock. Pour over chicken, add remaining stock, and cook about 20 minutes until chicken is tender and sauce fairly thick. Adjust seasoning and amount of vinegar, if necessary. Serve garnished with fresh herbs.

Makes 4 servings.

CHICKEN PEPITORIA

2 tablespoons olive oil
3½ lb. chicken, cut into 8 pieces, or 4 large chicken portions, halved
½ Spanish onion, finely chopped
4 oz. serrano ham, cut into strips
1 cup chicken stock
4 cloves garlic, crushed
15 almonds or hazelnuts, lightly roasted
pinch ground cloves
3 tablespoons fresh, chopped parsley
3 egg yolks
salt and freshly ground black pepper

Heat oil in a flameproof casserole, add chicken, and fry until lightly browned all over. Using a slotted spoon, remove chicken from casserole and set aside. Add onion to casserole and cook about 4 minutes, stirring occasionally. Stir in ham, cook 1 minute, then return chicken to casserole. Pour in stock, cover tightly, and simmer gently about 45 minutes until chicken is tender.

Meanwhile, pound together garlic, almonds or hazelnuts, ground cloves, and parsley. Place in a small bowl and gradually work in egg yolks. Stir a little hot chicken liquid into the bowl, then stir mixture into the casserole. Continue to cook gently, stirring, until sauce thickens; do not allow to boil. Season with salt and pepper.

Makes 4 servings.

TARRAGON CHICKEN

CHICKEN WITH YOGURT

2 tablespoons butter
1 tablespoon oil
4 large chicken fillets
2 large leeks
2 tablespoons tarragon vinegar
⅔ cup dry white wine
1 cup chicken stock
1 large carrot, peeled
⅔ cup sour cream
1 teaspoon cornstarch
1 teaspoon Dijon mustard
2 teaspoons fresh, chopped tarragon
salt and pepper
tarragon sprigs, to garnish

⅔ cup dry white wine
2 teaspoons English mustard
3 tablespoons fresh, chopped tarragon
4 chicken fillets, cut into strips
1 tablespoon oil
1 tablespoon cornstarch
3 tablespoons brandy
⅔ cup plain yogurt
salt and pepper

In a bowl, mix white wine with mustard and tarragon. Add chicken, mix well, cover, and refrigerate 3 to 4 hours. Drain and reserve marinade.

In a skillet, heat butter and oil and fry chicken until golden on both sides, remove from the pan, and allow to drain on absorbent paper towels. Coarsely chop one leek and fry gently until slightly softened, add vinegar, and boil rapidly until quantity is reduced by half. Pour in wine and stock and return chicken to the pan, then cover and simmer 25 minutes. Cut remaining leek and carrot into matchstick strips and cook 4 or 5 minutes in separate pans of boiling, salted water; drain and rinse under cold water, then drain again.

Heat oil in a pan and cook chicken quickly without browning. Mix cornstarch to a paste with a little water and add to the pan with brandy and reserved marinade.

Remove chicken from the pan and arrange on a warmed serving dish. Strain cooking liquid into a clean pan and bring to boil. In a bowl, whisk together sour cream, cornstarch, mustard, and 2 tablespoons of the pan juices. Return mixture to the pan and add carrots, leeks, and tarragon. Heat gently until sauce thickens and season to taste. Spoon over chicken and garnish with tarragon sprigs.

Makes 4 servings.

Cook over medium heat 12 to 15 minutes until chicken is cooked through. Add yogurt, heat through, and season with a little salt and pepper. Serve hot.

Makes 4 servings.

MOROCCAN CHICKEN

3 lb. chicken, cut into 8 pieces
¼ cup olive oil
grated zest and juice 1 lemon
1 teaspoon each ground cinnamon, ground ginger,
  and ground cumin
½ teaspoon salt
½ teaspoon cayenne pepper (or to taste)
1 onion, chopped
3 or 4 cloves garlic, finely chopped
1 red bell pepper, diced
1 tomato, peeled (see page 174), seeded, and chopped
1 cup chicken stock or water
16 pitted prunes
¼ cup honey
1 large lemon, thinly sliced
toasted almonds and fresh, chopped parsley, to garnish

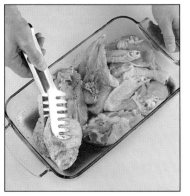

In a large, shallow baking dish, combine chicken pieces with 2 tablespoons olive oil, lemon zest and juice, cinnamon, ginger, cumin, salt, and cayenne pepper to taste. Work spices into chicken pieces, cover, and let marinate in the refrigerator 4 to 6 hours or overnight. Heat a wok or pan until hot. Add 1 tablespoon oil and swirl to coat. Arrange marinated chicken pieces on bottom and side of pan in a single layer and stir-fry 6 to 8 minutes until golden brown. Remove chicken pieces to the cleaned baking dish.

Add remaining oil, onion, garlic, and bell pepper to pan. Stir-fry 2 or 3 minutes. Add tomato and stock or water and bring to simmering point, stirring. Return chicken and marinade to sauce. Simmer, covered, 35 to 40 minutes until chicken is tender, adding prunes, honey, and lemon slices after 20 minutes cooking. Remove chicken to serving dish, spoon sauce over, and sprinkle with almonds and parsley. Serve with couscous.

Makes 4 servings.

SMOKED CHICKEN & LEEK BAKE

8 oz. dried, tricolor trompetti or fusilli
salt and freshly ground black pepper
¾ stick butter
3 leeks, washed and sliced
8 oz. mushrooms, sliced
1 yellow bell pepper, seeded and sliced
½ cup all-purpose flour
2 cups chicken stock
2 cups milk
1 heaping cup shredded cheddar cheese
8 oz. cooked smoked chicken fillet, diced
3 tablespoons fresh, chopped parsley
parsley sprigs, to garnish

Preheat oven to 400°F. Lightly butter an ovenproof dish and set aside. Cook pasta in a large saucepan of lightly salted boiling water 10 minutes or until al dente. Drain thoroughly. Meanwhile, melt 2 tablespoons butter in a skillet, add leeks, mushrooms, and bell pepper, and cook over fairly high heat 5 minutes, stirring occasionally, until softened. Remove pan from heat and set aside. Put remaining butter, flour, stock, and milk in a saucepan and heat gently, whisking, until sauce is thickened. Simmer gently 3 minutes, stirring.

Remove pan from heat and stir in chicken, chopped parsley, salt and pepper, and most of the cheese. Add pasta to chicken sauce with leeks, mushrooms, and bell pepper and mix well. Transfer to prepared dish and sprinkle with remaining cheese. Bake 25 to 30 minutes or until golden brown and bubbling. Garnish with parsley sprigs and serve.

Makes 4 servings.

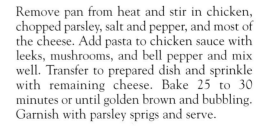

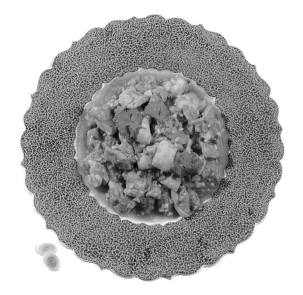

MALAYSIAN SPICED CHICKEN

MUGHLAI CHICKEN

8 chicken thighs, boned and chopped
3 tablespoons vegetable oil
1 clove garlic, finely chopped
2 tablespoons fish sauce
6 shallots, finely chopped
cilantro, to garnish
MARINADE:
2 small fresh red chilies, cored, seeded, and chopped
1 stalk lemongrass, chopped
1 clove garlic, crushed
1½ in. piece fresh ginger, chopped
1 tablespoon ground turmeric
8 oz. can tomatoes
1 tablespoon light brown sugar
salt

6 cloves garlic, peeled
½ cup blanched almonds
1 in. piece ginger, peeled and chopped
⅓ cup vegetable oil
2¼ lb. chicken pieces, diced
9 whole cardamom pods
1 stick cinnamon
6 whole cloves
1 onion, finely chopped
2½ teaspoons ground cumin
1 teaspoon cayenne pepper
⅔ cup plain yogurt
1¼ cups heavy cream
1 tablespoon golden raisins
½ teaspoon each garam masala and salt

To make marinade, put chilies, lemongrass, garlic, ginger, turmeric, tomatoes, sugar, and salt in a blender and mix together well. Put chicken in a nonreactive bowl and pour marinade over. Stir together, cover, and refrigerate overnight. Return bowl of chicken to room temperature 1 hour. In a wok or heavy sauté pan, heat oil over high heat. Add garlic and fry 30 seconds. Add chicken and marinade. Stir and toss together, then stir in fish sauce and ¼ cup hot water. Cover, lower heat, and simmer 5 minutes.

Put garlic, almonds, ginger, and ¼ cup water into a blender and blend to form a paste. Heat oil in a flameproof casserole or saucepan and fry chicken until golden. Set aside. Put cardamom, cinnamon, and cloves into the pan and fry a few seconds. Add chopped onion and fry until beginning to turn golden brown. Add paste from the blender together with cumin and cayenne pepper and fry 2 minutes or until mixture is lightly browned.

Add shallots and continue to cook, uncovered, stirring occasionally, about 10 minutes until chicken juices run clear. Serve garnished with cilantro.

Makes 4 servings.

Still on the heat, add 1 tablespoon yogurt and cook about 20 seconds, then add an additional tablespoon. Continue adding yogurt in this way until incorporated. Put chicken pieces and any juices into the pan with salt and cream and gently bring to simmer, stirring. Cover and cook gently about 20 minutes. Add golden raisins and cook an additional 10 minutes or until chicken is tender. Stir in garam masala and salt to taste.

Makes 4 servings.

THAI CHICKEN CURRY

1 small onion, chopped
1 clove garlic, peeled
1 stalk lemongrass, chopped
1 teaspoon ground coriander
½ teaspoon dried chili flakes
1 teaspoon grated lime zest
1 teaspoon paprika
½ teaspoon ground cumin
2 teaspoons vegetable oil
1 lb. raw chicken meat, sliced
1 tablespoon light soy sauce
⅔ cup coconut milk
2 lime leaves
¼ cup chicken stock
2 red bell peppers, seeded and sliced
10 scallions, sliced into matchstick strips

Blend or process onion, garlic, lemongrass, ground coriander, dried chili flakes, lime zest, paprika, and cumin in a blender or food processor until smooth. Heat oil in a large skillet, stir in paste, and cook 1 or 2 minutes. Add chicken and stir gently, coating well in curry paste.

Stir in soy sauce, coconut milk, lime leaves, chicken stock, bell peppers, and scallions. Cover and cook 20 to 25 minutes. Serve with plain rice and garnish with cilantro sprigs.

Makes 4 servings.

CHICKEN & PLUM CASSEROLE

1 oz. dried Chinese mushrooms, soaked in hot water
  20 minutes
1 lb. skinless, boneless chicken thighs
1 tablespoon sunflower oil
2 cloves garlic, thinly sliced
1 oz. prosciutto, trimmed and diced
4 or 5 plums, halved and pitted
1 tablespoon brown sugar
3 tablespoons light soy sauce
2 tablespoons rice wine
3 tablespoons plum sauce
1 tablespoon chili sauce
2½ cups chicken stock
2 teaspoons cornstarch mixed with 4 teaspoons
  water

Drain mushrooms and squeeze out excess water. Discard mushroom stems and thinly slice caps. Trim fat from chicken thighs and cut meat into 1 in. strips. Heat oil in a nonstick or well-seasoned wok and stir-fry chicken, garlic, and prosciutto 3 or 4 minutes. Add mushrooms and stir-fry 1 minute.

Add plums, brown sugar, soy sauce, rice wine, plum sauce, and chili sauce and simmer 20 minutes or until plums have softened. Add cornstarch mixture and cook, stirring, until thickened. Serve on a bed of rice.

Makes 4 servings.

CHICKEN IN SANFAINA SAUCE

¼ cup olive oil
3 lb. chicken, cut into 8 pieces
2 Spanish onions, chopped
2 cloves garlic, chopped
1 green bell pepper, seeded and sliced
1 red bell pepper, seeded and sliced
2 eggplants, cut into strips
4 oz. serrano ham, diced
2 or 3 beefsteak tomatoes, peeled (see page 174),
    seeded, and chopped
½ cup dry white wine
½ cup chicken stock
bouquet garni of 1 bay leaf, 1 thyme sprig, and
    1 parsley sprig
salt and freshly ground black pepper
1 tablespoon fresh, chopped parsley, to garnish

Heat oil in a large, heavy, flameproof casserole, add chicken, and fry about 10 minutes until lightly browned. Using a slotted spoon, remove chicken and reserve. Add onions and garlic to casserole and fry 1 minute. Add bell peppers and eggplant and cook, stirring occasionally, 5 minutes. Stir in ham, tomatoes, wine, stock, bouquet garni, and salt and pepper.

Bring casserole to boil, then reduce heat so liquid barely simmers. Return chicken to casserole and bury in sauce. Cover casserole and cook gently about 45 minutes until chicken juices run clear when pierced with a sharp knife and sauce is slightly thickened. Discard bouquet garni. Taste and adjust seasoning. Serve sprinkled with parsley.

Makes 4 servings.

Note: Use 4 large chicken portions, halved, instead of whole chicken, if preferred.

POULET AU VINAIGRE

1 tablespoon oil
1 tablespoon butter
4 chicken legs
1 onion, finely chopped
bouquet garni
4 ripe tomatoes, peeled, seeded, and chopped
2 teaspoons tomato paste
1¼ cups red wine vinegar
1¼ cups chicken stock
salt and freshly ground black pepper
fresh, chopped parsley, to garnish

Heat oil and butter in a heavy, flameproof casserole. Add chicken and cook until lightly browned all over.

Remove chicken and set aside. Add onion to casserole and cook, stirring occasionally, 5 minutes until soft. Return chicken to casserole, add bouquet garni, cover, and cook gently 20 minutes, turning occasionally.

Add tomatoes to casserole and cook, uncovered, until liquid has evaporated. Combine tomato paste and vinegar and add to casserole. Simmer until most of liquid has evaporated. Add stock and salt and pepper and simmer until reduced by half. Sprinkle with parsley and serve.

Makes 4 servings.

CHICKEN CACCIATORE

CHICKEN WITH PARSLEY

2 tablespoons olive oil
4 large chicken breasts, with bones
1 large or 2 small red onions, thinly sliced
2 cloves garlic, thinly sliced
⅔ cup red wine
⅔ cup chicken stock
14½ oz. can chopped tomatoes
1 tablespoon tomato paste
1 red bell pepper, seeded and sliced
1 yellow bell pepper, seeded and sliced
2 tablespoons fresh, chopped basil
salt and pepper
pinch sugar
pasta noodles, to serve

3 tablespoons olive oil
3½ lb. chicken, cut into 8 pieces
3 cloves garlic, lightly crushed
½ fresh red chili, seeded and finely chopped
⅓ cup dry white wine
salt and freshly ground black pepper
juice ½ lemon
3 tablespoons fresh, chopped parsley

Heat oil in a flameproof casserole. Add chicken and cook about 10 minutes until lightly browned. Cook in batches, if necessary. Remove and reserve.

Preheat oven to 350°F. In a pan, heat oil and fry chicken breasts all over until golden brown, then transfer to a shallow casserole. Gently fry onion and garlic in the pan without browning. Add wine, stock, tomatoes, tomato paste, bell peppers, 1 tablespoon basil, salt and pepper, and sugar and bring to boil.

Add garlic and chili to casserole and cook 5 minutes without browning, stirring occasionally. Return chicken to casserole, sprinkle with wine, and allow to boil 2 or 3 minutes.

Pour sauce over chicken, cover, and cook in the oven 45 minutes. Serve on a bed of pasta noodles and sprinkle with remaining basil and plenty of black pepper.

Makes 4 servings.

Season lightly, cover, and cook gently about 40 minutes until chicken juices run clear when pierced with a sharp knife. Transfer chicken to a warmed plate and keep warm. Stir lemon juice and parsley into casserole. Boil if necessary to lightly concentrate juices, then pour it over chicken.

Makes 4 servings.

Note: Use 4 large chicken portions, halved, instead of whole chicken, if preferred.

TURKEY RISOTTO

½ stick butter
1 large onion, sliced
1 clove garlic, crushed
4 oz. button mushrooms, sliced
1 cup arborio (Italian risotto) rice
1 teaspoon saffron threads
1 teaspoon salt
½ teaspoon ground black pepper
2 cups turkey stock
⅔ cup white wine
1 small red bell pepper
1 small yellow bell pepper
10 oz. cooked turkey
2 tablespoons shredded Gruyère cheese
1 tablespoon fresh, chopped parsley
small bell pepper rings and parsley, to garnish

Melt butter in a flameproof dish or saucepan. Add onion, garlic, and mushrooms and cook 2 minutes or until tender. Stir in rice and cook an additional 2 minutes. Add saffron, salt, pepper, stock, and wine. Bring to boil, stirring constantly, then cover and cook very gently 15 minutes. Broil bell peppers until skin is charred and peppers are tender. Remove stalk, seeds, and skin and cut bell peppers into fine strips. Cut turkey into bite-sized pieces.

Add turkey and peppers to risotto. Stir carefully to distribute ingredients. Cover and cook an additional 5 minutes or until rice is tender and mixture is creamy but not dry. Arrange risotto on a warmed serving plate. Sprinkle with cheese and parsley. Garnish with pepper rings and parsley and serve hot.

Makes 4 to 6 servings.

TURKEY PARMIGIANA

¼ cup olive oil
1 onion, chopped
1 clove garlic, crushed
14½ oz. can chopped tomatoes
1 teaspoon dried oregano
salt and freshly ground black pepper
small eggplant, weighing about 9 oz., thinly sliced
4 turkey steaks
4 oz. mozzarella cheese, thinly sliced
⅓ cup finely grated Parmesan cheese

Heat 1 tablespoon of olive oil in a saucepan. Add onion and garlic and cook 5 minutes until soft. Add tomatoes, oregano, and salt and pepper.

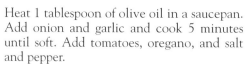

Bring to boil and simmer 2 minutes. Pour into a shallow, ovenproof dish and set aside. Preheat oven to 375°F. Preheat broiler. Brush eggplant with 2 tablespoons oil. Broil for a few minutes on each side until soft and lightly browned. Set aside.

Heat remaining oil in a skillet, add turkey steaks, and cook 2 or 3 minutes on each side until browned. Put turkey steaks on top of tomato sauce. Arrange eggplant and mozzarella slices on top, overlapping. Sprinkle with Parmesan cheese and bake 30 minutes or until turkey is cooked through and topping is browned.

Makes 4 servings.

TURKEY & BAMBOO CURRY

3 tablespoons unsweetened shredded coconut, soaked in ⅔ cup boiling water 30 minutes
1 lb. lean turkey fillet
1 tablespoon sunflower oil
1 clove garlic, finely chopped
½ in. piece fresh ginger, peeled and finely chopped
4 scallions, chopped
6 oz. baby corn
2 tablespoons dark soy sauce
1 whole cinnamon stick, broken
1 teaspoon ground coriander
⅔ cup chicken stock
4 oz. can bamboo shoots, drained

Pour coconut mixture through a fine strainer placed over a bowl, pressing coconut with the back of a spoon to extract all liquid. Reserve liquid and discard coconut. Cut turkey into ½ in. strips. Heat oil in a nonstick or well-seasoned wok or pan and stir-fry turkey, garlic, ginger, scallions, and baby corn 2 minutes or until turkey is lightly colored.

Stir in soy sauce, cinnamon stick, ground coriander, coconut water, and stock. Bring to boil and simmer 20 minutes. Stir in bamboo shoots and simmer an additional 5 minutes. Discard cinnamon stick and serve curry with rice and salad.

Makes 4 servings.

CILANTRO TURKEY RICE

1 tablespoon sunflower oil
2 shallots, chopped
2 cloves garlic, finely chopped
1 oz. prosciutto, trimmed and cut into strips
1¼ cups long-grain white rice, rinsed
1 teaspoon ground coriander
salt and freshly ground pepper
3¾ cups chicken stock
4 or 5 fresh asparagus spears, cut into 1 in. pieces, blanched
1½ cups frozen peas
8 oz. cooked turkey, skinless and diced
¼ cup fresh, chopped cilantro

Heat oil in a nonstick or well-seasoned wok or pan and stir-fry shallots, garlic, prosciutto, rice, and ground coriander 2 minutes. Season with salt and pepper.

Pour in stock and bring to boil. Reduce heat and simmer 20 minutes. Gently stir in asparagus, peas, turkey, and coriander and cook over low heat 5 minutes or until heated through, stirring to prevent sticking. Serve immediately.

Makes 4 servings.

TURKEY KORMA

1 teaspoon turmeric
1 teaspoon ground cumin
1 teaspoon ground coriander
½ teaspoon ground ginger
⅔ cup plain yogurt
2 teaspoons lemon juice
½ cup coconut milk
½ cup chicken stock
1 cup unsweetened dried coconut
3 cups diced cooked turkey meat
cilantro sprigs, to garnish

Preheat oven to 375°F. Dry-fry turmeric, cumin, coriander, and ginger in a flameproof casserole 2 or 3 minutes.

Add yogurt, lemon juice, coconut milk, stock, dried coconut, and salt and pepper and mix well. Stir in turkey.

Bring to boil, cover, and cook in the oven 30 to 40 minutes. Garnish with cilantro sprigs and serve with rice.

Makes 4 servings.

GINGER TURKEY & CABBAGE

1¼ cups red wine
2 tablespoons red wine vinegar
⅔ cup golden raisins
2 cups dried apricots, halved
1 in. piece fresh ginger, peeled and grated
2 cloves garlic, crushed
salt and freshly ground black pepper
4 turkey fillets, each weighing 6 oz.
½ red cabbage, shredded
Italian parsley sprigs, to garnish

In a large bowl, mix together red wine, vinegar, golden raisins, apricots, ginger, garlic, and salt and pepper. Add turkey fillets.

Cover and marinate at least 2 hours, preferably overnight. Preheat oven to 400°F. Arrange red cabbage in a shallow, ovenproof dish. Remove turkey fillets from marinade and mix marinade with cabbage. Place turkey on top.

Cook in the oven 45 to 50 minutes until turkey is tender and cooked through. Garnish with Italian parsley and serve.

Makes 4 servings.

DUCK
& GAME

DUCK WITH APPLES & PRUNES

MEDITERRANEAN DUCK

1 tablespoon olive oil
4 boneless duck breasts, each weighing 4 oz.
2 cooking apples, peeled, cored, and sliced
1¼ cups prunes
2½ cups dry cider
salt and freshly ground black pepper

Preheat oven to 400°F. Heat oil in a shallow, flameproof dish, add duck, and cook 3 or 4 minutes on each side, until browned.

1 tablespoon olive oil
4 lb. duck, quartered
1 large onion, thinly sliced
1 clove garlic, crushed
½ teaspoon ground cumin
1¾ cups chicken stock
juice ½ lemon
1 or 2 teaspoons harissa
1 cinnamon stick
1 teaspoon saffron threads
½ cup black olives
½ cup green olives
peel from 1 preserved lemon, rinsed and cut into strips
salt and freshly ground black pepper
2 tablespoons chopped cilantro
cilantro sprigs, to garnish

Cover with apple slices and prunes. Pour cider over duck and season with salt and pepper. Bring to boil, cover with a lid or piece of aluminum foil, and cook in the oven 55 to 60 minutes until duck is cooked through. Remove duck from the dish with a slotted spoon, leaving behind apples and prunes, and keep warm.

Heat oil in a flameproof casserole. Add duck and cook until browned all over. Remove with a slotted spoon and set aside. Add onion and garlic to the casserole and cook 5 minutes until soft. Add cumin and cook, stirring, 2 minutes.

Bring cooking juices in the dish to boil and boil 5 minutes until liquid has reduced and thickened. Pour sauce, apples, and prunes over duck and serve.

Makes 4 servings.

Add stock, lemon juice, harissa, cinnamon stick, and saffron. Bring to boil. Return duck to the casserole and add olives and lemon peel. Season with salt and pepper. Simmer gently, partially covered, 45 minutes until duck is cooked through. Discard cinnamon stick. Stir in chopped cilantro, garnish, and serve.

Makes 4 servings.

Note: If preserved lemons are unavailable, use grated zest of 1 fresh lemon instead.

DUCK & OLIVES

3 tablespoons olive oil
4 to 5 lb. duck, quartered
1 Spanish onion, finely chopped
1 tablespoon flour
2 beefsteak tomatoes, peeled (see page 174), seeded, and chopped
¼ cup dry white wine
3 tablespoons water
4 bay leaves
3 parsley sprigs
3 cloves garlic, crushed
salt and freshly ground black pepper
2 cups green olives

Heat half the oil in a heavy, flameproof casserole. Add duck in batches, brown evenly, then transfer to absorbent paper towels to drain. Heat remaining oil in casserole, add onion, and cook 6 to 8 minutes, stirring occasionally, until golden and translucent. Stir in flour, then tomatoes, wine, water, bay leaves, parsley, and garlic. Season with salt and pepper. Bring to boil, stirring. Add duck pieces, cover, and cook gently 30 minutes.

Put olives into a bowl, pour over boiling water, then drain well. Add to casserole, cover tightly, and cook about 30 minutes until juices run clear when thickest part of duck is pierced with a skewer. Skim excess fat from surface and adjust seasoning if necessary.

Makes 4 servings.

DUCK & COCONUT CURRY

4 duck portions, skinless
2 tablespoons vegetable oil
1 teaspoon mustard seeds
1 onion, finely chopped
3 cloves garlic, crushed
2 in. piece fresh ginger, grated
2 fresh green chilies, seeded and chopped
1 teaspoon ground cumin
1 tablespoon ground coriander
1 teaspoon turmeric
1 tablespoon white wine vinegar
salt and cayenne pepper
1¼ cups coconut milk
2 tablespoons shredded coconut, toasted, and lemon wedges, to garnish

Wash duck and pat dry with absorbent paper towels. Heat oil in a large skillet, add duck, and fry, stirring, over high heat 8 to 10 minutes until browned all over, then remove from pan. Pour off all but 2 tablespoons fat from pan, add mustard seeds, and fry 1 minute or until they begin to pop.

Add onion to pan and cook, stirring, over medium heat 8 minutes or until soft and golden. Stir in garlic, ginger, chilies, cumin, coriander, and turmeric and fry 2 minutes. Stir in vinegar and season with salt and cayenne pepper. Return duck to pan and turn pieces to coat them in spice mixture. Stir in coconut milk and bring to boil. Cover and cook over low heat about 40 minutes or until duck is tender. Garnish and serve hot.

Makes 4 servings.

DUCK WITH BEETS & BEANS

1 tablespoon olive oil
2 large duckling breast fillets, each weighing 8 oz.,
    fat removed and skin left on
4 shallots, finely chopped
1 clove garlic, finely sliced
12 oz. wild or field mushrooms, trimmed
1 tablespoon all-purpose flour
2 tablespoons fruity red wine
⅔ cup duck or chicken stock
8 oz. fresh or frozen fava beans
1 tablespoon red currant jelly
freshly ground black pepper
1 teaspoon cornstarch
½ teaspoon dry mustard powder
grated zest and juice 1 large orange
1 lb. fresh baby beets, cooked and peeled

Heat a wok or pan until hot. Add oil and swirl to coat. With a sharp knife, remove skin and make two or three diagonal slashes across duckling breasts, ½ in. deep. Add to pan and cook over moderate heat 5 or 6 minutes until golden, turning and stirring. Remove to a plate and keep warm. Add shallots and garlic to pan. Stir-fry 1 minute, add mushrooms, and stir-fry an additional 2 or 3 minutes. Sprinkle with flour and stir to blend. Add wine and stock and bring to boil. Add beans.

Simmer, covered, 15 to 20 minutes until beans are tender and sauce is thickened. (If using frozen beans, add 5 minutes before end of cooking time.) Stir in red currant jelly and season with pepper. Meanwhile, in a saucepan, combine cornstarch, mustard powder, orange zest and juice, and beets. Bring to boil and simmer 1 minute until glaze thickens and beets are hot. Slice duck thinly and arrange slices on four plates with beans and beets.

Makes 4 servings.

THAI DUCK CURRY

⅓ cup coconut cream
⅓ cup Thai green curry paste
3 lb. duck, skinless, well-trimmed of excess fat,
    divided into 8 portions
2½ cups coconut milk
1 tablespoon fish sauce
8 kaffir lime leaves, shredded
2 fresh green chilies, seeded and thinly sliced
12 Thai holy basil leaves
leaves from 5 cilantro sprigs
cilantro sprigs, to garnish

Heat coconut cream in a wok or pan over medium heat, stirring, until it thickens and oil begins to separate and boil.

Stir in curry paste and cook about 5 minutes until mixture darkens. Stir in duck pieces to coat with curry mixture. Lower heat, cover, and cook 15 minutes, stirring occasionally. If necessary, using a bulb baster, remove excess fat from the surface, or carefully spoon it off. Stir in coconut milk, fish sauce, and lime leaves. Heat to just simmering point, then cook gently without boiling, turning duck over occasionally, 30 to 40 minutes until meat is very tender. Remove surplus fat from surface, then stir in chilies.

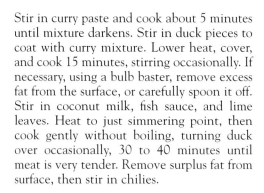

Cook an additional 5 minutes. Stir in basil and cilantro and cook an additional 2 minutes. Garnish with cilantro sprigs.

Makes 4 servings.

DUCK WITH TURNIPS

4 to 5 lb. duck
salt and freshly ground black pepper
1 tablespoon olive oil
1 cup chicken stock
½ cup dry white wine
bouquet garni
pinch sugar
5 small turnips, halved or quartered
sage sprigs, to garnish

Season duck generously inside and out with salt and pepper and prick fatty areas of breasts with a fork.

Heat oil in a heavy, flameproof casserole, add duck, and cook over low heat, turning, until browned all over. Pour fat from casserole, reserving 2 tablespoons. Add stock, wine, and bouquet garni to casserole, cover tightly, and cook gently 30 minutes.

Meanwhile, heat reserved duck fat in a skillet, add turnips, sprinkle with sugar, and cook until browned all over. Add turnips to casserole, baste with cooking liquid, and cook, uncovered, 25 minutes until duck and turnips are tender. Transfer duck and turnips to a warmed serving plate. Skim fat from sauce, then boil sauce to thicken slightly. Season with salt and pepper and remove bouquet garni. Carve duck, garnish, and serve with turnips and sauce.

Makes 4 servings.

DUCK TAGINE WITH PEARS

1 tablespoon olive oil
3 duck breasts, total weight about 2¼ lb.
4 onions, thickly sliced
3 cloves garlic, crushed
1 teaspoon sugar
2 teaspoons ground cinnamon
½ teaspoon saffron threads
1¼ cups chicken stock
salt and freshly ground black pepper
¾ cup dried pears
3 tablespoons fresh, chopped cilantro

Heat oil in a large nonstick skillet. Add duck, skin-side up, and cook 1 or 2 minutes until lightly browned.

Turn duck breasts and cook, as gently as possible, until skin is browned and crisp. Remove and drain on absorbent paper towels. Pour off all but 3 tablespoons fat. Add onions and cook 15 minutes until completely soft. Slice duck breasts crosswise into ½ in. slices. Place onion and duck in a heavy, flameproof casserole.

Stir in garlic, sugar, cinnamon, saffron, and stock. Season with salt and pepper. Cover and simmer gently 30 minutes. Cut pears into pieces, add to the casserole, cover, and cook gently an additional 30 minutes. Stir in cilantro and serve with couscous.

Makes 6 servings.

PAN-FRIED GAME HEN

1 tablespoon olive oil
2 game hens
4 slices bacon, chopped
6 oz. button mushrooms
10 shallots
2 tablespoons brandy
1 cup red wine
2½ cups chicken stock
3 tablespoons red currant jelly
salt and freshly ground black pepper
marjoram sprigs, to garnish

GAME HEN FRICASSEE

2 cloves garlic, crushed
1 teaspoon paprika
1 teaspoon ground ginger
salt and freshly ground black pepper
2 game hens, quartered
2 tablespoons oil
1 large onion, coarsely chopped
8 scallions, sliced
3 tomatoes, peeled (see page 174) and chopped
1 Scotch bonnet chili
1 fresh bay leaf
chicken stock, if required
fresh, chopped parsley, to garnish

Preheat oven to 350°F. Heat oil in an ovenproof dish. Add game hens and brown all over.

In a bowl, mix together garlic, paprika, ginger, and seasoning. Rub over game hen portions and place in a dish. Cover and chill overnight. Scrape off and reserve marinade. Pat game hen portions dry with absorbent paper towels. Heat oil in a large, heavy skillet and fry game hen pieces, in batches, until golden all over. Transfer to a casserole. Add onion to skillet and cook 10 minutes until soft.

Cover and cook in the oven 35 to 40 minutes. Remove and keep warm. Add bacon, mushrooms, and shallots to the dish and cook, stirring, 4 to 5 minutes until golden brown. Remove with a slotted spoon and keep warm. Add brandy, wine, stock, and red currant jelly to cooking juices and stir well. Bring to boil, stirring, and boil 20 to 25 minutes, stirring occasionally, until sauce is reduced and thickened.

Return game hens, bacon, mushrooms, and shallots to the casserole and season well. Bring to boil and simmer 4 to 5 minutes to warm through. Cut game hens in half with kitchen scissors or a sharp knife. Garnish with marjoram sprigs and serve.

Makes 4 servings.

Transfer onion to casserole and add scallions, tomatoes, chili, bay leaf, and reserved marinade. Cover and simmer gently 30 to 40 minutes until game hen is thoroughly cooked. Add a little chicken stock if necessary, although there should not be a large quantity of liquid. Remove and discard chili and bay leaf. Serve garnished with chopped parsley.

Makes 4 servings.

GAME HEN IN BEETS

1 lb. uncooked beets
1 onion, chopped
1¾ cups chicken stock
3 tablespoons butter
1 teaspoon ground cumin
½ teaspoon ground allspice
½ teaspoon ground cinnamon
1 large game hen, quartered
1 teaspoon cornstarch
¼ cup plain yogurt
fresh, chopped mint, to garnish

Place beets in a pan of boiling water. Cover and simmer 30 to 60 minutes until tender. Drain.

Preheat the oven to 325°F. As soon as beets are cool enough to handle, remove skin. Cut beets into chunks and place in a blender or food processor with onion and chicken stock. Blend until completely smooth. In a flameproof casserole, melt butter. Add cumin, allspice, and cinnamon and cook 1 minute. Add game hen portions and cook until lightly browned.

Stir in beet purée and season with salt and pepper. Heat to simmering point, then cover and cook in the oven 1 hour or until game hen is very tender. Place game hen portions on a heated serving plate. Blend cornstarch with a little cold water and pour into sauce. Bring to boil and simmer a minute until slightly thickened. Pour sauce over game hens; drizzle with yogurt and sprinkle with chopped mint. Serve with rice.

Makes 4 servings.

GAME HEN CASSEROLE

¼ cup olive oil
1 large game hen, quartered
1 large onion, finely sliced
1 clove garlic, crushed
14½ oz. can chopped tomatoes
1 tablespoon fresh, chopped oregano
salt and pepper
1 lb. small okra
halved black olives, to garnish

In a flameproof casserole, heat oil. Add game hen pieces. Cook on both sides until browned. Transfer to a plate.

Add onion and garlic to casserole and cook until soft. Add tomatoes, oregano, 1¼ cups water, salt, and pepper. Bring to boil, then add game hen and coat well with sauce. Cover pan and simmer gently 40 minutes.

Trim ends of okra without cutting pods. Put into a bowl of cold water, rinse gently, and strain. Repeat until water is clear. Spread okra over game hens. Cover and simmer an additional 30 minutes until okra is tender. Sprinkle the top with black olives and serve.

Makes 4 servings.

SPANISH PARTRIDGE

2 partridges, halved along backbone
2 tablespoons brandy
salt and freshly ground black pepper
3 tablespoons olive oil
1 Spanish onion, chopped
3 cloves garlic, finely chopped
2 tablespoons all-purpose flour
¼ cup red wine vinegar
1 cup red wine
1 cup chicken stock
6 black peppercorns
2 cloves
1 bay leaf
2 carrots, cut into short lengths
8 shallots
¼ cup grated unsweetened chocolate

Rub partridges with brandy, salt, and pepper and set aside 30 minutes. Heat oil in a heavy, flameproof casserole into which the birds fit snugly. Add onion and fry, stirring occasionally, 3 minutes. Stir in garlic and cook 2 minutes.

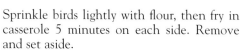

Sprinkle birds lightly with flour, then fry in casserole 5 minutes on each side. Remove and set aside.

Stir vinegar into casserole and boil 1 or 2 minutes. Add wine and boil 1 or 2 minutes, then add stock, peppercorns, cloves, bay leaf, and partridges. Heat to simmering point, cover tightly, and cook gently 40 minutes. Add carrots and shallots, cover again, and continue to cook gently 20 minutes.

Transfer partridges, shallots, and carrots to a warmed dish. If necessary, boil cooking juices until reduced to 1¼ cups, then purée in a blender or food processor.

Return juices to casserole, heat gently, and stir in grated chocolate until melted. Return partridges and vegetables to casserole and turn them over in sauce so they are well coated.

Makes 4 servings.

PHEASANT IN PARSLEY SAUCE

SQUAB STIFADO

½ stick butter
2 pheasants
3 oz. fresh parsley
3 onions, thinly sliced
¼ cup all-purpose flour
1¼ cups chicken stock
⅔ cup sour cream
salt and freshly ground black pepper
Italian parsley sprigs, to garnish

Preheat oven to 350°F. Melt butter in a large, flameproof dish. Add pheasants and cook until browned all over. Remove and keep warm.

Separate thick parsley stalks from the leaves and tie stalks together with string. Chop leaves and set aside. Add onions to the dish and cook, stirring occasionally, 7 minutes until soft and lightly colored. Add flour and cook, stirring, 1 minute. Gradually add chicken stock, stirring constantly until smooth. Bring to boil and add bundle of parsley stalks. Add pheasants, cover, and cook in the oven 1 hour.

Remove pheasants from the dish and keep warm. Remove and discard parsley stalks. Add chopped parsley and sour cream to sauce and season with salt and pepper. Heat gently to warm through. Cut pheasants in half with kitchen scissors. Garnish with Italian parsley sprigs and serve with parsley sauce.

Makes 4 servings.

4 squabs
2 tablespoons seasoned flour
⅓ cup olive oil
1 lb. tiny pearl onions, peeled
1 clove garlic, crushed
1 tablespoon tomato paste
¾ cup red wine
1 cup chicken stock
1 fresh bay leaf
2 thyme sprigs
salt and freshly ground black pepper
2 slices white bread, crusts removed
2 tablespoons fresh, chopped parsley

Toss squabs in seasoned flour.

Preheat the oven to 325°F. Heat half the oil in a flameproof casserole. Add squabs and cook until browned all over. Remove and set aside. Add onions to the casserole and cook 7 minutes until beginning to brown. Add garlic and tomato paste and stir in wine and stock. Add bay leaf, thyme, and salt and pepper. Return squabs to the casserole, cover, and cook in the oven 1½ to 2 hours until squabs are cooked through and tender. Transfer squabs to a warmed serving dish and keep warm.

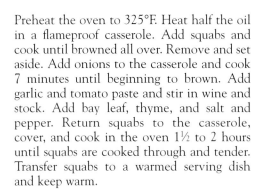

Remove herbs from cooking liquid and, reduce cooking liquid by boiling over high heat 1 or 2 minutes. Cut each slice of bread into four triangles. Heat remaining oil in a skillet, add bread, and fry until golden brown on both sides. Dip one edge of each triangle into parsley. Pour sauce over squabs, garnish with fried bread, and serve.

Makes 4 servings.

QUAIL WITH FIGS & ORANGES

3 tablespoons olive oil
8 quails
1 onion, thinly sliced
2 stalks celery, thinly sliced
⅔ cup dry white wine
⅔ cup hot chicken stock
salt and freshly ground black pepper
2 oranges
4 figs

Preheat oven to 325°F. Heat 2 tablespoons of the olive oil in a heavy casserole. Add quails and cook until browned all over. Remove and set aside.

Add onion and celery to the casserole and cook gently 7 minutes until soft and lightly browned. Replace quails and pour over wine and hot stock. Season with salt and pepper. Cover and cook in the oven 30 to 40 minutes until quails are cooked through. Just before the end of the cooking time, preheat the broiler. Peel oranges, removing all the pith, and cut each one into four thick slices. Cut figs in half.

Brush orange slices with olive oil and broil 2 or 3 minutes. Turn, add figs, and broil cut sides 2 minutes. Set aside and keep warm. Transfer quails, onion, and celery to a warmed serving dish. Pour over cooking juices, arrange oranges and figs around the birds, and serve.

Makes 4 servings.

QUAIL IN RUM & RAISIN SAUCE

¼ cup dark rum
¼ cup raisins
1 tablespoon oil
8 quails
1 onion, sliced
1 clove garlic, sliced
1 teaspoon molasses
⅔ cup chicken stock
1 teaspoon hot pepper sauce
salt and freshly ground black pepper
2 teaspoons arrowroot
chopped cilantro, to garnish

Put rum and raisins in a bowl and let soak 2 hours.

Heat oil in a flameproof casserole. Add quails and cook, turning frequently, until evenly browned. Remove and set aside. Add onion and garlic to casserole and cook 10 minutes until soft. Strain rum from raisins and put in a ladle or small saucepan. Heat gently, then ignite with a taper and pour into casserole.

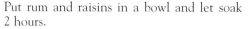
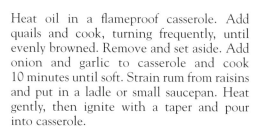

When flames die down, stir in molasses, stock, hot pepper sauce, and seasoning. Return quails to casserole. Cover and cook 20 to 30 minutes until cooked through. Remove to a serving dish and keep warm. In a bowl, mix arrowroot with a little water and stir into sauce in casserole. Cook, stirring, a few minutes until thickened, then pour over quails. Garnish with chopped cilantro and serve.

Makes 4 servings.

QUAIL IN MASALA SAUCE

8 quails
1 tablespoon melted butter
mint sprigs and lettuce leaves, to garnish
MARINADE:
1¼ cups plain yogurt
1 small onion, finely chopped
1 tablespoon fresh, finely chopped mint leaves
1 tablespoon fresh, finely chopped cilantro
1 clove garlic, crushed
1 in. piece fresh ginger, peeled and grated
1 tablespoon garam masala
juice 1 lemon
1 teaspoon salt

Put quails in a large dish. Mix together marinade ingredients and pour over quails.

Cover and marinate for at least 2 hours, preferably overnight. Preheat oven to 425°F. Remove quails from marinade, reserving marinade. Thread quails onto skewers and sit skewers over an ovenproof dish.

Cook in the oven 40 minutes, basting with melted butter, until quails are cooked through. Remove quails and keep warm. Add reserved marinade to dish and stir to combine with cooking juices. Bring to boil, stirring. Garnish quails with mint sprigs and lettuce leaves and serve with masala sauce.

Makes 4 servings.

QUAIL WITH GRAPES

3 tablespoons olive oil
1 Spanish onion, finely chopped
2 small carrots, finely chopped
salt and freshly ground black pepper
8 quails
8 slices bacon
4 black peppercorns
2 cloves garlic
9 oz. moscatel grapes, peeled and seeded
pinch freshly grated nutmeg
1 cup medium-bodied dry white wine
¼ cup Spanish brandy

Preheat oven to 375°F. Heat oil in a heavy, flameproof casserole that will hold quails in a single layer. Add onion and carrots and cook, stirring occasionally, 4 or 5 minutes. Season quails inside and out, lay a slice of bacon over each one, and tie in place with string. Place on vegetables, then cook in the oven 30 minutes.

Meanwhile, using a mortar and pestle, crush peppercorns and garlic, then work in half the grapes and the nutmeg, wine, and brandy. Pour mixture over quails and cook 30 minutes, basting occasionally. Add remaining grapes, then carefully pour cooking liquid into a saucepan; keep casserole warm. Boil liquid until lightly thickened, then season to taste. Transfer quails, bacon, vegetables, and grapes to a warmed serving plate and pour sauce on top.

Makes 4 to 6 servings.

PROVENÇAL RABBIT

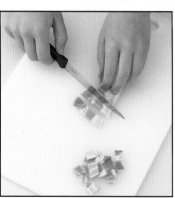

3 oz. pancetta
2 tablespoons olive oil
1 onion, chopped
4 rabbit portions
1 tablespoon seasoned flour
3 tablespoons tapenade
1¾ cups chicken stock
⅔ cup dry white wine
2 fresh bay leaves
2 thyme sprigs
salt and freshly ground black pepper
1 small fennel bulb, roughly chopped
black olives and fennel leaves, to garnish

Roughly chop half the pancetta.

Preheat the oven to 350°F. Heat half the oil in a flameproof casserole. Add onion and chopped pancetta and cook 3 minutes. Remove with a slotted spoon and set aside. Dust rabbit portions with seasoned flour. Heat remaining oil in the casserole, add rabbit, and cook until browned all over. Mix together tapenade, stock, and wine and pour over rabbit. Add onion, pancetta, bay leaves, and thyme. Season with salt and pepper and bring to boil. Cover and cook in the oven 45 minutes.

Add fennel and cook 45 minutes or until rabbit is cooked through and tender. Broil remaining pancetta until crisp, then snip into small pieces and sprinkle over rabbit. Garnish with olives and fennel leaves and serve.

Makes 4 servings.

RABBIT IN MUSTARD SAUCE

½ stick butter
8 rabbit portions
1 cup dry white wine
½ cup Dijon mustard
1 thyme sprig
salt and freshly ground black pepper
½ cup plain yogurt
fresh, chopped Italian parsley and thyme sprigs, to garnish

Melt butter in a flameproof casserole. Add rabbit and cook 5 to 10 minutes, turning, until browned all over. Remove with a slotted spoon.

Stir in wine, mustard, thyme, and salt and pepper and bring to boil. Return rabbit to the casserole, cover, and simmer 25 minutes. Remove rabbit with a slotted spoon and keep warm.

Boil sauce until reduced by half. Remove and discard thyme sprig and stir in yogurt. Heat gently to warm through. Garnish rabbit with chopped parsley and thyme sprigs, pour over sauce, and serve.

Makes 4 servings.

RABBIT & RED BELL PEPPER STEW

CALYPSO RABBIT

2¼ lb. rabbit pieces
2 tablespoons fresh, chopped thyme
2 tablespoons fresh, chopped rosemary
2 fresh bay leaves
juice 1 lemon
1 tablespoon balsamic vinegar
salt and freshly ground black pepper
2 tablespoons olive oil
4 red bell peppers, seeded and roughly diced
14½ oz. can strained crushed tomatoes

Place rabbit in a plastic bag with thyme, rosemary, bay leaves, lemon juice, vinegar, salt, and pepper. Seal and let marinate in the refrigerator 2 to 3 hours or overnight.

Heat half the oil in a saucepan. Add bell peppers and cook over gentle heat about 10 minutes until soft. Stir in tomatoes and season with salt and pepper. Cover and cook 30 minutes. Remove rabbit from marinade, reserving marinade, and pat dry with absorbent paper towels.

Heat remaining oil in a skillet, add rabbit pieces, and fry on all sides until golden. Add rabbit to bell pepper sauce. Deglaze skillet with reserved marinade and add to rabbit. Cover and simmer 20 to 30 minutes until rabbit is tender. Serve with pasta.

Makes 4 servings.

juice 1 lime
salt and freshly ground black pepper
½ teaspoon fresh, chopped thyme
2 cloves garlic, crushed
6 boneless rabbit portions
3 tablespoons oil
2 teaspoons brown sugar
¾ cup cashews
2 large onions, chopped
4 oz. mushrooms, sliced
1 in. piece fresh ginger, grated
¼ cup chicken stock
few drops Angostura bitters
2 teaspoons arrowroot
thyme sprigs and lime slices, to garnish

In a dish, mix together lime juice, seasoning, thyme, and 1 garlic clove. Add rabbit pieces and turn in marinade to coat thoroughly. Cover and leave in a cool place 3 hours. In a flameproof casserole, heat half the oil. Add sugar and cook gently until bubbling. Add rabbit and fry, turning until evenly browned. Meanwhile, in a skillet, heat remaining oil. Add cashews and cook gently until lightly browned. Remove with a slotted spoon and set aside.

Add onions to pan and cook 5 minutes. Stir in remaining garlic, mushrooms, and ginger and cook 5 minutes. Stir in stock and Angostura bitters and pour over rabbit. Stir in half the cashews. Cover casserole and simmer gently 30 to 40 minutes until rabbit is cooked through. In a bowl, mix arrowroot with a little water. Stir into rabbit mixture and simmer 3 minutes. Sprinkle with remaining cashews and garnish with thyme and lime slices. Serve with rice.

Makes 6 servings.

RABBIT STIFADO

2 tablespoons all-purpose flour
salt and pepper
1½ to 2¼ lb. rabbit portions
⅓ cup olive oil
1 lb. tiny pearl onions, peeled
1 clove garlic, crushed
1 tablespoon tomato paste
1¼ cups red wine
1¼ cups chicken stock
1 bay leaf
2 thyme sprigs
2 slices bread, crusts removed
2 tablespoons fresh, chopped parsley

VENISON RAGOUT

1 tablespoon all-purpose flour
salt and freshly ground black pepper
2 lb. stewing venison, diced
1 tablespoon olive oil
1 clove garlic, chopped
1¼ cups beef stock
1 tablespoon balsamic vinegar
8 juniper berries
8 black peppercorns
4 cloves
14½ oz. can chopped tomatoes
8 oz. baby carrots, trimmed
4 oz. button mushrooms
1 tablespoon fresh, chopped parsley

On a plate, mix together flour, salt, and pepper. Toss rabbit pieces in seasoned flour. Heat half the oil in a skillet. Fry rabbit pieces until browned on both sides. Transfer to a flameproof casserole. Add onions to skillet and cook until they begin to brown. Add garlic and tomato paste to pan, then stir in wine and stock. Add bay leaf, thyme, salt, and pepper. Add to casserole, cover, and cook over low heat 1½ to 2 hours or until rabbit is tender.

Preheat oven to 350°F. Season flour with salt and pepper and use to coat venison. Heat oil in a large, flameproof casserole. Add venison, remaining seasoned flour, and garlic and cook, stirring, 4 or 5 minutes.

Cut each slice of bread into four triangles. In a skillet, heat remaining oil and fry bread until golden brown on both sides. Dip one edge of each triangle into chopped parsley. To serve, place rabbit on a shallow plate and arrange onions around edge. Pour sauce over rabbit and garnish with fried bread.

Makes 6 servings.

Add stock, vinegar, juniper berries, peppercorns, cloves, tomatoes, and carrots. Bring to boil, cover, and cook in the oven 1 hour. Add mushrooms and cook 15 minutes. Sprinkle with chopped parsley and serve.

Makes 6 to 8 servings.

LAMB

CHUMP CHOP BOULANGÈRE

1 tablespoon olive oil
4 lamb loin chops, each weighing 6 oz.
2 large onions, sliced
8 oz. Savoy cabbage, shredded
5 medium potatoes, thinly sliced
salt and freshly ground black pepper
fresh bouquet garni
2¼ cups lamb or chicken stock
2 tablespoons butter, melted
fresh, chopped parsley, to garnish

Heat oil in a flameproof casserole. Add chops and cook 2 or 3 minutes on each side until browned. Remove and set aside.

Preheat oven to 400°F. Add onions and cabbage to the casserole and cook gently 10 minutes until soft. Remove half the mixture and set aside. Place chops on top of remaining onion and cabbage mixture. Mix two thirds of the potatoes with reserved onion and cabbage mixture. Season with salt and pepper. Arrange on top of chops, placing bouquet garni in the middle. Pour over stock.

Arrange remaining potatoes on top and brush with melted butter. Cook in the oven 15 minutes. Remove from the oven and press potatoes down. Brush again with melted butter and season with salt and pepper. Lower oven temperature to 350°F and cook 1 hour. Garnish with chopped parsley and serve.

Makes 4 servings.

SAGE LAMB COBBLER

2 lb. neck of lamb, boned and diced
¼ cup all-purpose flour
1 tablespoon olive oil
1 large onion, chopped
¼ cup dried peas, soaked overnight
2 or 3 carrots
1¼ cups diced rutabaga
2¼ cups lamb or chicken stock
salt, pepper, and large pinch paprika
TOPPING:
2 cups all-purpose flour
1½ teaspoons baking powder
½ stick butter
1 teaspoon dried sage
1 egg
2 tablespoons milk, plus extra for brushing

Preheat oven to 325°F. Coat lamb in flour. Heat oil in a flameproof casserole. Add lamb and cook until browned all over. Remove and set aside. Add onion and cook, stirring occasionally, 7 minutes until lightly browned. Return lamb and add peas, carrots, and rutabaga. Pour in stock and season with salt, pepper, and paprika. Bring to boil, cover, and cook in the oven 2 hours.

Sift flour, baking powder, and salt into a bowl. Cut in butter until mixture resembles fine bread crumbs. Stir in sage. Add egg and milk and bind to a soft dough. Knead on a lightly floured surface and roll out to ½ in. thick. Using a cookie cutter, cut out 1½ in. rounds. Arrange scones on top of the casserole and brush with milk. Increase oven temperature to 400°F. Return casserole to the oven and cook, uncovered, 15 to 20 minutes until scones are risen and golden.

Makes 6 to 8 servings.

BRAISED LAMB & VEGETABLES

LAMB CHILINDRON

5 medium, firm, yellow-fleshed potatoes, cut into
¼ in. slices
2 cloves garlic, pounded to a paste
6 to 8 scallions, thinly sliced
2 medium to large artichoke bottoms, sliced
5 oz. chestnut mushrooms, chopped
handful parsley, finely chopped
1 tablespoon mixed, fresh herbs, chopped
salt and freshly ground black pepper
3 tablespoons olive oil
4 lamb shoulder or loin chops
¾ cup full-bodied dry white wine

¼ cup olive oil
1½ lb. lean lamb, diced
salt and freshly ground black pepper
1 Spanish onion
2 cloves garlic, chopped
3 large red bell peppers, peeled, seeded, and cut into
strips
4 beefsteak tomatoes, peeled (see page 174), seeded,
and chopped
1 dried red chili, chopped
fresh, chopped herbs, to garnish

Heat oil in a flameproof casserole. Season
lamb and add to casserole.

Preheat oven to 375°F. In a bowl, combine
potatoes, garlic, scallions, artichoke bottoms,
mushrooms, parsley, mixed herbs, and
seasoning. Place half the mixture in a heavy,
flameproof casserole. Heat oil in a skillet, add
lamb, and brown on both sides. Drain on
absorbent paper towels, then season and place
in casserole.

Cook, stirring, until evenly browned, then
with a slotted spoon, transfer to a bowl. Add
onion to casserole and cook about 4 minutes,
stirring occasionally, until softened but not
colored. Stir in garlic, cook 1 or 2 minutes,
then stir in bell peppers, tomatoes, and chili.
Simmer 5 minutes.

Over heat, stir wine into pan to dislodge
cooking juices, bring to boil, and pour over
lamb. Cover with remaining vegetables and
add sufficient water to come almost to the
level of the vegetables. Bring to boil, cover,
and cook in the oven about 30 minutes.
Uncover and cook an additional 1 hour. Add
a little water if it seems to be drying out.

Makes 4 servings.

Return lamb, and any juices that have
collected in bowl, to casserole. Cover tightly
and cook gently about 1½ hours until lamb is
tender. Season if necessary. Serve garnished
with chopped herbs.

Makes 6 servings.

LAMB WITH BLACK OLIVES

¼ cup olive oil
1½ lb. lean lamb, cut into small cubes
4 oz. side of pork, cut into small strips
2 cloves garlic, sliced
½ or 1 teaspoon fresh, chopped oregano
¾ cup full-bodied white wine
1 fresh red chili, seeded and finely chopped
12 to 15 pitted black olives

Heat oil in a wide, shallow, flameproof casserole. Add lamb, pork, and garlic and cook over high heat to seal and brown meat.

In a small saucepan, boil oregano and wine 2 or 3 minutes. Stir into casserole, cover, and cook 30 minutes.

Stir chili and olives into casserole. Cover again and cook about 30 minutes until lamb is tender. If necessary, uncover casserole toward end of cooking time so liquid can evaporate to make a light sauce.

Makes 4 servings.

SPICE-COATED LAMB

4 cloves garlic
¼ teaspoon cumin seeds
1 tablespoon paprika
¼ teaspoon saffron threads, crushed
salt and freshly ground black pepper
1½ lb. lean boned lamb, cut into 1 to 1½ in. cubes
3 tablespoons olive oil
⅔ cup full-bodied dry white wine

Using a mortar and pestle, pound together garlic, cumin, paprika, saffron, salt, and pepper.

Put lamb into a bowl, add spice mixture, and stir well, but gently, to coat lamb. Set aside 30 minutes.

Heat oil in a flameproof casserole, add lamb, and cook 5 to 7 minutes, stirring occasionally, until lamb has browned. Stir in wine and heat to simmering point. Cover tightly and cook gently about 30 to 40 minutes until meat is tender and sauce thickened.

Makes 4 servings.

LAMB IN GREEN SAUCE

2 tablespoons olive oil
1½ lb. boneless lamb, cut into pieces
1 Spanish onion, chopped
2 green bell peppers, seeded and chopped
3 cloves garlic, crushed
¾ cup dry white wine
⅔ cup water
1½ teaspoons fresh, chopped thyme
salt and freshly ground black pepper
1 small iceberg lettuce, shredded
2 tablespoons fresh, chopped parsley
2 tablespoons fresh, chopped mint
½ cup pine nuts
mint sprigs and pine nuts, to garnish

In a flameproof casserole, heat oil, add lamb, and fry, stirring occasionally, until evenly browned. Using a slotted spoon, remove lamb and set aside. Stir onion into casserole and cook about 4 minutes, stirring occasionally, until softened but not browned. Stir in bell peppers and garlic, cook 2 or 3 minutes, then stir in wine. Boil 1 minute.

Pour in water and bring to boil. Lower heat so liquid is just simmering, then add lamb, thyme, and seasoning. Cover and cook gently about 1 hour. Stir in lettuce, parsley, mint, and pine nuts, cover, and cook an additional 10 to 15 minutes. Serve garnished with mint sprigs and pine nuts.

Makes 4 servings.

LAMB WITH LEMON & GARLIC

3 tablespoons olive oil
2¼ lb. lean, boneless lamb, cut into 1 in. pieces
1 Spanish onion, finely chopped
3 cloves garlic, crushed
1 tablespoon paprika
3 tablespoons fresh, finely chopped parsley
3 tablespoons lemon juice
salt and freshly ground black pepper
3 tablespoons dry white wine (optional)

Heat oil in a heavy, flameproof casserole, add lamb, and cook, stirring occasionally, until lightly browned. Do this in batches, if necessary, so pieces are not crowded. Using a slotted spoon, transfer meat to a plate or bowl and reserve.

Stir onion into casserole and cook about 5 minutes, stirring occasionally, until softened. Stir in garlic, cook 2 minutes, then stir in paprika. When well blended, stir in lamb and any juices on plate or in bowl, parsley, lemon juice, and seasoning. Cover tightly and cook over very low heat 1¼ to 1½ hours, shaking casserole occasionally, until lamb is very tender. If necessary, add 3 tablespoons wine or water.

Makes 4 to 6 servings.

SPICED RACK OF LAMB

1 tablespoon all-purpose flour
salt and pepper
2 racks of lamb
1 clove garlic, finely chopped
2 tablespoons extra-virgin olive oil
5 medium tomatoes, coarsely chopped
½ lemon, cut into small pieces
1 cinnamon stick
3 whole cloves
1 small red chili, seeded and chopped
½ cup dry white wine
2 tablespoons tomato paste
lemon slices, to garnish

Preheat oven to 350°F. Mix together flour, salt, and pepper. Rub over lamb. Press garlic into gaps between bones. Heat oil in a flameproof baking pan. Put lamb, skin-side down, in oil to brown. Remove lamb from baking pan and add tomatoes, lemon, cinnamon, cloves, and chili. Return lamb, skin-side up, to pan.

In a bowl, mix together wine, ½ cup water, and tomato paste. Pour over lamb. Cover baking pan loosely with aluminum foil and roast in the oven 1 hour. Remove foil and roast an additional 30 minutes or until lamb is cooked. Cut lamb into individual chops and keep warm. Place baking pan over direct heat and boil liquid to reduce to a thick sauce. Pour over meat. Garnish with lemon slices.

Makes 6 servings.

ROAST LAMB & VEGETABLES

1 clove garlic, crushed
1 teaspoon fresh, chopped mint
1 teaspoon fresh, chopped rosemary
1 teaspoon fresh, chopped oregano
salt and freshly ground black pepper
4 lb. shoulder of lamb, boned
1½ lb. potatoes, thinly sliced
1 large onion, thinly sliced
5 medium tomatoes, sliced
½ cup dry white wine
mint, rosemary, and oregano sprigs, to garnish

Preheat the oven to 425°F. Mix together garlic, mint, rosemary, oregano, and salt and pepper.

Spread herb mixture over inside of lamb, then roll up and tie into a neat shape. Put in a large baking pan. Reduce the oven temperature to 350°F and roast lamb 30 minutes. Spoon off any fat from the baking pan and add potatoes, onion, and tomatoes.

Pour over wine and season with salt and pepper. Cook 1 hour, turning vegetables occasionally. Carve lamb and arrange on warmed serving plates with vegetables. Pour over cooking juices. Garnish with mint, rosemary, and oregano sprigs and serve.

Makes 6 servings.

LAMB EN PAPILLOTTE

4 lamb leg steaks, each weighing about 6 oz.
1 tablespoon Dijon mustard
4 scallions, sliced
1 teaspoon fresh, chopped rosemary
3 medium sweet potatoes, cut into chunks
3 medium zucchini, thickly sliced
1 tablespoon olive oil
rosemary sprigs, to garnish

Preheat oven to 400°F. Cut four large squares of aluminum foil and place a lamb steak on each one. Spread lamb with mustard and sprinkle with scallions and rosemary. Season with salt and pepper.

Bring the foil up over steaks to make packets and twist the edges together to seal. Put packets in an ovenproof dish. Arrange sweet potatoes and zucchini around packets.

Drizzle vegetables with oil and season with salt and pepper. Cook in the oven 1 hour, basting and turning vegetables at least twice. Remove lamb from packages, garnish with rosemary, and serve with vegetables.

Makes 4 servings.

ONE-POT MOUSSAKA

1 tablespoon olive oil
2 onions, chopped
2 cloves garlic, chopped
1½ lb. (3 cups) lean ground lamb
14½ oz. can chopped or crushed tomatoes
3 or 4 zucchini, sliced into ½ in. pieces
1 tablespoon capers, rinsed and drained
2 tablespoons fresh, chopped or 1 tablespoon dried
  oregano or basil
salt and freshly ground black pepper
1½ cups orzo (rice-shaped pasta)
1 cup feta cheese, crumbled

Heat a wok or pan until hot. Add oil and swirl to coat. Add onions and garlic and stir-fry 2 or 3 minutes until softened. Add lamb and stir-fry 4 or 5 minutes until browned.

Add tomatoes, zucchini, capers, oregano or basil, and salt and pepper. Stir in 1½ cups water and orzo and bring to boil. Reduce heat to low and cook, covered, 8 to 10 minutes until orzo is cooked and most of the liquid absorbed. Remove pan from heat and stir in feta cheese. Serve with a green salad.

Makes 6 to 8 servings.

POMEGRANATE LAMB

3 tablespoons vegetable oil
1 large onion, sliced
2 cloves garlic, finely chopped
1 in. piece fresh ginger, peeled and finely chopped
2¼ lb. lean lamb, diced
salt and freshly ground black pepper
juice 2 pomegranates, about 1¼ cups
1 teaspoon ground cumin
½ teaspoon ground cinnamon
¼ teaspoon ground nutmeg
3 cardamom pods, lightly crushed
⅓ cup plain yogurt
pomegranate seeds and fresh, chopped mint, to
    garnish

Heat oil in a large, flameproof casserole. Add onion, garlic, and ginger and cook 10 minutes until soft. Remove from the pan and set aside. In the same pan, brown lamb, in batches and set aside. Return onion, garlic, ginger, and lamb to the pan. Season with salt and pepper. Gradually stir in pomegranate juice, allowing each addition to be absorbed before adding more. There should be very little liquid left.

Add cumin, cinnamon, nutmeg, and cardamom pods to the pan and stir 1 minute. Stir in yogurt. Cover the pan tightly and cook very gently, preferably on a heat diffuser, 30 to 40 minutes until lamb is tender. Check from time to time that the meat is not sticking and drying out too much. Add a little water if necessary. Garnish with pomegranate seeds and chopped mint and serve with rice.

Makes 4 to 6 servings.

LAMB STEAKS WITH PASTA

4 thick lamb leg steaks
salt and pepper
2 cloves garlic, sliced
14½ oz. can chopped tomatoes
⅓ cup olive oil
1 tablespoon fresh, chopped marjoram
1 tablespoon fresh, chopped parsley
1½ to 2 cups orzo (rice-shaped pasta)
lettuce leaves, to serve

Preheat oven to 400°F. Season meat with salt and pepper. Place in a large baking pan.

Sprinkle meat with garlic. Add ⅔ cup water and tomatoes. Stir in olive oil, salt, pepper, marjoram, and parsley. Cook 40 minutes, basting from time to time and turning pieces of lamb over.

Add 1¼ cups boiling water and pasta. Stir in more salt and pepper. Cook an additional 40 minutes until pasta is cooked. If necessary, add more hot water. Serve with lettuce leaves.

Makes 4 servings.

CURRIED LAMB WITH ONIONS

1½ lb. shoulder of lamb, boned
1 teaspoon turmeric
1 teaspoon ground cumin
1 teaspoon ground coriander
1 in. piece fresh ginger, grated
2 cloves garlic, crushed
3 tablespoons vegetable oil
1 tablespoon sugar
4 large onions, sliced into thin rings
5 medium potatoes, cut into large chunks
salt and cayenne pepper
1 teaspoon garam masala
rosemary sprigs, to garnish

Wipe lamb, trim, and dice.

Put lamb in a nonmetallic dish. Mix together turmeric, cumin, coriander, ginger, and garlic and add to lamb. Stir well, then cover loosely and leave in a cool place 2 to 3 hours. Heat oil in heavy-bottomed pan until smoking. Stir in sugar, then add onions and cook over medium to high heat 10 minutes, stirring frequently, until a rich brown. Remove onions with a slotted spoon and set aside.

Add lamb to pan and fry until browned all over. Add potatoes and fry, stirring, 2 minutes. Return onions to pan, add 1 cup water, and season with salt and cayenne pepper. Bring to boil and simmer, covered, 1¼ hours or until lamb is tender, stirring occasionally. Stir in garam masala and serve, garnished with rosemary sprigs.

Makes 4 servings.

CURRIED LAMB WITH RAITA

3 tablespoons olive oil
2 onions, finely chopped
½ in. piece fresh ginger, peeled and grated
3 cloves garlic, crushed
1 teaspoon chili powder
1½ teaspoons turmeric
1½ teaspoons ground coriander
½ teaspoon each ground cumin and garam masala
1 lb. lamb fillet, diced
½ cup plain yogurt
salt and freshly ground black pepper
mint sprigs, to garnish
RAITA:
1¼ cups plain yogurt
1 small or ½ large cucumber, diced
1 tablespoon fresh, chopped mint

Heat oil in a flameproof casserole. Add onions and cook, stirring occasionally, 5 minutes until soft. Add ginger, garlic, chili powder, turmeric, coriander, cumin, and garam masala and cook, stirring, 2 minutes. Add lamb and cook, stirring, an additional 2 minutes until browned.

Add yogurt, ½ cup water, and salt and pepper and stir well. Bring to boil and simmer gently 45 minutes. Meanwhile, make raita. Mix together yogurt, cucumber, and chopped mint. Season with salt and pepper. Chill until required. Garnish lamb with mint sprigs and serve with raita.

Makes 4 servings.

LAMB & FLAGEOLET BEANS

4 lamb shanks, each weighing 8 oz.
4 cloves garlic, thinly sliced
2 tablespoons olive oil
1 onion, finely chopped
1½ cups flageolet kidney beans, soaked overnight
6 or 7 medium tomatoes, peeled (see page 174),
    seeded, and chopped
1 tablespoon tomato paste
⅔ cup red wine
bouquet garni
1 small bunch parsley, chopped
Italian parsley and bay leaves, to garnish

Cut four incisions in each lamb shank. Insert a slice of garlic in each incision.

Heat oil in a heavy, flameproof casserole, add lamb, and cook until browned all over. Remove and set aside. Add onion and remaining garlic to casserole and cook, stirring occasionally, 5 minutes until soft but not browned.

Drain and rinse beans and add to casserole with tomatoes, tomato paste, wine, bouquet garni, and salt and pepper. Return lamb to casserole, cover tightly, and cook gently 1 to 2 hours, until lamb and beans are tender. Discard bouquet garni and stir in parsley. Garnish and serve.

Makes 4 servings.

MEDITERRANEAN LAMB

1 eggplant, sliced
2 teaspoons salt
2 tablespoons olive oil, plus extra for brushing
1 lb. lamb fillet, diced
2 leeks, sliced
1 green bell pepper, chopped
14½ oz. can chopped tomatoes
1 clove garlic, crushed
2 zucchini, sliced
1 tablespoon tomato paste
1 tablespoon fresh, chopped rosemary

Place eggplant in a colander, sprinkle with salt, and let stand 30 minutes.

Preheat oven to 375°F. Heat oil in a flameproof dish. Add lamb and cook, stirring, 3 or 4 minutes until browned all over. Add leeks and cook, stirring, 4 or 5 minutes until soft. Stir in bell pepper, tomatoes, garlic, zucchini, tomato paste, and rosemary. Simmer 5 to 10 minutes.

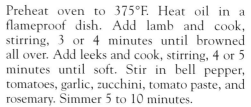

Rinse eggplant in cold water and pat dry with absorbent paper towels. Arrange eggplant slices on top of lamb mixture and brush with olive oil. Bake 30 to 40 minutes until eggplant slices are golden brown and tender.

Makes 4 servings.

NAVARIN OF LAMB

1 tablespoon olive oil
2¼ lb. boneless lamb, diced
1 onion and 1 large carrot, finely chopped
pinch sugar
2 teaspoons all-purpose flour
½ cup dry white wine
2½ cups veal or chicken stock
bouquet garni
salt and freshly ground black pepper
3 ripe tomatoes, peeled, seeded, and chopped
3 small turnips, quartered
12 baby onions
12 small new potatoes
12 baby carrots, halved or quartered
1 cup shelled fresh peas or small fava beans
parsley sprigs, to garnish

Heat oil in a heavy, flameproof casserole, add lamb, and cook until browned all over. Remove with a slotted spoon and set aside. Add chopped onion and carrot and cook, stirring occasionally, 10 minutes until browned. Sprinkle with sugar and flour and cook, stirring, until lightly browned. Add wine, stock, bouquet garni, and salt and pepper. Add tomatoes and bring to boil, stirring. Return lamb to casserole, cover tightly, and cook gently 30 minutes.

Add turnips, onions, and potatoes, cover, and cook 20 minutes. Add carrots and cook 10 minutes. Add peas or beans and cook 5 to 7 minutes. Remove meat and vegetables with a slotted spoon, transfer to a warmed plate, and keep warm. Boil cooking juices to thicken slightly. Return lamb and vegetables to casserole and turn in sauce. Garnish with parsley and serve.

Makes 4 servings.

ROAST LEG OF LAMB WITH WINE

2¼ lb. lean leg of lamb
2 tablespoons olive oil
2 oz. can anchovies in oil, drained
2 cloves garlic, chopped
1 tablespoon fresh, chopped rosemary
8 juniper berries
2 tablespoons balsamic vinegar
salt and freshly ground pepper
⅔ cup dry white wine

Trim lamb of any excess fat. Heat oil in a flameproof casserole in which lamb will fit snugly. Add lamb and brown all over. Remove and let cool.

In a mortar, pound anchovies, garlic, rosemary, and 4 juniper berries to a paste. Stir in vinegar. Make small incisions all over lamb with a small, sharp knife. Spread paste all over lamb, working it into the slits. Season. Replace lamb in casserole and pour in wine. Crush remaining juniper berries and add to the casserole. Cover and simmer 1½ to 2 hours, until very tender, turning lamb every 20 minutes.

Carefully remove lamb from casserole and keep warm. Skim fat from sauce. Add a little water, if necessary, and bring to boil, scraping the bottom of the pan to mix in the brown bits. Serve sauce with lamb.

Makes 8 servings.

CARIBBEAN LAMB CURRY

1¾ lb. trimmed shoulder of lamb, cut into
    1 in. cubes
finely grated zest and juice 1 lime
3 cloves garlic, crushed
3 tablespoons oil
1 large onion, chopped
2 teaspoons curry powder
1 teaspoon ground cumin
1 tablespoon hot pepper sauce
2 teaspoons molasses
2 tablespoons tomato paste
2 oz. creamed coconut
salt
1 tablespoon chopped cilantro

MOROCCAN LAMB

1 cup dried apricots
2 tablespoons olive oil
1 large onion, chopped
2¼ lb. boneless shoulder of lamb, diced
1 teaspoon ground cumin
½ teaspoon each ground coriander and cinnamon
salt and freshly ground black pepper
grated zest and juice ½ orange
1 teaspoon saffron threads
1 tablespoon ground almonds
1¼ cups lamb or chicken stock
1 tablespoon sesame seeds
Italian parsley sprigs, to garnish

Cut apricots in half and put in a bowl.

Place lamb in a bowl with lime zest and juice and garlic. Mix well, cover, and leave in a cool place 2 hours. In a flameproof casserole, heat oil. Add onion and cook 10 minutes until soft. Remove and set aside. Drain meat (reserve any marinade) and pat dry with absorbent paper towels. Add meat to hot oil, in batches, and fry until well browned. Return onions and browned meat to casserole.

Cover with ⅔ cup water and let soak overnight. Preheat the oven to 350°F. Heat olive oil in a flameproof casserole. Add onion and cook gently 10 minutes until soft and golden. Add lamb, cumin, coriander, cinnamon, and salt and pepper and cook, stirring, 5 minutes.

Stir in curry powder and cumin and cook an additional 1 minute. Add hot pepper sauce, molasses, tomato paste, and creamed coconut and cook an additional 5 minutes. Add salt and about ⅔ cup water, to just cover meat. Bring to boil, then reduce heat, cover, and simmer gently, stirring occasionally, 1½ to 2 hours until meat is tender. Stir in chopped cilantro. Serve with rice.

Makes 4 servings.

Add apricots and their soaking liquid. Stir in orange zest and juice, saffron, ground almonds, and enough stock to cover. Cover and cook in the oven 1 to 1½ hours until meat is tender, adding extra stock if necessary. Heat a skillet, add sesame seeds, and dry-fry, shaking the pan, until golden. Sprinkle meat with sesame seeds, garnish with parsley, and serve.

Makes 4 to 6 servings.

LAMB COUSCOUS

2¼ lb. trimmed shoulder of lamb, cut into pieces
2 onions, chopped
⅓ cup chickpeas, soaked overnight
1 teaspoon ground ginger
pinch saffron threads
4 small turnips, cut into large pieces
4 small carrots, cut into large pieces
2½ cups regular couscous (not instant)
2 tablespoons butter, melted
a little rosewater
⅓ cup raisins
4 medium zucchini, halved lengthwise
1 butternut squash, peeled and diced
2 tomatoes, quartered
2 tablespoons each chopped cilantro and parsley
harissa, to serve

Place lamb, onions, and chickpeas in the bottom of a large stockpot. Stir in ginger, saffron, and 1 teaspoon pepper. Cover with water, bring to a boil, and simmer, covered, 45 minutes. Add turnips and carrots.

Place couscous grains in a large bowl. Dissolve 1 teaspoon salt in ⅔ cup water and sprinkle over couscous. Stir with your fingers, rubbing to separate grains and break up any lumps. When couscous has soaked up all the water, place in a colander lined with cheesecloth. Set the colander on top of the simmering stew.

If any steam escapes, wrap a strip of cloth around the top of the pan before placing couscous on top. Steam, covered, for 20 minutes, occasionally drawing a fork through couscous grains to separate them. Turn couscous out onto a large wooden or earthenware dish. Sprinkle with a little soaked water, as before, and separate grains with your fingers.

Lightly rub in melted butter and rosewater and put couscous back in the top part of the colander. Add raisins, zucchini, squash, tomatoes, salt, coriander, and parsley to simmering stew, then replace couscous over the pan. Steam for another 30 minutes, occasionally fluffing couscous grains with a fork.

To serve, pile couscous onto a large wooden or earthenware serving dish. With a slotted spoon, transfer lamb and vegetables to the center of the dish. Pour over some of the broth. Stir some harissa into remaining broth and serve it separately.

Serves 6.

Note: In this traditional Moroccan dish, seven vegetables are used. The selection of vegetables may vary to include beans, peas, and eggplant.

RED-COOKED LAMB FILLET

1 lb. lean lamb fillet
3 tablespoons dry sherry
½ in. piece fresh ginger, peeled and finely chopped
2 cloves garlic, thinly sliced
1 teaspoon five-spice powder
3 tablespoons dark soy sauce
1¼ cups vegetable stock
2 teaspoons sugar
2 teaspoons cornstarch mixed with 4 teaspoons water
salt and freshly ground pepper
shredded scallions, to garnish

Trim any excess fat and skin from lamb and discard. Cut lamb into ¾ in. cubes.

Cook lamb in a saucepan of boiling water 3 minutes. Drain well. Heat a nonstick or well-seasoned wok and add lamb, sherry, ginger, garlic, five-spice powder, and soy sauce. Bring to boil, reduce heat, and simmer 2 minutes, stirring. Pour in stock, return to boil, then simmer 25 minutes.

Add sugar, cornstarch mixture, salt, and pepper and stir until thickened. Simmer 5 minutes. Garnish with shredded scallions and serve on a bed of rice.

Makes 4 servings.

MALAYSIAN LAMB CURRY

2 onions, chopped
3 cloves garlic, smashed
4 fresh red chilies, cored, seeded, and chopped
1 stalk lemongrass, chopped
1½ tablespoons fresh, chopped ginger
2 teaspoons ground coriander
1 teaspoon ground cumin
3½ cups coconut milk
2¼ lb. lean mature lamb or mutton shoulder, cut into 2 in. cubes
juice 1 lime
1½ teaspoons light brown sugar
salt

Put onions, garlic, chilies, lemongrass, ginger, coriander, and cumin in a blender. Add about ⅔ cup coconut milk and mix together well. Pour into a large saucepan. Stir in 1¼ cups coconut milk and 3 cups water and bring to a simmer. Add lamb and lime juice. Simmer gently, uncovered, stirring occasionally, about 2 hours, until meat is tender and liquid has evaporated.

Add a little boiling water if liquid evaporates too quickly. Stir in remaining coconut milk and sugar. Add salt to taste and simmer about 5 minutes. Serve with rice.

Makes 4 to 6 servings.

PORK

MARINATED SPICED PORK

PORK WITH PRUNES

3½ lb. leg of pork, skin and fat removed
1 tablespoon olive oil
4 oz. brown cap or shiitake mushrooms, sliced
thyme sprigs and celery leaves, to garnish
MARINADE:
2 tablespoons olive oil
1 onion, finely chopped
1 carrot, finely chopped
1 stalk celery, chopped
2 cups full-bodied red wine
6 juniper berries, crushed
8 peppercorns, crushed
¼ teaspoon ground allspice
bouquet garni
salt

1 cup large prunes
2½ cups dry white wine
3 tablespoons butter
4 pork chops
1½ cups mixed chopped onion, carrot, and celery
1 cup veal or pork stock
bouquet garni
salt and freshly ground black pepper
squeeze of lemon juice

Put prunes in a bowl, pour over half the wine, and let soak overnight.

To make marinade, heat oil in a heavy skillet, add onion and carrot, and cook, stirring occasionally, 5 minutes. Add celery and cook, stirring occasionally, until vegetables are browned. Add wine, juniper berries, peppercorns, allspice, bouquet garni, and salt. Let cool. Put pork in a nonmetallic dish, pour over marinade, cover, and leave in a cool place 24 hours, turning pork occasionally. Preheat oven to 350°F. Remove pork and vegetables with a slotted spoon and drain pork on absorbent paper towels. Strain marinade and set aside.

Heat 2 tablespoons butter in a heavy, flameproof casserole, add chops, and cook quickly until browned on both sides. Remove and set aside. Add mixed chopped onion, carrot, and celery to casserole and cook, stirring occasionally, 5 to 7 minutes until lightly browned. Stir in remaining wine and bring to boil 2 or 3 minutes, then add stock and bring to boil again. Return chops to casserole, add bouquet garni and salt and pepper, cover tightly, and cook gently 45 minutes.

Heat oil in a heavy, flameproof casserole just large enough to hold pork. Add pork and cook until browned all over. Remove and set aside. Add mushrooms and cook 5 minutes. Add reserved vegetables and put pork on top. Pour over marinade. Heat to almost simmering, cover, and cook in the oven, turning occasionally, 2 to 2½ hours. Transfer to a warmed plate. Skim excess fat from sauce, then boil to thicken and season. Carve pork, garnish, and serve with sauce.

Add prunes and soaking liquid to casserole, bring to boil, cover, and cook 30 minutes. Transfer pork and prunes to warmed serving plates and keep warm. Discard bouquet garni and boil sauce to thicken slightly. Reduce heat and gradually stir in remaining butter. Add lemon juice to taste, pour over pork and prunes, and serve.

Makes 4 servings.

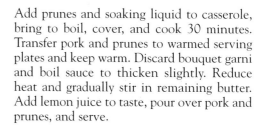

Makes 4 to 6 servings.

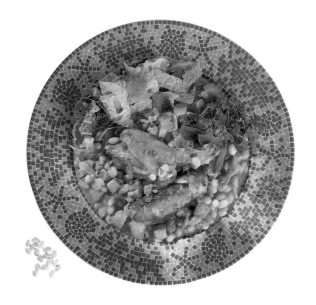

PORK WITH CIDER

2 tablespoons butter
4 pork chops
1 onion, finely chopped
2 teaspoons Calvados or brandy
1¼ cups dry cider
1 bay leaf
2 small cooking apples, peeled, cored, and sliced
1 tablespoon lemon juice
2 tablespoons sour cream
salt and freshly ground black pepper
thyme sprigs and leaves, to garnish

Heat butter in a heavy, flameproof casserole, add chops, and cook quickly until browned on both sides. Remove and set aside.

Preheat oven to 350°F. Add onion to casserole and cook, stirring occasionally, 5 minutes until soft. Add Calvados or brandy and ignite. When flames die down, stir in cider and bring to boil. Return chops to casserole, add bay leaf and salt and pepper, cover tightly, and cook in the oven 20 minutes.

Toss apples in lemon juice. Add to casserole, cover again, and cook 10 to 15 minutes. Remove pork and apples from casserole with a slotted spoon, transfer to warmed serving plates, and keep warm. Boil cooking liquid until lightly syrupy. Stir in sour cream, pour over pork and apples, garnish with thyme, and serve.

Makes 4 servings.

CASSOULET

1½ cups kidney beans, soaked overnight
2 tablespoons olive oil
6 slices thick-cut smoked bacon, chopped
6 coarse-cut pork sausages
3 duck leg portions, halved
2 large onions, chopped
2 cloves garlic, crushed
3 or 4 medium ripe tomatoes, peeled and chopped
1½ tablespoons tomato paste
½ cup dry white wine
large bunch fresh herbs
fresh herbs and fresh, chopped parsley, to garnish

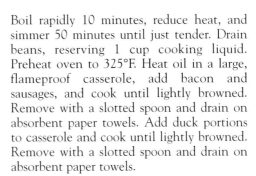

Drain and rinse beans. Put in a saucepan, cover with cold water, and bring to boil.

Boil rapidly 10 minutes, reduce heat, and simmer 50 minutes until just tender. Drain beans, reserving 1 cup cooking liquid. Preheat oven to 325°F. Heat oil in a large, flameproof casserole, add bacon and sausages, and cook until lightly browned. Remove with a slotted spoon and drain on absorbent paper towels. Add duck portions to casserole and cook until lightly browned. Remove with a slotted spoon and drain on absorbent paper towels.

Add onions to casserole and cook, stirring occasionally, 7 minutes until beginning to color. Return meats to casserole with beans, reserved cooking liquid, garlic, tomatoes, tomato paste, wine, and bunch of fresh herbs. Bring to boil, cover, and cook in oven 1 to 1¼ hours, uncovering toward end of cooking to thicken juices. Garnish with herb sprigs and chopped parsley and serve.

Makes 6 servings.

MEXICAN PORK

1 lb. lean pork fillet, diced
2 tablespoons seasoned flour
2 tablespoons butter
2 onions, sliced
2 cloves garlic, crushed
1¼ cups tomato juice
14½ oz. can chopped tomatoes
15 oz. can red kidney beans, rinsed and drained
1 teaspoon ground cumin
½ teaspoon ground coriander
½ teaspoon hot chili powder
½ teaspoon each dried basil and oregano
salt and freshly ground black pepper
3 zucchini, sliced
basil sprigs, to garnish

SPICED PORK & SPAGHETTINI

1 tablespoon sunflower oil
2 red onions, chopped
1 large red bell pepper, seeded and diced
12 oz. (1½ cups) lean ground pork
1 tablespoon all-purpose flour
2 teaspoons ground cumin
1½ teaspoons hot chili powder
1 teaspoon ground coriander
14½ oz. can chopped tomatoes
2 tablespoons tomato paste
1¼ cups pork or vegetable stock
salt and freshly ground black pepper
8 oz. chestnut mushrooms, sliced
1 lb. 2 oz. fresh spaghettini
herb sprigs, to garnish

Toss pork fillet in seasoned flour. In a large saucepan, melt butter over low heat. Cook onions and garlic 3 minutes. Add pork and cook gently 3 to 5 minutes, stirring occasionally, until meat is browned all over. Stir in tomato juice, tomatoes, kidney beans, cumin, coriander, chili powder, basil, oregano, and salt and pepper and mix well. Bring slowly to boil, cover, and simmer gently 1 to 1½ hours, until meat is tender, stirring occasionally.

Heat oil in a large saucepan, add onions and bell pepper, and cook gently 5 minutes, stirring occasionally. Add ground pork and cook until browned all over, stirring frequently. Add flour and ground spices and cook 1 minute, stirring. Stir in tomatoes, tomato paste, stock, and salt and pepper and mix well. Bring to boil, then reduce the heat, cover, and simmer 30 minutes, stirring occasionally.

Add zucchini 10 minutes before the end of cooking time. Garnish with basil sprigs and serve with freshly cooked tagliatelle.

Makes 6 servings.

Note: For authentic flavors and aromas, use a mortar and pestle to crush your own spices.

Stir in mushrooms, cover, and simmer an additional 30 minutes, stirring occasionally. Meanwhile, cook pasta in a large pan of lightly salted boiling water 3 minutes or until al dente. Drain thoroughly and serve on warmed plates. Spoon sauce over pasta and garnish with herb sprigs.

Makes 4 to 6 servings.

Variation: Use lean ground lamb or turkey instead of pork.

STUFFED CABBAGE LEAVES

STUFFED BAKED PAPAYA

18 large cabbage leaves
2 onions, finely chopped
¼ cup fresh, finely chopped parsley
2 cloves garlic, crushed
1½ cups shredded young spinach leaves
8 oz. (1 cup) ground pork
1 lb. pork sausage meat
¼ cup all-purpose flour
2 eggs, beaten
salt and freshly ground black pepper
12 slices bacon
2¼ cups chicken stock

Blanch cabbage leaves in boiling water 2 minutes. Remove and drain.

Preheat oven to 350°F. In a large bowl, mix together onions, parsley, garlic, spinach, ground pork, and sausage meat. Add flour and eggs and mix well. Season with salt and pepper. Divide into six portions. Trim tough central core from each cabbage leaf. Arrange leaves in six piles of three leaves each.

1 green papaya, weighing about 4½ lb.
2 tablespoons oil
1 onion, finely chopped
1 clove garlic, crushed
1 lb. (2 cups) lean ground pork
3 tomatoes, peeled (see page 174) and chopped
1 fresh green chili, seeded and finely chopped
¼ teaspoon dried thyme
¼ teaspoon ground allspice
salt and freshly ground black pepper
¼ cup shredded Parmesan cheese
1 tablespoon fresh bread crumbs
lime wedges, to garnish

Preheat oven to 350°F. Cut papaya in half lengthwise and remove seeds (peel papaya if you prefer). Place papaya halves in a pan of boiling salted water and simmer 10 minutes. Remove, drain thoroughly, and pat dry with absorbent paper towels. Place in a baking dish. Meanwhile, heat oil in a saucepan. Add onion and garlic and cook 10 minutes until soft. Add pork and stir until browned.

Divide portions of filling among cabbage leaves. Fold each one into a package and wrap each with 2 slices of bacon. Put into a flameproof casserole and pour over stock. Bring to boil, cover, and cook in the oven 1½ hours. Remove with a slotted spoon, pour over a little of the cooking liquid, and serve.

Makes 6 servings.

Add tomatoes, chili, thyme, allspice, and seasoning and cook, stirring several times, 15 to 20 minutes until thickened. Stir in half the cheese. Fill papaya halves with meat mixture. Mix together bread crumbs and remaining cheese and sprinkle on top. Bake 30 to 40 minutes until browned on top and the papaya is tender. Garnish with lime slices and serve.

Makes 6 servings.

CARIBBEAN MEATBALLS

PORK WITH TAMARIND

3 tablespoons oil
1 onion, finely chopped
1 lb. (2 cups) lean ground pork
1 cup fresh bread crumbs
1 egg, beaten
¼ to ½ teaspoon chili powder
1 teaspoon ground coriander
salt and freshly ground black pepper
TOMATO SAUCE:
2 tablespoons oil
1 onion, finely chopped
1 clove garlic, crushed
3 stalks celery, chopped
14½ oz. can chopped tomatoes
1 teaspoon molasses
chopped cilantro, to garnish

4 dried red chilies, cored and seeded
1 large onion, chopped
4 cashews
2 tablespoons vegetable oil
1½ lb. shoulder of pork, cut into large bite-sized
    pieces
2 tablespoons tamarind paste
2 tablespoons dark soy sauce
1 tablespoon yellow bean sauce
1 tablespoon light brown sugar
sliced fresh chilies, to garnish (optional)

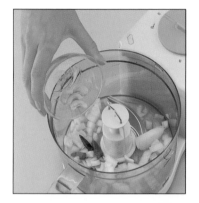

Put chilies in a blender. Add ¼ cup hot
water and leave until slightly softened. Add
onion and nuts; mix to a smooth paste.

In a saucepan, heat half the oil. Add onion
and cook 10 minutes until soft. Set aside to
cool. In a bowl, mix together onion, pork,
bread crumbs, egg, chili powder, ground
coriander, and seasoning until thoroughly
combined. Divide mixture into twenty-four
and form into balls. Set aside.

In a sauté pan, preferably nonstick, heat oil
over medium-high heat. Add meat in
batches and fry until an even light brown.
Using a slotted spoon, transfer to absorbent
paper towels to drain.

To make sauce, heat oil in a saucepan.
Add onion, garlic, and celery and cook
10 minutes until soft. Add tomatoes,
molasses, and seasoning. Bring to boil, cover,
and simmer 15 minutes. Meanwhile, in a
skillet, heat remaining oil. Fry meatballs,
in batches if necessary, until browned
on all sides. With a slotted spoon,
transfer meatballs to sauce. Simmer gently
20 minutes. Serve garnished with chopped
cilantro.

Makes 4 to 6 servings.

Add chili paste to pan and fry about
5 minutes. Stir in pork, tamarind paste, soy
sauce, yellow bean sauce, sugar, and 1½ cups
water. Bring to a simmer, cover pan, then
cook gently 30 to 40 minutes, stirring
occasionally, until pork is very tender. Serve
garnished with sliced, fresh chilies.

Makes 4 servings.

DRY PORK CURRY

PORK IN CIDER & ORANGE

12 oz. lean boneless pork, trimmed and cut into
  ¾ in. cubes
1 tablespoon light brown sugar
2 or 3 medium potatoes
2 carrots
8 shallots
1 tablespoon sunflower oil
1 in. piece fresh ginger, peeled and finely chopped
2 tablespoons Madras curry paste
⅔ cup coconut milk
1¼ cups chicken stock
salt and freshly ground pepper
2 tablespoons chopped cilantro

3 tablespoons olive oil
flour for coating
salt and freshly ground black pepper
1½ lb. boned and rolled loin of pork
1 small Spanish onion, sliced
1¼ cups well-flavored dry cider
juice 1 large orange
peel from ¼ orange, cut into fine strips
pinch ground cinnamon
pinch sugar (optional)
thin orange slices, parsley sprigs, and slivered,
  toasted almonds, to garnish

In a bowl, mix together pork and brown sugar and set aside. Cut potatoes and carrots into ¾ in. chunks. Peel and halve shallots.

Heat oil in a heavy, flameproof casserole. Put flour on a plate and season with salt and pepper. Roll pork in seasoned flour to coat evenly and lightly. Add to casserole and brown evenly about 10 minutes. Remove and keep warm. Stir onion into casserole and cook over low heat about 20 minutes, stirring occasionally, until very soft and lightly browned. Stir in cider, orange juice and strips of peel, and cinnamon. Bring to boil and simmer 2 or 3 minutes.

Heat oil in a nonstick or well-seasoned wok and stir-fry pork, ginger, potatoes, carrots, and shallots 2 or 3 minutes or until lightly browned. Blend curry paste with coconut milk, stock, salt, and pepper. Stir into pork mixture and bring to boil. Reduce heat and simmer 40 minutes. Sprinkle with cilantro and serve on a bed of rice.

Makes 4 servings.

Return pork to casserole, turn it in sauce, cover, and cook gently about 45 minutes until pork is tender. Transfer pork to a serving dish and boil sauce, if necessary, to thicken lightly. Adjust seasoning and level of cinnamon, and add a pinch of sugar. Pour sauce over pork and garnish with orange slices, parsley sprigs, and slivered almonds.

Makes 4 servings.

TOAD IN THE HOLE

1 cup all-purpose flour
pinch salt
1 teaspoon dried, mixed herbs
1 egg, beaten
1¼ cups milk
1 tablespoon sunflower oil
1 small onion, chopped
1 lb. herby sausages

Preheat oven to 400°F. In a large bowl, mix together flour, salt, and herbs. Make a well in the center and add egg and half the milk. Beat to a smooth batter. Stir in remaining milk and mix until smooth.

Heat oil in a shallow, flameproof dish. Add onion and cook, stirring occasionally, 3 minutes. Add sausages and cook until browned all over.

Pour batter into dish and cook in the oven 30 minutes until batter is risen and golden. Serve immediately.

Makes 4 servings.

PORK & CLAMS

2¼ lb. loin pork, diced
3 tablespoons olive oil
1 onion, chopped
2 teaspoons tomato paste
salt and freshly ground black pepper
2¼ lb. clams or cockles, cleaned
cilantro and lemon wedges, to garnish
MARINADE:
2 teaspoons balsamic vinegar
1¼ cups dry white wine
2 cloves garlic, crushed
1 fresh bay leaf
pinch saffron threads
cilantro sprig

To make marinade, mix together vinegar, wine, garlic, bay leaf, saffron, and cilantro. Add pork and mix well to coat with marinade. Cover and leave in a cool place overnight. Remove pork with a slotted spoon and dry on absorbent paper towels. Reserve marinade.

Heat oil in a flameproof casserole. Add onion and cook gently 5 minutes until soft. Add pork and cook over high heat 10 minutes or until cooked through. Add strained marinade, tomato paste, salt and pepper, and clams or cockles. Cover tightly and cook over medium heat 5 minutes until all clams or cockles have opened. Discard any that remain closed. Garnish with cilantro and lemon wedges and serve.

Makes 4 to 6 servings.

STUFFED PORK SHOULDER

3 lb. shoulder of pork, boned and skinned
3 medium potatoes, cut into chunks
1 lb. rutabaga, cut into chunks
4 medium parsnips, cut into chunks
1 tablespoon olive oil
salt and freshly ground black pepper
1 tablespoon cornstarch
2¼ cups vegetable stock
1 tablespoon mango and lime chutney
sage leaves, to garnish
STUFFING:
6 oz. can corned beef, finely chopped
2 cups fresh white bread crumbs
1 onion, finely chopped
1 teaspoon dried sage
1 tablespoon mango and lime chutney

Preheat oven to 350°F. Open out shoulder of pork and flatten. To make stuffing, mix together corned beef, bread crumbs, onion, and sage. Add chutney and bind mixture together. Spread stuffing along the center of the inside of the pork. Roll pork into a round shape and tie securely with string. Season with salt and pepper. Put in a flameproof dish, cover with a lid or piece of aluminum foil, and cook in the oven 2 hours, basting meat every 45 minutes. Increase the oven temperature to 400°F.

Place potatoes, rutabaga, and parsnips around meat. Drizzle vegetables with oil and season with salt and pepper. Cook, uncovered, 45 to 55 minutes, turning vegetables occasionally, until tender. Remove meat and vegetables and keep warm. Add cornstarch and stir into cooking juices. Gradually add stock and bring to boil, stirring. Add chutney and simmer 3 or 4 minutes. Slice pork, garnish, and serve with vegetables and sauce.

Makes 6 to 8 servings.

PROVENÇAL PORK CHOPS

2 teaspoons capers, chopped
¼ cup pitted black olives, chopped
8 sun-dried tomatoes, chopped
2 oz. can anchovies, drained and chopped
juice 2 lemons
2 cloves garlic, crushed
⅓ cup olive oil
¼ cup fresh, chopped parsley
4 pork loin chops, each weighing about 6 oz.
basil sprigs, to garnish

Mix together capers, olives, sun-dried tomatoes, anchovies, and lemon juice. Add garlic, all but 1 tablespoon of olive oil, parsley, and salt and pepper.

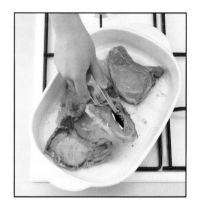

Heat remaining oil in a flameproof dish. Add chops and cook 10 minutes on each side until cooked through.

Pour tomato mixture over chops and bring to boil. Simmer 5 minutes. Garnish with basil sprigs and serve.

Makes 4 servings.

CARAWAY POT ROAST

1 tablespoon olive oil
2½ lb. arm shoulder of pork, boned
2 large onions, chopped
4 medium parsnips, cut into chunks
¼ cup caraway seeds
½ teaspoon freshly grated nutmeg
salt and freshly ground black pepper
1 cup chicken stock
1 cup red wine
thyme sprigs, to garnish

Preheat oven to 350°F. Heat oil in a large, flameproof casserole. Add pork and cook until browned all over.

Remove meat from the casserole. Add onions and parsnips and cook, stirring occasionally, 7 minutes until golden. Lay pork on top of vegetables. Mix together caraway seeds and nutmeg and sprinkle on top of pork. Season with salt and pepper. Pour stock and wine around pork. Cover tightly and cook in the oven 2 hours or until pork is cooked through and tender. Remove pork from the casserole and keep warm.

Remove vegetables from the casserole with a slotted spoon. Bring sauce to boil and boil until reduced and thickened. Season with salt and pepper. Slice meat, garnish with thyme sprigs, and serve with vegetables and sauce.

Makes 6 to 8 servings.

Note: Skim any fat from the surface of the sauce before serving.

HARVEST CASSEROLE

2 tablespoons olive oil
4 sparerib pork chops
1 large onion, sliced
2 leeks, chopped
1 clove garlic, crushed
2 medium parsnips, cut into chunks
2 carrots, cut into chunks
1 teaspoon dried sage
2 tablespoons all-purpose flour
1¼ cups beef stock
1¼ cups apple juice
salt and freshly ground black pepper
2 small dessert apples
1½ cups self-rising flour
⅔ cup shredded suet
1 teaspoon mixed, dried herbs

Preheat oven to 325°F. Heat the oil in a large, flameproof casserole. Add chops and cook 2 or 3 minutes on each side until browned. Remove from the casserole and drain on absorbent paper towels. Add onion, leeks, and garlic and cook, stirring occasionally, 5 minutes until soft. Add parsnips, carrots, and sage and cook 2 minutes. Add all-purpose flour and cook, stirring, 1 minute. Gradually stir in stock and apple juice. Season with salt and pepper and bring to boil.

Replace chops, cover, and cook in the oven 1¼ hours or until pork is tender. Meanwhile, core and roughly chop apples and set aside. Mix together self-rising flour, suet, dried herbs, and salt and pepper. Add ¾ cup water and bind to a firm dough. Divide dough into 8 small dumplings. Stir apples into the casserole. Place dumplings on top, return to the oven, and cook, uncovered, 20 minutes.

Makes 4 servings.

PORK WITH APPLE BALLS

2 tablespoons olive oil
4 boneless pork loin chops, each weighing 6 oz.
3 medium onions, sliced
2 cloves garlic, crushed
12 plum tomatoes, peeled (see page 174) and
  chopped
⅔ cup beef stock
¼ cup red wine vinegar
5 crisp dessert apples
2 tablespoons lemon juice
salt and freshly ground black pepper

Preheat oven to 350°F. Heat olive oil in an ovenproof casserole. Add chops and cook 3 minutes on each side, until browned.

Remove chops and keep warm. Add onions to the casserole and cook, stirring occasionally, 5 minutes until soft. Add garlic and tomatoes. Return chops to the casserole and pour in stock and red wine vinegar. Bring to boil. Meanwhile, peel apples and use a melon baller to cut out ball-shaped pieces. Put balls into a bowl of water with lemon juice, to prevent apple discoloring. Chop remaining apple and add to the casserole. Cover and cook in the oven 1 hour.

Remove chops from the casserole and keep warm. Pour sauce into a blender or food processor and process 1 minute. Season with salt and pepper. Return to the pan with chops and apple balls. Cook gently 15 minutes until apple balls are just tender.

Makes 4 servings.

FRAGRANT HAM

3 lb. piece ham
2 medium parsnips, halved lengthwise
5 carrots, cut into chunks
1 lb. rutabaga, cut into chunks
2 stalks celery, cut into chunks
1 tablespoon brown sugar
1 tablespoon red wine vinegar
1 tablespoon black peppercorns
6 cloves
oregano sprigs, to garnish

Put ham in a flameproof casserole. Cover with cold water and let soak 1 hour. Drain and cover with fresh water.

Add parsnips, carrots, rutabaga, celery, brown sugar, red wine vinegar, peppercorns, and cloves to casserole. Bring to boil, cover, and simmer gently 1½ hours, until ham is cooked through.

Lift out ham, slice, and arrange on warmed serving plates. Remove vegetables with a slotted spoon, arrange around ham, garnish with oregano sprigs, and serve.

Makes 6 to 8 servings.

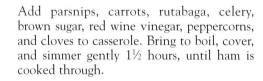

FRUITY HAM STEAKS

ZUCCHINI & BACON SLICE

½ in. piece fresh ginger, peeled and grated
2 tablespoons ketchup
1 tablespoon brown sugar
1 tablespoon light soy sauce
1 tablespoon malt vinegar
1 tablespoon lemon juice
2 tablespoons olive oil
4 ham steaks, each weighing about 6 oz.
1 green bell pepper, chopped
1 red bell pepper, chopped
1 onion, chopped
8 oz. can pineapple pieces, drained, with
  2 tablespoons juice reserved
1 tablespoon cornstarch
watercress, to garnish

3 medium zucchini, finely shredded
1 large onion, finely chopped
6 slices bacon, chopped
1¼ cups shredded cheddar cheese
1¼ cups self-rising flour
⅓ cup sunflower oil, plus extra for greasing
5 eggs, beaten
salt and freshly ground black pepper

In a bowl, mix together ginger, soy sauce, ketchup, brown sugar, vinegar, and lemon juice. Set aside. Heat oil in a flameproof dish. Add ham and cook 5 minutes on each side.

Preheat oven to 400°F. In a large bowl, mix together zucchini, onion, bacon, cheese, flour, oil, and eggs. Season with salt and pepper.

Remove ham from the dish and keep warm. Add bell pepper and onion to the dish and cook, stirring occasionally, 5 minutes until soft. Stir in ketchup mixture and pineapple pieces. Blend reserved pineapple juice with cornstarch. Add to the dish and bring to boil, stirring. Return steaks to the dish and simmer 5 minutes. Garnish and serve.

Makes 4 servings.

Lightly butter a shallow, flameproof dish. Add zucchini mixture and level surface. Bake 50 to 60 minutes until golden brown and firm. Cut into wedges and serve hot or cold.

Makes 4 to 6 servings.

PANCETTA & CHILI PENNE

PEA, HAM, & PARSLEY BAKE

6 plum tomatoes
3 tablespoons butter
6 shallots, finely chopped
1 large clove garlic, crushed
2 fresh red chilies, seeded and finely chopped
2 stalks celery, finely chopped
8 oz. pancetta, diced
6 oz. mushrooms, finely chopped
⅔ cup red wine
4 sun-dried tomatoes in oil, drained and chopped
salt and freshly ground black pepper
1 lb. 2 oz. fresh penne rigate
2 tablespoons fresh, chopped oregano
oregano sprigs, to garnish

8 oz. dried rigatoni
salt and freshly ground black pepper
3 tablespoons butter
⅓ cup all-purpose flour
3¾ cups milk
1½ cups lean smoked ham, diced
1½ cups frozen peas
¼ cup fresh, chopped parsley
½ cup shredded cheddar cheese (optional)
Italian parsley sprigs, to garnish

Preheat the oven to 400°F. Lightly butter an
ovenproof dish; set aside.

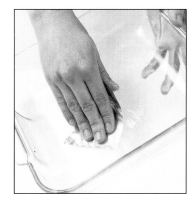

Put plum tomatoes in a large bowl and cover
with boiling water. Leave 30 to 60 seconds,
then drain and peel, remove seeds and pith,
and chop flesh. Set aside. Melt butter in a
saucepan, add shallots, garlic, chilies, celery,
and pancetta, and cook 5 minutes, stirring.
Add chopped plum tomatoes, mushrooms,
wine, sun-dried tomatoes, and salt and pepper
and stir to mix. Bring to boil, then cover and
simmer 10 minutes, stirring occasionally.
Uncover pan, increase heat slightly, and cook
10 to 15 minutes, stirring occasionally, until
sauce has thickened slightly.

Cook pasta in a large saucepan of lightly
salted boiling water about 10 minutes or
until al dente. Drain well, set aside, and keep
warm. Meanwhile, put butter, flour, and milk
in a separate saucepan. Heat gently, whisking
continuously, until sauce is thickened and
smooth. Simmer gently 3 minutes, stirring.
Remove pan from the heat, add pasta, ham,
peas, chopped parsley, and salt and pepper,
and stir gently to mix.

Meanwhile, cook pasta in a large saucepan
of lightly salted boiling water 3 to 5 minutes
or until al dente. Drain thoroughly and
return to the rinsed-out pan. Add tomato
sauce and chopped oregano and toss well to
mix. Garnish with oregano sprigs and serve.

Makes 4 servings.

Variation: Use chorizo instead of pancetta.

Transfer to prepared dish and sprinkle with
cheddar cheese, if using. Bake in the oven
20 to 25 minutes or until lightly browned
and bubbling. Garnish with parsley sprigs
and serve with cooked vegetables such as
green beans and broiled tomatoes.

Makes 4 servings.

Variations: Use cooked smoked chicken or
turkey instead of ham. Use fresh Parmesan
cheese instead of cheddar.

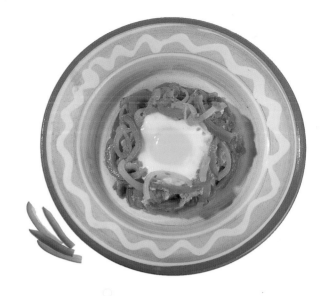

PISTO MANCHEGO

CHAKCHOUKA

2 tablespoons olive oil
2 slices bacon, chopped
2 large Spanish onions, chopped
1 clove garlic, chopped
2 zucchini, chopped
4 red bell peppers, peeled and chopped
2 beefsteak tomatoes, peeled (see page 174), seeded, and chopped
bunch mint, parsley, and basil, chopped
salt and freshly ground black pepper
4 poached or fried eggs, to serve (optional)

2 tablespoons olive oil
1 onion, thinly sliced
1 clove garlic, crushed
1 red bell pepper, seeded and sliced
1 green bell pepper, seeded and sliced
4 merguez sausages, sliced
6 tomatoes, peeled (see page 174) and quartered
salt and freshly ground black pepper
1 teaspoon harissa
2 teaspoons fresh, chopped mint
4 eggs

Heat oil in a large skillet. Add onion, garlic, and bell peppers and cook gently 10 minutes.

In a large skillet, heat oil, add bacon, onions, and garlic, and cook gently about 15 minutes, stirring occasionally, until onions are very soft and lightly colored.

Add sausages, cook for a few minutes, then stir in tomatoes. Season with salt, pepper, and harissa and cook slowly 10 minutes until vegetables are well blended. Stir in mint.

Add zucchini and bell peppers to pan and fry about 4 minutes until soft. Stir in tomatoes and herbs and cook 20 to 30 minutes until thickened. Season to taste. Serve topped with poached or fried eggs.

Makes 4 servings.

Make four indentations in mixture and break an egg into each one. Cover pan and cook gently 6 or 7 minutes until eggs are set. Divide into four and serve straight from the pan.

Makes 4 servings.

Variation: Eggs may be omitted and double the quantity of sausages used instead.

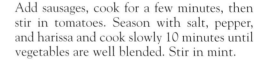

POTATOES WITH CHORIZO

¼ cup olive oil
4 oz. chorizo, chopped
4 or 5 medium potatoes, coarsely chopped
1 Spanish onion, chopped
1 red bell pepper, chopped
2 beefsteak tomatoes, peeled (see page 174), seeded, and chopped
salt and freshly ground black pepper
chicken or veal stock, or water, to cover
mint sprigs, to garnish

Heat oil in a flameproof casserole. Add chorizo and cook, stirring occasionally, until fat runs. Remove chorizo.

Add potatoes and onion and cook, stirring occasionally, 5 minutes. Stir in red bell pepper, fry 5 minutes, then add tomatoes and return chorizo to pan. Season with salt and pepper.

Just cover with stock or water and simmer about 15 minutes until potatoes are tender and most of the liquid has been absorbed. Garnish with mint sprigs and serve.

Makes 4 servings.

CHORIZO & BEAN CASSEROLE

1 tablespoon olive oil
1 onion, thinly sliced
10 chorizo sausages, cut into chunks
15 oz. can pinto beans, drained
15 oz. can cannellini beans, drained
14½ oz. can chopped tomatoes
1 cup vegetable stock
salt and freshly ground black pepper
3 potatoes, thinly sliced

Preheat oven to 400°F. Heat oil in a flameproof casserole. Add onion and cook, stirring occasionally, 5 minutes until soft. Add chorizo sausages and cook 4 or 5 minutes.

Add pinto and cannellini beans, tomatoes, stock, and salt and pepper and bring to boil. Remove from the heat and arrange sliced potatoes on top. Bake 40 or 45 minutes until potatoes are tender and golden brown.

Makes 4 servings.

SAUSAGE & BELL PEPPERS

2 tablespoons olive oil
1½ lb. hot, sweet, or mixed Italian sausages
2 onions, halved lengthwise, then cut lengthwise
    into "petals"
4 to 6 cloves garlic, finely chopped
1 each large red, green, and yellow bell pepper, cut
    in half lengthwise, then into strips
8 oz. can peeled tomatoes
1 tablespoon fresh shredded or 1 teaspoon dried
    oregano or basil
½ teaspoon crushed chilies
½ teaspoon dried thyme
½ teaspoon rubbed sage
salt and freshly ground black pepper
fresh oregano or basil leaves, to garnish
fresh Parmesan cheese, to serve

Heat a wok or pan until hot, add olive oil, and swirl to coat. Add sausages and cook over moderate heat 8 to 10 minutes until golden brown on all sides, turning them frequently during cooking. Remove sausages to a plate and pour off all but 2 tablespoons oil from the pan. Add onions and garlic and stir-fry 2 minutes until golden. Add bell pepper strips and stir-fry 1 or 2 minutes until just beginning to soften.

Add tomatoes and their liquid, fresh or dried oregano or basil, crushed chilies, thyme, sage, salt, and pepper. Stir to break up tomatoes and mix well. Return sausages to pan and cover with vegetable mixture. Simmer 15 to 20 minutes until vegetables are tender and sauce is thickened. Garnish with fresh oregano or basil leaves and sprinkle with shaved or grated Parmesan cheese. Serve with spaghetti.

Makes 6 servings.

SAUSAGE RAGU WITH POLENTA

1 lb. fresh Italian sausages
1 tablespoon olive oil
1 medium onion, chopped
2 cups passata or tomato sauce
⅔ cup dry red wine
6 sun-dried tomatoes, soaked in hot water, then
    sliced
salt and freshly ground pepper
2 cups quick-cook cornmeal
freshly grated Parmesan cheese, to serve (optional)

Squeeze sausage meat out of skins into a bowl and break up meat. Heat oil in a medium saucepan and add chopped onion. Cook 5 minutes until soft and golden.

Stir in sausage meat and brown it all over, breaking up lumps with a wooden spoon. Pour in passata and wine and bring to a boil. Add sun-dried tomatoes and simmer 30 minutes or until well reduced, stirring occasionally. Season with salt and pepper. Meanwhile, bring 6¼ cups water to boil in a pan with 2 teaspoons salt, then sprinkle in cornmeal, stirring or whisking to keep lumps from forming. Simmer, stirring constantly, 5 to 10 minutes according to package directions, until cornmeal has thickened.

Spoon polenta into six large soup plates and make a dip in the center of each. Top with sausage ragu and serve at once, with grated Parmesan cheese.

Makes 6 servings.

Note: If you can't buy fresh Italian sausages, use good-quality sausages mixed with a little crushed garlic, black pepper, and fennel.

SPICY SAUSAGE & TOMATO

SPICY PORK STEW

1 lb. sausages
1 teaspoon sunflower oil
1 onion, sliced
1 clove garlic, crushed
1 fresh green chili, seeded and finely chopped
2 teaspoons dried thyme
2 teaspoons garam masala
1 teaspoon turmeric
½ teaspoon chili powder
6 oz. mushrooms, sliced
⅔ cup pork or vegetable stock
14½ oz. can chopped tomatoes
salt and freshly ground black pepper
fresh thyme and parsley, to garnish

1 tablespoon vegetable oil
2 cloves garlic, chopped
2 shallots, chopped
1 lb. lean pork, cut into bite-sized pieces
3 tablespoons sugar
3 tablespoons fish sauce
1 teaspoon five-spice powder
about 1 cup chicken stock or water
salt and freshly ground black pepper
2 or 3 scallions, cut into short sections, to garnish

Heat oil in a flameproof casserole and stir-fry garlic and shallots about 1 minute or until fragrant.

Heat a skillet and cook sausages 8 to 10 minutes until browned all over. Cut into 1 in. pieces. In a saucepan, heat oil and cook onion, garlic, and chili 5 minutes. Add thyme, garam masala, turmeric, and chili powder and cook, stirring, 1 minute.

Add pork pieces and stir-fry about 2 minutes or until pork turns almost white in color.

Add sausages, mushrooms, stock, tomatoes, and salt and pepper. Mix gently but thoroughly and bring mixture to boil. Cover and simmer 20 minutes, stirring occasionally, until sausages are cooked through. Garnish with thyme and parsley and serve with freshly cooked penne.

Makes 6 servings.

Add sugar, fish sauce, and five-spice powder, stir 1 minute, then add stock or water, bring to boil, reduce heat, cover, and simmer 15 to 20 minutes. Adjust seasoning and garnish with scallions. Serve with snow peas and bell peppers.

Makes 4 servings.

Variation: Chicken, lamb, veal, or beef can all be cooked in this way; increase the cooking time by 10 to 15 minutes for lamb and veal and 20 to 25 minutes for beef.

SPICY RIBS

2¼ lb. spareribs
1 large onion, finely chopped
3 cloves garlic, crushed
2 bay leaves
1 teaspoon ground cumin
1 teaspoon mild chili powder
3 tablespoons cider vinegar
2 tablespoons ketchup
1 tablespoon soy sauce
2 tablespoons honey
14½ oz. can chopped tomatoes

Preheat oven to 400°F. Put spareribs in a flameproof casserole and cook in the oven 30 minutes.

Remove ribs with a slotted spoon and set aside. In a bowl, mix together onion, garlic, bay leaves, cumin, chili powder, cider vinegar, ketchup, soy sauce, honey, and tomatoes. Season with salt and pepper.

Stir tomato mixture into the casserole. Bring to boil and simmer 5 minutes. Add ribs, turn to coat with sauce, and cover. Return to the oven and cook an additional 30 minutes.

Makes 4 servings.

PORK WITH PEARS

2 tablespoons olive oil
2 onions, chopped
2¼ lb. boned lean pork, diced
1 cup red wine
grated zest ½ orange
½ cinnamon stick
salt and pepper
2 pears
2 teaspoons honey
chopped cilantro, strips of orange peel, and pita
  bread, to garnish

In a flameproof casserole, heat oil. Add onions; cook until soft. Push to side of pan, turn up heat, and brown meat in batches.

Add wine, orange zest, cinnamon stick, salt, pepper, and 1¼ cups water. Bring to simmering point, then cover casserole and cook 1 hour.

Peel, core, and slice pears and place on top of meat. Drizzle pears with honey. Cover pan and simmer gently 30 to 40 minutes until meat is tender. Garnish with chopped cilantro, strips of orange peel, and pieces of pita bread.

Makes 6 servings.

Note: This recipe is traditionally made with quinces. If quinces are available, use them instead of pears.

PORK IN SPINACH SAUCE

1½ lb. fresh spinach, well rinsed
salt
1½ lb. lean boneless pork
3 tablespoons vegetable oil
2 onions, finely sliced
4 cloves garlic, crushed
1 in. piece fresh ginger, grated
3 tablespoons garam masala
½ teaspoon turmeric
1 bay leaf
2 tomatoes, peeled (see page 174) and chopped
2 fresh green chilies, seeded and chopped
⅔ cup plain yogurt
tomato slices and bay leaves, to garnish

Trim stems from spinach and cook leaves in boiling salted water 2 or 3 minutes until tender. Drain thoroughly and rinse under cold running water. Put in a blender or food processor fitted with a metal blade and process to a smooth purée. Set aside. Preheat oven to 325°F. Cut pork into 1 in. cubes. Heat oil in a large skillet and fry pork until browned all over. Transfer to a casserole with a slotted spoon.

Add onions to pan and cook, stirring, 10 to 15 minutes until a rich brown. Add garlic, ginger, garam masala, turmeric, bay leaf, tomatoes, and chilies. Cook, stirring, 2 or 3 minutes until tomatoes have softened. Add yogurt and ⅔ cup water and stir. Pour over pork, cover, and cook 1¼ to 1½ hours, until pork is cooked through. Remove bay leaf, stir in spinach and salt, cover, and cook an additional 10 minutes. Garnish and serve.

Makes 4 servings.

INDONESIAN-STYLE PORK

1 tablespoon seasoned flour
1¼ lb. pork fillet, cut into small cubes
2 or 3 tablespoons vegetable oil
1 onion, cut lengthwise in half and thinly sliced
2 cloves garlic, finely chopped
1 in. piece fresh ginger, peeled and cut into matchstick strips
½ teaspoon sambal oelek (see Note) or Chinese chili sauce
¼ cup Indonesian soy sauce or dark soy sauce sweetened with 1 tablespoon sugar
cilantro, to garnish

In a medium bowl, combine seasoned flour and pork cubes and toss to coat well.

Heat the wok until very hot. Add 2 tablespoons oil and swirl to coat wok. Shake pork cubes to remove any excess flour, then add to wok and stir-fry 3 to 4 minutes until browned on all sides, adding a little more oil if necessary. Push pork to one side, add onion, garlic, and ginger, and stir-fry 1 minute, tossing all ingredients.

Add sambal oelek or chili sauce, soy sauce, and ⅔ cup water; stir. Bring to boil, reduce heat to low, and simmer gently, covered, 20 to 25 minutes, stirring occasionally, until pork is tender and sauce thickened. Garnish with cilantro and serve with fried rice or noodles.

Makes 4 servings.

Note: Sambal oelek is a very hot, chili-based Indonesian condiment available in specialty and Asian markets.

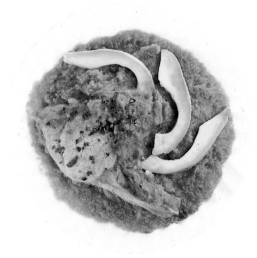

COASTAL-STYLE PORK

2 tablespoons oil
2¼ lb. pork fillet, cut into 1 in. cubes
¾ cup seasoned flour
1 large onion, chopped
2 cups beef stock
1 teaspoon ground coriander
1 clove garlic, finely chopped
1 fresh green chili, seeded and chopped
2 tomatoes, peeled (see page 174) and chopped
1 red bell pepper, seeded and chopped
½ fresh pineapple, peeled, cored, and cut into chunks
2 medium sweet potatoes, peeled and diced
1 tablespoon fresh, finely chopped cilantro, to garnish

Preheat oven to 350°F. Heat oil in a large, heavy skillet. Toss pork in seasoned flour and fry until evenly browned, turning frequently. Transfer meat to a large, flameproof casserole. Add onion to skillet and fry gently until soft, adding a little more oil if necessary. Stir in stock and bring to boil, stirring. Add ground coriander, garlic, chili, tomatoes, and bell pepper. Simmer 5 minutes. Pour over pork. Bring to boil, cover, and bake 1½ to 2 hours until tender.

Add pineapple and sweet potatoes. Return to the oven and bake an additional 20 to 25 minutes until fruit and vegetables are tender. Garnish with cilantro.

Makes 6 servings.

MEXICAN PORK CHOPS

2 cloves garlic, peeled and halved
4 pork chops
2 tablespoons oil
1 medium avocado, to garnish
1 tablespoon lemon juice
SAUCE:
3 fresh green chilies
6 tomatoes, peeled (see page 174) and chopped
2 small onions, chopped
1 clove garlic
salt

Rub garlic over chops; cover and leave in the refrigerator 5 hours. To make sauce, put chilies in a saucepan, cover with water, bring to boil, and cook 3 minutes. Drain. Remove stems and cut chilies in half lengthwise. Discard white pith and seeds. Put chilies in a blender or food processor, add tomatoes, onions, garlic, and salt, and process until smooth; set aside. Heat oil in a skillet. Fry chops 5 minutes on each side or until browned.

Pour over chili mixture and simmer, uncovered, 15 minutes. Peel avocado. Cut in half and remove pit. Slice and sprinkle with lemon juice. Put chops on a warmed serving plate, spoon over sauce, and garnish with avocado slices.

Makes 4 servings.

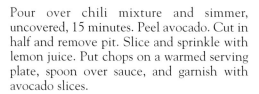

BEEF & VEAL

BELGIAN HODGEPODGE

8 oz. brisket of beef, diced
8 oz. shoulder of lamb, diced
3 oz. side of pork, diced
2¼ cups chicken stock
2 bay leaves
4 oz. rutabaga, diced
10 small onions
2 cups Brussels sprouts
4 or 5 medium potatoes, diced
1 carrot, diced
8 oz. pork chipolata sausages
⅔ cup sour cream

POT ROAST OF BRISKET

3 lb. brisket of beef
2 leeks, thickly sliced
1 bay leaf
2 parsley stalks
1 celery leaf
5 medium carrots, thickly sliced
3 medium sweet potatoes, cut into chunks
¼ cup cider vinegar
½ small white cabbage, thickly shredded
salt and freshly ground black pepper

Put beef, lamb, and pork in a flameproof casserole and pour in stock.

Heat a large, flameproof casserole, add brisket, and cook, turning, 3 to 4 minutes until browned all over.

Add 2¼ cups water, bay leaves, and 1 teaspoon salt. Bring to boil, skimming any scum from the surface. Cover tightly and simmer 2 hours. Add rutabaga, onions, Brussels sprouts, potatoes, and carrots and cook 30 minutes until meat is tender. Remove meat and vegetables from the casserole with a slotted spoon and keep warm. Put sausages in the casserole and cook 10 minutes. Remove with a slotted spoon and add to meat and vegetables.

Remove from the casserole. Add leeks and mix into cooking juices. With a piece of string, tie together bay leaf, parsley stalks, and celery leaf and add to the casserole with carrots and sweet potatoes. Stir well. Add vinegar and ½ cup water. Put meat on top.

Bring sauce to boil and boil until reduced by one third. Season with salt and pepper, stir in sour cream, and heat gently to warm through. Pour sauce over meat and vegetables and serve.

Makes 4 to 6 servings.

Cover and cook very gently 2½ hours. Remove beef from the casserole and keep warm. Remove vegetables with a slotted spoon and keep warm. Bring sauce to boil and add white cabbage. Season and simmer 5 minutes. Carve beef and serve with vegetables.

Makes 6 to 8 servings.

BOEUF EN DAUBE PROVENÇAL

2¼ lb. braising steak, diced
1 Spanish onion, chopped
3 cloves garlic, chopped
bouquet garni
3 cups full-bodied red wine
1 teaspoon black peppercorns
2 tablespoons olive oil
8 slices bacon, cut into strips
3 tomatoes, peeled, seeded, and chopped
2 in. wide strip of orange peel, oven-dried
12 black olives
Italian parsley sprigs, to garnish

Put steak, onion, garlic, bouquet garni, wine, and peppercorns in a nonmetallic bowl.

Cover and let marinate 12 to 24 hours. Preheat oven to 325°F. Remove meat from marinade with a slotted spoon, reserving marinade, and drain beef on absorbent paper towels. Heat oil in a heavy, flameproof casserole, add bacon, and cook until browned. Remove with a slotted spoon and set aside. Add beef and cook over moderately high heat until browned all over. Add tomatoes and cook 2 or 3 minutes.

Add reserved marinade, bacon, and orange peel and season with salt and pepper. Heat to almost simmering, cover tightly, and cook in the oven 3¼ hours. Add olives and cook 15 minutes. Discard bouquet garni and orange peel, garnish with parsley, and serve.

Makes 4 to 6 servings.

Note: To dry orange peel, put in a very low oven and leave until hard.

BOEUF BOURGUIGNON

1 or 2 tablespoons olive oil
2 slices thick-cut bacon, chopped
12 each baby onions and button mushrooms
2¼ lb. braising steak, diced
1 large onion, finely chopped
1 carrot, finely chopped
3 cloves garlic, chopped
1 tablespoon all-purpose flour
3 cups red Burgundy wine
bouquet garni
salt and freshly ground black pepper
fresh parsley and bay leaves, to garnish

Heat 1 tablespoon oil in a heavy, flameproof casserole and cook bacon 2 or 3 minutes.

Remove with a slotted spoon and set aside. Add baby onions to casserole and cook, stirring occasionally, until browned. Remove with a slotted spoon and set aside. Add mushrooms to casserole and cook, stirring occasionally, until lightly browned, adding more oil if necessary. Remove with a slotted spoon and set aside. Add beef to casserole and cook over moderately high heat until browned all over. Remove with a slotted spoon and set aside.

Add chopped onion and carrot to casserole and cook, stirring occasionally, until beginning to brown. Return bacon and beef to casserole, add garlic, and stir in flour. Stir in wine, bouquet garni, salt, and plenty of pepper. Heat to almost simmering, cover, and cook very gently 2¾ hours, stirring occasionally. Add reserved onions and mushrooms, cover, and cook 10 minutes to warm through. Garnish with parsley and bay leaves and serve.

Makes 4 servings.

BLACK-BEAN BEEF & RICE

1 tablespoon sunflower oil
2 shallots, chopped
2 cloves garlic, finely chopped
1 whole cinnamon stick, broken
2 star anise
8 oz. lean beef, trimmed and cut into ¾ in. cubes
3 tablespoons fermented black beans
1¼ cups long-grain white rice, rinsed
3½ cups beef stock
salt and freshly ground pepper
2 tablespoons fresh, chopped chives, to garnish

ROAST HOISIN BEEF

1½ lb. lean beef round
freshly ground pepper
2 cloves garlic, finely chopped
½ in. piece fresh ginger, peeled and finely chopped
2 teaspoons sesame oil
¼ cup hoisin sauce
2 cups beef stock
4 carrots
1 daikon
1 large green bell pepper
1 large yellow bell pepper
4 scallions, shredded
scallion rings, to garnish

Heat oil in a nonstick or well-seasoned wok or pan and stir-fry shallots, garlic, cinnamon stick, star anise, beef, black beans, and rice 2 or 3 minutes or until beef is browned and rice is opaque.

Preheat oven to 350°F. Trim any fat from beef and place in a nonstick roasting pan. Season with pepper. Mix together garlic, ginger, sesame oil, and hoisin sauce and spread over beef. Pour half the stock into the roasting pan and roast 1 hour, basting beef occasionally to keep it from drying out.

Pour in stock and bring to boil. Reduce heat and simmer 25 minutes or until liquid is absorbed and beef is tender. Discard cinnamon stick and star anise. Garnish with chives and serve with a salad.

Makes 4 servings.

Meanwhile, peel carrots and daikon. Halve carrots and slice lengthwise, slice daikon crosswise, and quarter bell peppers. Arrange vegetables around beef, pour in remaining stock, and cook 45 to 60 minutes or until tender. Drain beef and vegetables. Slice beef and serve with vegetables, topped with shredded scallions and garnished with scallion rings.

Makes 4 servings.

SHABUSHABU

1 lb. beef sirloin or round
2 leeks, white part only
8 fresh or dried shiitake or 12 button mushrooms,
  stalks removed
9 oz. (1 cake) firm tofu
4 to 6 Chinese cabbage leaves
10 oz. spinach, trimmed
4 in. piece dried konbu (kelp)
10 oz. udon noodles, cooked (optional)
finely chopped scallion, to garnish
CITRUS DIP:
½ daikon, peeled
1 dried or fresh red chili
2 scallions, finely chopped
juice ½ lemon and ½ lime
½ cup shoyu

SESAME DIP:
¼ cup sesame paste or smooth peanut butter
½ cup dashi
3 tablespoons shoyu
1 tablespoon mirin or sweet sherry
1 tablespoon sugar
2 tablespoons sake or white wine
2 teaspoons chili oil or chili powder (optional)

Trim off any fat from beef and cut into
3 × 1½ in. flat pieces (any length). Place in
separate freezer bags and freeze 1 to 2 hours.

Remove beef from the freezer and leave until
half thawed, then cut into wafer-thin slices
and arrange in a circular fan on a large
platter. Slice leeks diagonally. If shiitake
mushrooms are large, cut in half. If using
dried shiitake, soak in warm water with a
pinch sugar 45 minutes, then remove stalks
before use. Cut tofu into sixteen cubes. Cut
Chinese cabbage leaves and spinach into
bite-sized pieces. Arrange vegetables and
tofu on a large platter.

To prepare citrus dip, first make "autumn
maple leaf" relish: Grate daikon very finely
and chop fresh red chili, then mix together.
Put relish, chopped scallion, a mixture of
lemon and lime juices, and shoyu in separate
small bowls. To make sesame dip, mix
together sesame paste or peanut butter,
dashi, shoyu, mirin or sweet sherry, sugar,
sake or white wine, and chili oil or chili
powder and stir until of a smooth, runny
consistency. Divide between four to six
individual dipping bowls.

Put konbu in a large pot (ideally a clay pot or
an enameled cast-iron casserole) and fill two
thirds full with water. Bring to boil and
remove konbu. Put in some of the leek,
Chinese cabbage, shiitake mushrooms,
spinach, and tofu and when it begins to
come back to boil, transfer the pot to a
portable burner on the dining table. Diners
make their own citrus dip in individual
dipping bowls by mixing 1 or 2 teaspoons
each of the relish, scallion, and citrus juice
with some shoyu.

Diners serve themselves by cooking meat in
the pot, adding more vegetables, and eating
them dipped in either of the sauces. When
ingredients are finished, skim and season
soup with shoyu and a little salt and sugar. If
using noodles, warm them in soup, seasoned
with a little shoyu to taste, so that diners can
end the meal with plain noodles garnished
with chopped scallion.

Makes 4 to 6 servings.

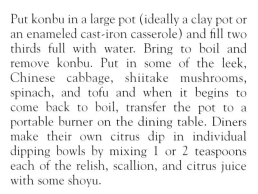

BEEF IN CHILI SAUCE

DRY BEEF WITH COCONUT

8 dried red chilies, cored, seeded, and chopped
2 small onions, chopped
2 in. piece fresh ginger, chopped
1½ lb. lean beef, cut into bite-sized pieces
1 tablespoon ground coriander
1 tablespoon ground cumin
1 tablespoon ketchup
2 teaspoons turmeric
2 teaspoons paprika
2 tablespoons vegetable oil
2 cloves garlic, crushed
1 in. stick cinnamon
seeds from 3 cardamom pods, crushed
½ star anise
sugar and salt
1 onion, sliced into thick rings

¼ cup vegetable oil
6 shallots, finely chopped
3 cloves garlic, finely chopped
1 fresh red chili, cored, seeded, and finely chopped
1½ lb. lean beef, thinly sliced and cut into
 ½ in. strips
1 tablespoon light brown sugar
1½ teaspoons ground cumin
1 teaspoon ground coriander
squeeze of lime juice
salt
½ fresh coconut, shredded, or 2⅔ cups dried
 coconut

Put chilies in a small blender. Add ¼ cup hot water and leave until slightly softened. Add half of small onions and half of ginger to blender and mix to a paste. Put beef in a large bowl. Add spice paste from blender, coriander, cumin, ketchup, turmeric, and paprika. Stir together. Cover and let marinate at least 1 hour.

In a wok or sauté pan, heat 1 tablespoon oil over medium heat. Add shallots, garlic, and chili and fry about 5 minutes, stirring occasionally, until softened but not browned. Add beef, sugar, cumin, coriander, lime juice, salt to taste, and ⅔ cup water. Cover pan tightly and simmer gently 30 minutes, stirring occasionally.

Heat oil in a wok and add remaining onion and ginger and garlic. Fry, stirring, 3 minutes until lightly browned. Stir in cinnamon stick, cardamom, and star anise and cook 1 minute. Add meat and marinade and cook over medium to high heat, stirring, 5 minutes. Add 1½ cups water, and sugar and salt to taste. Cover pan. Simmer very gently 1¼ hours or until beef is tender, stirring occasionally. Add onion rings and cook 3 to 5 minutes or until soft.

Uncover pan and stir in coconut until all liquid has been absorbed. Stir in remaining oil and continue stirring until coconut begins to brown.

Makes 6 servings.

Makes 4 to 6 servings.

CURRIED COCONUT BEEF

6¾ cups coconut milk
4 fresh bay leaves
3 lb. braising steak, cut into 2 in. cubes
CURRY PASTE:
6 shallots, chopped
6 cloves garlic, smashed
6 fresh red chilies, cored, seeded, and chopped
3 in. piece galangal, chopped
2 stalks lemongrass, chopped
1 in. piece cinnamon stick
12 whole cloves
1 teaspoon ground turmeric

Mix all curry paste ingredients in a blender. Add a little coconut milk, if necessary.

In a saucepan, combine curry paste and coconut milk. Add bay leaves and bring to boil over high heat, stirring occasionally. Lower heat to medium and cook sauce, stirring occasionally, 15 minutes.

Stir in beef. Simmer, uncovered, stirring occasionally, 2 hours. Reduce heat to very low and cook beef an additional 1½ to 2 hours until sauce is quite thick. Stir frequently to prevent sticking. Skim fat and oil from surface. Serve with rice.

Makes 8 servings.

GARLIC BEEF CASSEROLE

1 tablespoon peanut oil
1 lb. lean beef chuck, trimmed and cut into
   ¾ in. cubes
2 shallots, chopped
4 cloves garlic, thinly sliced
2 large carrots, sliced
6 oz. baby corn, halved lengthwise
8 oz. button mushrooms
1¼ cups beef stock
2 tablespoons dark soy sauce
1 tablespoon rice wine
2 teaspoons five-spice powder
2 tablespoons hoisin sauce
1 teaspoon chili sauce

Heat oil in a nonstick or well-seasoned wok and stir-fry beef, shallots, garlic, carrots, baby corn, and mushrooms 5 minutes. Add stock, soy sauce, rice wine, five-spice powder, hoisin sauce, and chili sauce and bring to boil. Reduce to a simmer, cover, and simmer 1 hour.

Remove from heat and blot surface with paper towels to absorb surface fat. Increase the heat and boil 10 minutes to reduce and thicken sauce. Serve with rice.

Makes 4 servings.

BEEF IN BAROLO WINE

2¼ lb. braising beef joint
6 cloves garlic, crushed
1 onion, roughly chopped
1 carrot, chopped
1 stalk celery, chopped
2 bay leaves
2 large thyme sprigs
2 or 3 peppercorns, lightly crushed
2 cloves
2 allspice berries, crushed
½ cup Barolo wine, or other full-bodied red wine
2 tablespoons olive oil
2 tablespoons tomato paste
⅔ cup strong beef stock
salt and freshly ground black pepper

Place meat in a plastic bag with garlic, onion, carrot, celery, bay leaves, cloves, thyme, peppercorns, allspice, and wine. Shake the bag, seal, and refrigerate several hours or overnight, turning meat occasionally. Preheat oven to 325°F. Open bag, remove meat from marinade, and pat dry with absorbent paper towels. Heat oil in a large, flameproof casserole and brown meat all over. Pour in reserved marinade, tomato paste, and stock. Cover tightly and bake in oven 2 to 3 hours until beef is tender.

Lift meat out of casserole and keep warm. Skim off any fat and remove bay leaves from sauce. Purée sauce in a blender or food processor until smooth. Taste and season. The sauce should be quite thick; if it is not, boil to reduce it. Slice meat thinly and serve with sauce.

Makes 8 servings.

CARBONNADE DE BOEUF

2 tablespoons olive oil
2¼ lb. braising steak, diced
3 or 4 medium onions, sliced
2 tablespoons all-purpose flour
2½ cups brown ale
1 clove garlic, crushed
bouquet garni
4 thick slices French bread
salt and freshly ground black pepper
Dijon mustard, for spreading
Italian parsley and fresh, chopped parsley, to garnish

Heat oil in a heavy, flameproof casserole, add meat, and cook until browned all over. Remove with a slotted spoon and set aside.

Add onions to casserole and cook gently, stirring occasionally, 10 minutes until browned. Sprinkle in flour and cook, stirring, until lightly browned. Stir in beer and bring to boil, stirring. Return beef to casserole, add garlic and bouquet garni, cover tightly, and cook very gently 2 hours, stirring occasionally.

Preheat broiler to low. Toast bread slowly until crisp and golden. Spread thickly with mustard, baste lightly with sauce from casserole, and toast 5 to 10 minutes until topping is browned. Garnish casserole with parsley and serve with mustard croûtes.

Makes 4 servings.

BEEF WITH TOMATO SAUCE

2 cloves garlic, thinly sliced
1 tablespoon fresh, finely chopped thyme
1 tablespoon fresh, finely chopped marjoram
1½ lb. piece chuck steak
2 tablespoons olive oil
SAUCE:
2 tablespoons olive oil
8 cloves garlic, chopped
1 thyme sprig
2 marjoram sprigs
3 parsley sprigs
14½ oz. can chopped tomatoes
8 canned anchovy fillets, chopped
¾ cup dry white wine
24 small pitted black olives
salt and freshly ground black pepper

To make sauce, heat oil in a saucepan, add garlic, thyme, marjoram, and parsley, and cook gently 5 minutes. Add tomatoes with their juice, then stir in anchovies, wine, and olives. Simmer 15 minutes. Taste and adjust seasoning.

Meanwhile, mix sliced garlic with chopped thyme and marjoram. Using the point of a sharp knife, cut small slits in beef and push herb-covered slices of garlic deep into slits. Heat oil in a flameproof casserole, add beef, and cook until evenly browned, 10 minutes. Pour over sauce, cover tightly, and cook gently about 1½ hours, turning beef occasionally, until it is tender.

Makes 4 servings.

BEEF IN SPINACH SAUCE

2 tablespoons olive oil
1½ lb. chuck steak, cut into 1½ in. cubes
8 baby onions
1 tablespoon red wine vinegar
8 oz. fresh spinach, trimmed
1 tablespoon bread crumbs
3 cloves garlic
2 cups veal stock or water
salt and freshly ground black pepper
1 tablespoon black olive paste

In a large, flameproof casserole, heat oil, add beef, and brown on all sides. Remove and set aside. Add onions to casserole and cook, stirring frequently, until evenly browned. Stir in vinegar and boil 1 minute.

Put spinach, bread crumbs, garlic, and half the stock or water in a blender or food processor and mix until smooth. Return beef to casserole and pour over spinach mixture with remaining stock or water. Season. Heat to simmering point, then cover and simmer very gently 1½ to 2 hours until beef is tender. Stir in black olive paste and serve.

Makes 4 to 6 servings.

PASTITSIO

2 cups macaroni
2 tablespoons olive oil
1 onion, chopped
1 clove garlic, crushed
1 lb. (2 cups) ground beef
1¼ cups beef stock
2 teaspoons tomato paste
½ teaspoon ground cinnamon
1 teaspoon fresh, chopped mint
salt and pepper
½ stick butter
½ cup all-purpose flour
2 cups milk
½ cup plain yogurt
1½ cups shredded kefalotyri cheese

ZUCCHINI MOUSSAKA

3 tablespoons olive oil
3 zucchini, thinly sliced
1 large onion, finely chopped
1 clove garlic, crushed
1½ lb. (3 cups) ground beef or lamb
8 oz. can chopped tomatoes
1 tablespoon tomato paste
2 teaspoons dried oregano
1 teaspoon ground cinnamon
½ cup red wine
½ cup beef or lamb stock
salt and freshly ground black pepper
12 oz. (about 1⅔ cups) thinly sliced, cooked potato
4 tomatoes, thinly sliced
SAUCE:
½ stick butter
¼ cup all-purpose flour
2 cups milk
⅔ cup yogurt
¼ cup shredded kefalotyri cheese

Cook macaroni in a pan of boiling water 8 minutes until tender. Drain, rinse with cold water, and set aside. Meanwhile, preheat oven to 375°F. In a skillet, heat oil, add onion and garlic, and cook until soft. Add ground beef and stir until browned. Stir in stock, tomato paste, cinnamon, mint, salt, and pepper. Simmer 10 to 15 minutes until sauce is reduced.

Heat 2 tablespoons oil in a large saucepan. Add zucchini and cook 3 minutes. Remove with a slotted spoon and drain on absorbent paper towels. Heat remaining oil in the saucepan and cook onion and garlic until soft. Add ground beef or lamb and cook until browned. Add tomatoes, tomato paste, oregano, cinnamon, wine, stock, and salt and pepper. Cover and simmer 30 minutes.

In a saucepan, melt butter. Stir in flour and cook 1 minute. Gradually stir in milk and yogurt and simmer 5 minutes. Stir in half the cheese and season with salt and pepper. Mix macaroni into cheese sauce. Spread half the macaroni mixture over the bottom of a large gratin or soufflé dish. Cover with meat sauce, then top with remaining macaroni. Sprinkle with remaining cheese. Bake 45 minutes or until browned.

Makes 4 to 6 servings.

Uncover and cook until any liquid evaporates. Preheat the oven to 350°F. To make sauce, melt butter in a saucepan, add flour, and cook, stirring, 2 minutes. Remove from the heat and stir in milk and yogurt. Cook, stirring, until thickened. Simmer 5 minutes. Season. Put meat in an ovenproof dish. Top with layers of potato, zucchini, and tomato. Spoon over sauce and sprinkle with cheese. Bake 40 minutes.

Makes 6 servings.

MEATBALLS IN TOMATO SAUCE

PICADILLO

¼ cup milk
1 egg, beaten
½ teaspoon freshly grated nutmeg
2 slices white bread
2 onions, finely chopped
2 cloves garlic, crushed
1 teaspoon dried thyme
2 tablespoons fresh, chopped parsley
1 lb. (2 cups) ground beef
1 tablespoon olive oil
14½ oz. can chopped tomatoes
2 tablespoons tomato paste
salt and freshly ground black pepper
basil leaves, to garnish

2 tablespoons oil
2 onions, finely chopped
2 cloves garlic, crushed
1 green bell pepper, chopped
1 red bell pepper, chopped
1 green chili, finely chopped
1½ lb. (3 cups) ground beef
5 medium tomatoes, peeled (see page 174) and
  chopped
½ teaspoon cumin seeds
2 teaspoons dried oregano
2 tablespoons raisins
salt and freshly ground black pepper
15 pimiento-stuffed olives, sliced
1 tablespoon capers
rings of green and red bell peppers, to garnish

In a shallow dish, mix together milk, egg, and nutmeg. Add bread and let soak 5 minutes. In a bowl, mix half the onions and garlic with thyme, parsley, and ground beef. Squeeze liquid from bread and add bread to beef mixture. Mix well and shape into thirty balls. Heat oil in a flameproof casserole. Add meatballs in batches and cook, turning, about 8 minutes until browned all over. Remove with a slotted spoon, drain on absorbent paper towels, and keep warm.

Heat oil in a large heavy-bottomed skillet. Add onions, garlic, bell peppers, and chili and cook 10 minutes until soft. Add beef and cook, stirring, until browned.

Put remaining onion and garlic in the casserole with chopped tomatoes, tomato paste, and salt and pepper. Bring to boil and cook over medium heat, stirring constantly, until reduced and thickened. Add meatballs and heat gently to warm through. Garnish and serve.

Makes 4 servings.

Add tomatoes, cumin, oregano, raisins, and seasoning and simmer gently, uncovered, stirring frequently, 20 minutes until meat is cooked and mixture is well blended. Add olives and capers and cook 5 minutes. Transfer to a heated serving dish and garnish with bell pepper rings.

Makes 6 servings.

Note: Picadillo is traditionally served topped with a fried egg and fried plantains, with black beans and rice.

CHILI BEEF WITH NACHOS

1 tablespoon olive oil
1 onion, chopped
1 clove garlic, crushed
1 lb. (2 cups) ground beef
15 oz. can red kidney beans, drained
1 green bell pepper, chopped
2 tablespoons tomato paste
2 teaspoons chili powder
5 oz. tortilla chips
1 cup shredded mozzarella cheese
1 or 2 teaspoons paprika

BEEF TAGINE WITH PRUNES

1¼ cups pitted prunes
1 teaspoon ground ginger
1 tablespoon ground coriander
pinch saffron threads
salt and freshly ground black pepper
3 tablespoons olive oil
2½ lb. stewing beef, diced
2 onions, sliced
2 cloves garlic, crushed
chicken stock or water
1 cinnamon stick
1 tablespoon honey
1 teaspoon harissa
1 tablespoon sesame seeds
3 tablespoons fresh, chopped parsley
1 teaspoon orange flower water, to serve

Heat oil in a flameproof casserole. Add onion and garlic and cook, stirring occasionally, 5 minutes until soft. Add ground beef and cook 6 to 8 minutes until browned. Stir in kidney beans, bell pepper, tomato paste, chili powder, and ⅔ cup water. Cover and simmer 10 to 15 minutes. Preheat oven to 400°F.

Place prunes in a bowl and cover with boiling water. Let soak 2 hours. In a large bowl, mix together ginger, coriander, saffron, salt, bell pepper, and 2 tablespoons oil. Add beef and mix well, rubbing spices into meat with your fingers. Transfer to a tagine or casserole. In a large skillet, heat remaining oil. Add onions and garlic and cook 10 minutes until soft. Add to spiced beef, then pour in enough stock or water to barely cover meat. Add cinnamon.

Uncover and cook 5 minutes until sauce is reduced and thickened. Arrange tortilla chips over the top, sprinkle with mozzarella cheese and paprika, and cook in the oven 20 minutes until cheese is melted and golden.

Makes 4 servings.

Cover the tagine and simmer gently 2 hours until beef is tender. Check from time to time and add more liquid, if necessary. Drain prunes and add to the casserole; simmer an additional 20 minutes. Stir in honey and harissa and cook an additional 15 minutes. Dry-fry sesame seeds in a skillet until lightly browned. To serve, stir in parsley and sprinkle with orange flower water and sesame seeds. Serve with couscous.

Makes 6 servings.

JAMAICAN PEPPER STEW

2 tablespoons oil
2 onions, chopped
2 cloves garlic, crushed
1¼ lb. foreshank of beef, diced
2½ cups beef stock
2 cups fresh spinach leaves
1 teaspoon dried thyme
2 fresh green chilies, seeded and chopped
1 or 2 sweet potatoes
2 cups diced squash
1 green bell pepper, chopped
2 tomatoes, peeled (see page 174) and chopped
salt and 2 teaspoons hot pepper sauce
2 cups all-purpose flour
1 tablespoon baking powder
2 tablespoons butter

In a flameproof casserole, heat oil. Add onions and garlic and cook 10 minutes until soft. Remove and set aside. Add beef to hot oil and fry in batches until browned. Return onions and browned meat to casserole. Add stock, cover, and simmer gently 1½ hours. Cook spinach in a little water, then drain thoroughly and process in a food processor. Add to casserole with thyme, chilies, sweet potato, squash, bell pepper, tomatoes, salt, and hot pepper sauce. Cook an additional 30 minutes until beef and vegetables are tender.

Meanwhile, make dumplings: Sift flour, baking powder, and a little salt into a bowl. Cut in butter and add enough cold water to make a dough. Shape into balls about 1½ in. in diameter and flatten slightly. Drop into very gently simmering casserole about 10 minutes before end of cooking time.

Makes 4 to 6 servings.

MADRAS MEAT CURRY

1½ lb. braising steak
2 tablespoons vegetable oil
1 large onion, finely sliced
4 cloves
4 green cardamom pods, bruised
3 fresh green chilies, seeded and finely chopped
2 dry red chilies, seeded and crushed
1 in. piece fresh ginger, grated
2 cloves garlic, crushed
2 teaspoons ground coriander
2 teaspoons turmeric
¼ cup tamarind juice (see Note)
salt
lettuce leaves, to garnish

Cut beef into 1 in. cubes. Heat oil in a large, heavy-bottomed pan, add beef, and fry until browned all over. Remove with a slotted spoon and set aside. Add onion, cloves, and cardamom pods to pan and fry about 8 minutes, stirring, until onion is soft and golden brown. Stir in chilies, ginger, garlic, coriander, and turmeric and fry 2 minutes. Return beef to pan, add ¼ cup water, and simmer, covered, 1 hour.

Stir in tamarind juice, season with salt, and simmer, covered, 15 to 30 minutes until beef is tender. Serve garnished with lettuce leaves.

Makes 4 servings.

Note: Tamarind pulp, available in Indian markets, is used to make tamarind juice. Soak a walnut-sized piece in 1 cup boiling water 20 minutes, then squeeze pulp in cheesecloth to extract juice. Discard pulp.

PASTA BOLOGNESE

3 oz. pancetta or bacon, diced
1 medium onion, finely chopped
1 medium carrot, finely diced
1 stalk celery, finely chopped
8 oz. (1 cup) lean ground beef
4 oz. chicken livers, trimmed and chopped
1 medium potato, shredded
2 tablespoons tomato paste
½ cup white wine
1 cup beef stock or water
salt and freshly ground black pepper
freshly grated nutmeg
14 oz. dried spaghetti, fettuccine, or tagliatelle
freshly grated Parmesan cheese, to serve (optional)

Heat a saucepan and add pancetta. Cook in its own fat 2 or 3 minutes until browning. Add onion, carrot, and celery and brown. Stir in ground beef and brown over high heat, breaking it up with a wooden spoon. Stir in chicken livers and cook 2 or 3 minutes.

Add shredded potato and tomato paste, mix well, and pour in wine and stock. Season with salt, pepper, and nutmeg. Bring to boil, half cover, and simmer 35 minutes until reduced and thickened, stirring occasionally. Meanwhile, cook pasta in boiling salted water until tender. Drain well and toss with sauce. Serve with Parmesan cheese.

Makes 6 servings.

BEEF GOULASH WITH CHILI

2 tablespoons olive oil
1 onion, sliced
1 clove garlic, crushed
2 teaspoons paprika
1½ lb. lean stewing beef, diced
pinch caraway seeds
2 bay leaves
1 tablespoon balsamic vinegar
2 cups beef stock
salt and freshly ground black pepper
6 medium potatoes, diced
2 green bell peppers, sliced
1 fresh green chili, cored, seeded, and sliced
14½ oz. can chopped tomatoes
2 tablespoons tomato paste

Heat oil in a flameproof casserole. Add onion, garlic, and paprika and cook, stirring, 2 minutes. Add beef and cook 3 to 4 minutes until onion is soft and beef has browned. Add caraway seeds, bay leaves, vinegar, and half the stock. Season with salt and pepper and bring to boil. Cover and simmer 1 hour.

Stir in remaining stock, potatoes, bell peppers, chili, tomatoes, and tomato paste. Bring to boil, cover, and simmer 30 to 40 minutes until meat and vegetables are tender.

Makes 4 servings.

SPICY BRAISED BEEF

3 lb. beef round joint
2 cloves garlic, crushed
½ teaspoon ground cinnamon
¼ teaspoon ground cloves
salt and pepper
3 tablespoons olive oil
4 onions, thinly sliced
½ cup red wine
2 tablespoons tomato paste
1 lb. spaghetti
1 tablespoon balsamic vinegar
fresh herbs, to garnish

With a sharp knife, make slits in beef.

In a bowl, mix garlic, cinnamon, cloves, salt, and pepper. Press mixture into slits and leave beef in a cool place 1 hour. Heat oil in a flameproof casserole into which meat will just fit. Turn meat in hot oil until browned all over. Remove from casserole. Add onions and cook gently until soft and lightly browned. Replace meat. Add wine and enough hot water to barely cover it. Mix tomato paste with a little water, stir into casserole, and season.

Cover casserole and cook over gentle heat about 1½ hours, turning meat frequently, until tender. Bring a large pan of salted water to boil and cook spaghetti until al dente. Remove meat and keep hot. Add vinegar to sauce. Boil briskly until reduced to a smooth, glossy sauce. Slice beef. Garnish with herbs and serve with some sauce poured over beef and remainder stirred into spaghetti.

Makes 6 servings.

GARLIC BEEF

2 tablespoons olive oil
4 oz. piece unsmoked bacon, cut into 2 in. cubes
2¼ lb. chuck steak, cut into 1½ in. cubes
1 Spanish onion, chopped
1 head garlic, divided into cloves
1 cup red wine
2 cloves
bouquet garni of 1 marjoram sprig, 1 thyme sprig,
  2 parsley sprigs, and 1 bay leaf
salt and freshly ground black pepper

In a heavy, flameproof casserole, heat oil, add bacon, and cook over low heat until bacon gives off its fat. Increase heat, add beef, and cook about 5 minutes, stirring occasionally, until browned all over. Using a slotted spoon, transfer beef and bacon to a bowl.

Stir onion and garlic into casserole and cook gently 6 minutes, stirring occasionally. Stir in wine, cloves, bouquet garni, and salt and pepper. Return meat to casserole, cover tightly, and cook gently 2 hours, stirring occasionally, until meat is very tender. Check from time to time to ensure casserole is not drying out.

Makes 6 servings.

BOBOTIE

1 cup milk
1 thick slice white bread
1 tablespoon olive oil
1 large onion, chopped
2¼ lb. (4½ cups) ground beef
2 teaspoons apricot jelly
¼ cup lemon juice
½ cup raisins
10 dried apricots
2 tablespoons mild curry powder
12 blanched almonds, roughly chopped
1 teaspoon salt
freshly ground black pepper
6 bay leaves
2 eggs

Preheat oven to 350°F. Put half the milk in a shallow dish, add bread, and let soak 5 minutes. Heat oil in a flameproof casserole. Add onion and cook, stirring occasionally, 5 minutes until soft. Squeeze milk from bread and add bread to the casserole with ground beef, apricot jelly, lemon juice, raisins, dried apricots, curry powder, blanched almonds, salt and pepper, and bay leaves. Mix well, then level the surface. Bake 30 minutes.

Beat together remaining milk and eggs and pour over meat. Return to the oven and bake 20 to 25 minutes until custard has set.

Makes 6 to 8 servings.

Note: This dish is particularly good served with a fruity chutney.

JAPANESE BEEF & POTATOES

10 oz. piece lean beef
5 medium potatoes, peeled
2 Spanish onions
2 tablespoons vegetable oil
⅓ cup sugar
⅓ cup shoyu
dashi or water
parboiled mange-tout, to garnish (optional)

Put beef in the freezer about 1 hour to harden, then slice very thinly against the grain into bite-sized pieces.

Quarter each potato and boil until tender but still slightly hard in the center. Drain and set aside. Cut onions into thin half-moon slices. In a skillet or a shallow saucepan, heat a little vegetable oil and stir-fry beef slices over medium heat. When beef begins to change color, add potatoes and continue to stir. Add sugar and shoyu to the pan and lightly fold in. Pour in enough dashi or water to just cover ingredients and bring to boil. Skim the surface and lower the heat.

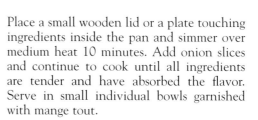

Place a small wooden lid or a plate touching ingredients inside the pan and simmer over medium heat 10 minutes. Add onion slices and continue to cook until all ingredients are tender and have absorbed the flavor. Serve in small individual bowls garnished with mange tout.

Makes 4 servings.

VEAL CHOPS WITH TOMATOES

2 tablespoons olive oil
4 veal chops or steaks
1 large onion, sliced
1 clove garlic, crushed
8 oz. can chopped tomatoes
1 teaspoon tomato paste
salt and pepper
1 teaspoon dried oregano
½ teaspoon ground cinnamon
toasted pine nuts and oregano sprigs, to garnish

In a skillet, heat olive oil. Add chops and cook on one side until browned, then turn and brown other side. Transfer to a plate and keep warm.

Add onion and garlic to pan and cook for a few minutes until soft. Stir in tomatoes, tomato paste, salt, pepper, oregano, cinnamon, and ⅔ cup water.

Return chops to pan. Spoon some of the sauce over. Simmer, uncovered, 20 minutes or until chops are cooked and sauce is thick. Sprinkle with toasted pine nuts and oregano before serving.

Makes 4 servings.

VIETNAMESE BEEF STEW

1 tablespoon vegetable oil
2 cloves garlic, chopped
1 onion, chopped
1 stalk lemongrass, chopped
1 lb. stewing beef, cut into bite-sized cubes
2½ cups beef stock or water
⅓ cup soy sauce or fish sauce
1 teaspoon chili sauce
2 teaspoons five-spice powder
1 tablespoon sugar
2 or 3 scallions, chopped
freshly ground black pepper
cilantro sprigs, to garnish

Heat oil in a flameproof casserole over high heat and stir-fry garlic, onion, and lemongrass about 1 minute. Add beef and stir-fry 2 or 3 minutes or until color of meat changes. Add stock or water, bring to boil, then add soy or fish sauce, chili sauce, five-spice powder, and sugar. Blend well, then reduce heat, cover, and simmer 45 to 50 minutes.

Add scallions, season with pepper, and cook an additional 5 minutes. Garnish with cilantro sprigs and serve straight from the pot, accompanied by carrots and baby corn.

Makes 4 servings.

Variation: Substitute curry powder for five-spice powder to make beef curry.

VEAL WITH MUSHROOMS

2 tablespoons olive oil
6 slices bacon, cut into thin strips
4 slices veal shank, each weighing 8 oz.
3 or 4 carrots, cut into thick strips
4 plum tomatoes, peeled, quartered, and seeded
2½ cups beef stock
½ cup red wine
1 lb. mixed mushrooms
½ stick butter, diced
1½ cups fresh, chopped parsley

Heat oil in a flameproof casserole. Add bacon and cook 3 to 4 minutes. Remove and drain on absorbent paper towels. Add veal and cook until browned on both sides.

Remove veal and drain on absorbent paper towels. Add carrots and tomatoes to the casserole and cook 2 or 3 minutes. Return veal to the casserole. Pour over stock and red wine. Bring to boil, cover, and simmer 40 minutes. Add mushrooms and bacon and cook 10 minutes until veal is cooked through and tender.

Lift out veal and remove carrots, mushrooms, and bacon with a slotted spoon. Keep warm. Strain sauce and return to the casserole. Bring to boil and boil until reduced by one third. Whisk in butter, a little at a time. Stir in parsley. Return bacon and vegetables to sauce and cook gently 2 minutes to warm through. Arrange veal on warmed serving plates, pour sauce over, and serve.

Makes 4 servings.

SOFRITO

¼ cup olive oil
1 onion, finely chopped
1 clove garlic, crushed
1½ lb. thin veal slices
seasoned flour
2 tablespoons brandy
⅔ cup white wine
1¼ cups beef stock
salt and pepper
3 tablespoons fresh, chopped parsley
parsley, to garnish

In a skillet, heat oil. Add onion and garlic and cook until soft. Transfer to a flameproof casserole.

Coat meat lightly with seasoned flour. Fry in skillet until browned on both sides. Add brandy. When brandy has stopped bubbling, transfer meat to casserole.

Add wine, stock, salt, and pepper. Cover and cook gently 45 minutes until meat is tender and sauce lightly thickened. Stir in parsley. Garnish with more parsley.

Makes 6 servings.

VEGETABLES & VEGETARIAN

LENTIL-STUFFED BELL PEPPERS

⅔ cup red split lentils
¼ cup vegetable oil
4 green or red bell peppers
1 teaspoon cumin seeds
2 onions, finely chopped
2 green chilies, seeded and chopped
1 in. piece fresh ginger, grated
1 tablespoon ground coriander
salt and pepper
2 tablespoons fresh, chopped cilantro
cilantro, to garnish

Wash lentils, then soak in cold water 30 minutes.

Heat half the oil in a skillet and fry bell peppers 3 to 5 minutes until golden brown on all sides. Drain on absorbent paper towels and let cool. Add remaining oil to pan, then add cumin seeds and fry until just beginning to pop. Add onions and chilies and fry, stirring, 8 minutes until onions are soft and golden brown. Stir in ginger and ground coriander. Drain lentils and add to pan with 1¼ cups water; stir well.

Cook, covered, over low heat 15 to 20 minutes until tender and liquid has been absorbed. Season with salt and pepper and add fresh cilantro. Preheat oven to 350°F. Cut tops from bell peppers and remove seeds. Stuff bell peppers with lentil mixture and replace tops. Stand in an ovenproof dish and cook 15 to 20 minutes until soft. Serve hot, garnished with cilantro.

Makes 4 servings.

CALLALOO GRATIN

butter for greasing
1 tablespoon oil
1 large onion, chopped
1 clove garlic, crushed
20 oz. can callaloo, drained
1 cup shredded cheddar cheese
2 eggs, beaten
½ teaspoon freshly grated nutmeg
salt and freshly ground black pepper
2 tablespoons fresh bread crumbs

Preheat oven to 350°F. Butter an ovenproof dish. Heat oil in a skillet. Add onion and garlic and cook 10 minutes until soft. Add callaloo and cook until excess moisture has evaporated. Let cool. Set aside 2 tablespoons cheese and place remainder in a bowl with eggs, nutmeg, and seasoning. Mix together thoroughly.

Stir cooled callaloo mixture into bowl. Pour into prepared dish. Sprinkle with reserved cheese and bread crumbs. Bake 45 minutes until firm and lightly browned.

Makes 4 servings.

RICE & PEAS

1¾ cups basmati rice, washed and soaked 1 hour
14 fl. oz. can coconut milk
1 fresh thyme sprig
1 Scotch bonnet chili
salt and freshly ground black pepper
1 tablespoon oil
4 scallions, sliced
1 clove garlic, crushed
14 oz. can gungo peas, drained and rinsed

GREEN BANANA CURRY

5 green bananas
2 tablespoons oil
1 onion, finely sliced
1 tablespoon curry paste
14 fl. oz. can coconut milk
salt and freshly ground black pepper
fresh, chopped cilantro and lime wedges, to garnish

Drain rice and put in a saucepan with coconut milk, thyme, chili, and salt. Bring to boil and stir once. Lower heat so liquid simmers gently, cover with a tightly fitting lid, and cook 10 to 12 minutes until rice is tender and liquid is absorbed.

Slice skin off bananas and cut flesh into 1 in. slices. Heat oil in a deep skillet and fry banana slices, in batches, until lightly browned on each side. Set aside. Add onion to pan and cook 10 minutes until soft. Return banana slices to pan and stir in curry paste.

Meanwhile, heat oil in a large pan. Add scallions and garlic and cook 2 or 3 minutes. Remove thyme and chili from rice and discard. Carefully stir scallion mixture, gungo peas, and freshly ground black pepper into rice and heat through gently.

Makes 6 servings.

Add half the coconut milk and stir well. Cook 10 minutes over low heat, then add seasoning. Pour in remaining coconut milk and simmer until mixture thickens and bananas break down a little. Garnish with chopped cilantro and lime wedges and serve immediately.

Makes 4 servings.

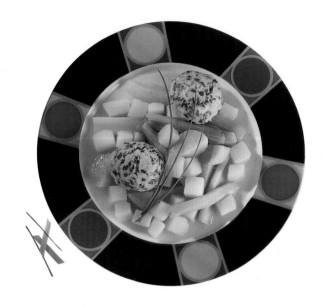

RATATOUILLE

2 eggplants, sliced
3 zucchini, sliced
¼ cup olive oil
1 Spanish onion, very thinly sliced
3 cloves garlic, crushed
2 large red bell peppers, thinly sliced
4 ripe beefsteak tomatoes, peeled, seeded, and
  chopped
few thyme, marjoram, and oregano sprigs
salt and freshly ground black pepper
2 tablespoons fresh, chopped parsley
2 tablespoons fresh, chopped basil

Put eggplant and zucchini in a colander, sprinkle with salt, and let stand 1 hour.

Rinse well, drain, and dry thoroughly with absorbent paper towels. Heat 2 tablespoons oil in a heavy, flameproof casserole, add eggplant, and cook, stirring occasionally, a few minutes. Add 1 tablespoon oil, onion, and garlic and cook, stirring occasionally, 2 to 3 minutes. Add bell peppers and cook, stirring occasionally, 1 or 2 minutes.

Add zucchini to casserole with more oil if necessary. Cook, stirring occasionally, 2 or 3 minutes, then add tomatoes and thyme, marjoram, and oregano leaves. Season lightly with salt and pepper, cover, and cook very gently 30 to 40 minutes, stirring occasionally. Stir in parsley and basil and cook, uncovered, 5 to 10 minutes until liquid has evaporated. Serve warm or cold.

Makes 4 servings.

LEEK STEW WITH DUMPLINGS

1½ lb. leeks, halved lengthwise
2 medium potatoes, diced
8 oz. Jerusalem artichokes, peeled and quartered
4 cups vegetable stock
salt
fresh chives, to garnish
DUMPLINGS:
1 cup self-rising flour
½ cup vegetable suet
2 or 3 cups fresh, chopped chives

Cut leeks into 3 in. lengths. Put leeks, potatoes, and artichokes in a large, flameproof casserole.

Add stock and season with salt. Bring to boil, cover, and simmer 45 to 60 minutes. Meanwhile, to make dumplings, put flour, suet, and chives in a large bowl, season with salt, and mix well. Stir in ¼ cup water and bind to a dough. Knead lightly and let rest 5 minutes.

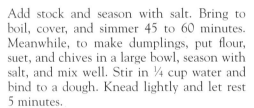

Shape dough into eight small dumplings. Place dumplings around the outside of the vegetable mixture. Cover and simmer 30 minutes. Garnish with chives and serve.

Makes 4 servings.

BRAISED FENNEL PROVENÇAL

3 fennel bulbs, trimmed
3 tablespoons olive oil
4 cloves garlic, peeled
5 ripe plum tomatoes, peeled, seeded, and diced (see page 174)
⅔ cup dry white wine
12 Niçoise olives
4 thyme sprigs
2 bay leaves
pinch sugar
salt and pepper
thyme sprigs, to garnish

Cut fennel bulbs lengthwise into ½ in. slices.

Heat oil in a large skillet and fry fennel slices and garlic 4 or 5 minutes on each side until golden. Remove from pan with a slotted spoon and reserve.

Add tomatoes and wine to the pan and boil rapidly 5 minutes. Stir in olives, thyme, bay leaves, and sugar and arrange fennel slices over the top, in a single layer if possible. Cover and simmer gently 20 minutes, season, and serve hot. Alternatively, let cool and serve at room temperature, garnished with thyme.

Makes 4 servings.

MUSHROOM RATATOUILLE

¼ cup dried porcini mushrooms
14½ oz. can chopped tomatoes
3 tablespoons olive oil
1 clove garlic, crushed
1 tablespoon fresh, chopped basil
1 large onion, chopped
2 teaspoons fresh, chopped thyme
1 lb. 2 oz. mixed mushrooms, wiped
salt and pepper
French bread, to serve

Place porcini in a small bowl and pour over ⅔ cup boiling water. Set aside 20 minutes to soak. Strain, reserving liquid, chop porcini, and reserve.

Place tomatoes, 1 tablespoon oil, garlic, and basil in a pan. Bring to boil and simmer 20 minutes.

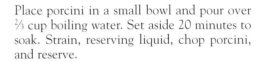

Meanwhile, heat remaining oil in a large skillet and fry onion and thyme 5 minutes. Add porcini and fresh mushrooms and stir-fry over high heat 3 or 4 minutes until golden. Add porcini liquid and simmer 3 minutes, stir in tomato sauce, and simmer gently an additional 5 minutes. Season and serve hot, warm, or cold with crisp French bread.

Makes 4 to 6 servings.

CAPONATA

½ cup olive oil
1 onion, chopped
4 stalks celery, sliced
3 or 4 tomatoes, peeled and chopped
3 tablespoons balsamic vinegar
1 tablespoon sugar
2 eggplants, diced
1 tablespoon capers, drained
12 green olives, pitted and roughly chopped
1 tablespoon pine nuts, lightly toasted
2 tablespoons fresh, chopped basil
red bell pepper strips and basil sprigs, to garnish

Heat 2 tablespoons oil in a saucepan. Add onion and cook 5 minutes.

Add celery and cook 3 minutes. Stir in tomatoes and simmer, uncovered, 5 minutes. Add vinegar and sugar and simmer 15 minutes. Heat remaining oil in a large skillet and cook eggplant until tender and golden.

Remove with a slotted spoon and add to tomato sauce. Add capers, olives, and pine nuts and season with salt and pepper. Simmer 2 or 3 minutes. Stir in basil, transfer to a serving dish, and let cool. Garnish with pepper strips and basil sprigs and serve.

Makes 4 to 6 servings.

PASTA NAPOLETANA

10 fresh ripe tomatoes, or 2 × 14½ oz. cans chopped
    tomatoes
1 medium onion, finely chopped
1 medium carrot, finely diced
1 stalk celery, diced
⅔ cup dry white wine (optional)
parsley sprig
salt and freshly ground pepper
pinch sugar
1 tablespoon fresh, chopped oregano
12 oz. dried pasta
freshly grated Parmesan cheese, to serve (optional)

Put tomatoes, onion, carrot, celery, wine, parsley, seasoning, and sugar in a saucepan.

Bring to boil and simmer, half covered, 45 minutes until very thick, stirring occasionally. Pass mixture through a strainer or purée in a blender and strain to remove tomato seeds. Stir in chopped oregano, then taste and adjust seasoning, if necessary. Reheat gently.

Bring a large pan of salted water to boil and cook pasta according to package directions until al dente. Drain well and toss with hot sauce. Serve at once, with grated Parmesan cheese.

Makes 4 servings.

BAKED MIXED VEGETABLES

1 eggplant, thinly sliced
salt and freshly ground black pepper
⅔ cup olive oil
3 cloves garlic, crushed
2 or 3 beefsteak tomatoes, peeled (see page 174), seeded, and chopped
1 tablespoon tomato paste
2 Spanish onions, thinly sliced
1 green bell pepper, sliced
1 red bell pepper, sliced
5 medium potatoes, boiled and sliced
½ cup fresh bread crumbs

Sprinkle eggplant slices with salt and leave in a colander 30 minutes. Rinse under cold running water and dry well on absorbent paper towels. Meanwhile, in a saucepan, heat 1 tablespoon oil, add garlic, and fry gently without browning. Add tomatoes, tomato paste, and salt and pepper. Cover and simmer 15 minutes. Preheat oven to 400°F.

In a skillet, heat ¼ cup oil. Add onions and bell peppers and cook gently 15 minutes. Using a slotted spoon, remove from pan and set aside. Add remaining oil to pan. Add eggplant slices in batches and fry until golden. Drain on absorbent paper towels. Layer all vegetables in a baking dish, seasoning each layer and moistening with tomato sauce. Finish with tomato sauce. Sprinkle with bread crumbs. Bake about 20 minutes until golden.

Makes 4 to 6 servings.

RED ROAST VEGETABLES

3 medium sweet potatoes
3 small turnips
3 large carrots
1 tablespoon sunflower oil
2 fresh red chilies, seeded and chopped
1 clove garlic, finely chopped
½ in. piece fresh ginger, finely chopped
2 tablespoons hoisin sauce
¼ cup dark soy sauce
⅓ cup vegetable stock
strips fresh ginger, to garnish

Cut sweet potato into 2 × ½ in. pieces and turnips and carrots into 1 in. pieces.

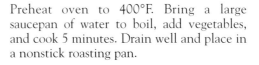

Preheat oven to 400°F. Bring a large saucepan of water to boil, add vegetables, and cook 5 minutes. Drain well and place in a nonstick roasting pan.

In a small bowl, mix together oil, chilies, garlic, ginger, hoisin sauce, soy sauce, and stock. Spoon over vegetables and stir to coat vegetables thoroughly. Roast in the oven for 30 minutes, basting occasionally, until vegetables are tender. Garnish with strips of ginger and serve.

Makes 4 servings.

BULGUR & VERMICELLI PILAF

2 tablespoons olive oil
1 onion, thinly sliced
1 green bell pepper, seeded and sliced
1 oz. cut vermicelli
1¼ cups bulgur wheat
1½ cups vegetable stock
2 tomatoes, roughly chopped
salt and freshly ground black pepper
2 tablespoons fresh, chopped Italian parsley
fried onions, to garnish (optional)

Heat olive oil in a large saucepan. Add onion and cook 5 minutes. Add sliced pepper and cook until onion is soft.

Add vermicelli and stir to coat with oil. Put bulgur wheat in a colander and rinse in cold water, then add to the pan. Pour in vegetable stock and bring to boil. Cover the pan and simmer 5 minutes.

Add tomatoes and simmer an additional 5 to 10 minutes until bulgur wheat is tender and stock is absorbed. Add more stock if necessary. Season with salt and pepper and stir in parsley. Serve, garnished with fried onions.

Makes 6 servings.

BLACK-EYED BEANS & SPINACH

1¼ cups black-eyed beans, soaked overnight
2 bay leaves
3 tablespoons vegetable oil
1 large onion, finely chopped
2 cloves garlic, crushed
1 teaspoon cumin seeds
2 teaspoons ground cumin
1 teaspoon ground coriander
4 plum tomatoes, peeled (see page 174) and roughly chopped
salt and freshly ground black pepper
4 cups fresh young spinach leaves, washed and dried
¼ cup plain yogurt
2 tablespoons fresh, chopped cilantro

Drain black-eyed beans and place in a saucepan with bay leaves. Cover with cold water and bring to boil. Boil rapidly 10 minutes, then skim off any scum from the surface. Cover and simmer 30 to 35 minutes until beans are tender. Drain, reserving cooking liquid. Heat oil in a large pan. Add onion and cook 10 minutes until soft and lightly colored. Add garlic and cumin seeds and cook until seeds begin to pop. Add ground cumin and coriander and cook, stirring, 1 minute.

Add tomatoes and drained beans and enough reserved cooking liquid just to cover. Season generously with salt and pepper and simmer until reduced and tomatoes are soft. Check seasoning, adding more salt if necessary. Stir in spinach and cook until leaves wilt. Stir in yogurt and chopped cilantro, bring to boil, and stir well. Serve immediately.

Makes 6 servings.

Note: To save time, you can use canned beans.

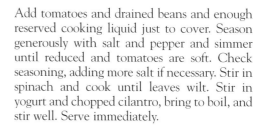

FENNEL SICILIANO

3 fennel bulbs
1 cup fresh bread crumbs
¼ cup pine nuts
3 tablespoons raisins
1 teaspoon fresh, chopped thyme
⅓ cup finely grated Parmesan cheese
¼ cup olive oil
salt and freshly ground black pepper
fennel leaves, to garnish

BAKED EGGS IN NESTS

4 or 5 waxy potatoes, halved
1 cup broccoli florets
2 zucchini
2 leeks, thinly sliced
1 tablespoon Worcestershire sauce
salt and freshly ground black pepper
vegetable oil for greasing
4 eggs

Preheat the oven to 375°F. Trim fennel and discard outer leaves, if necessary. Quarter bulbs and thinly slice.

Cook potatoes in boiling salted water for 5 to 10 minutes. Add broccoli and cook an additional 5 minutes. Drain.

Bring a saucepan of salted water to boil. Add fennel and simmer 3 to 5 minutes until just soft. Drain thoroughly. Brush an ovenproof dish with olive oil and arrange fennel slices inside in an even layer.

Coarsely grate potatoes. Using a vegetable peeler, cut zucchini lengthwise into ribbons. Mix together potatoes, broccoli, leeks, zucchini, and Worcestershire sauce. Season with salt and pepper. Lightly oil a flameproof casserole and add vegetable mixture.

Mix together bread crumbs, pine nuts, raisins, thyme, Parmesan, olive oil, and salt and pepper. Sprinkle mixture over fennel, making sure raisins are beneath the surface. Bake 20 to 30 minutes until golden. Garnish with fennel leaves and serve.

Makes 4 servings.

Make four wells in vegetable mixture and break an egg into each one. Cover and cook very gently 10 minutes until eggs have set. Serve immediately.

Makes 2 to 4 servings.

BELL PEPPER & EGGPLANT

2 eggplants, cut into large cubes
2 red bell peppers, diced
2 yellow bell peppers, diced
2 cloves garlic, crushed
1 bunch scallions, cut into ½ in. lengths
¾ cup tomato juice
1 cup canned chopped tomatoes
2 tablespoons fresh, chopped, mixed herbs
few drops Tabasco sauce
salt and freshly ground black pepper
oregano leaves, to garnish

Preheat oven to 350°F. Place eggplant cubes on a plate and sprinkle liberally with salt. Let stand 30 minutes.

Rinse eggplant, drain thoroughly, and pat dry with absorbent paper towels. Place eggplant, bell peppers, garlic, and scallions in an ovenproof casserole and mix well. Add tomato juice, chopped tomatoes, herbs, Tabasco sauce, and salt and pepper and stir to combine.

Cover and cook in the oven 45 minutes, stirring occasionally. Garnish with oregano leaves and serve with freshly cooked pasta.

Makes 6 servings.

VEGETABLE COUSCOUS

3 tablespoons olive oil
1 onion, chopped
2 cloves garlic, crushed
1 teaspoon ground cumin
1 teaspoon paprika
1¼ cups vegetable stock
14½ oz. can tomatoes
1 cinnamon stick
pinch saffron threads
4 baby eggplants, quartered
8 baby zucchini, trimmed
8 baby carrots
salt
15 oz. can chickpeas, drained
1 cup prunes
1¾ cups couscous
3 tablespoons fresh, chopped parsley
3 tablespoons chopped cilantro
2 or 3 tablespoons harissa

Heat olive oil in a large saucepan. Add onion and garlic and cook gently 5 minutes until soft. Add cumin and paprika and cook, stirring, 1 minute. Add stock, tomatoes, cinnamon, saffron, eggplant, zucchini, and carrots. Season with salt. Bring to boil, cover, and cook 20 minutes until vegetables are just tender.

Add chickpeas and prunes and cook 10 minutes. Meanwhile, put couscous in a bowl and cover generously with boiling water. Leave 10 minutes, then drain thoroughly and fluff up with a fork. Stir parsley and cilantro into vegetables. Heap couscous onto a warmed serving plate. Remove vegetables with a slotted spoon and arrange on top. Spoon over a little sauce. Stir harissa into remaining sauce and serve separately.

Makes 4 servings.

LENTIL & BEAN CHILI

1 tablespoon olive oil
1 onion, chopped
1 clove garlic, chopped
¾ cup green lentils
1¼ cups vegetable stock
1 teaspoon mild chili powder
14½ oz. can chopped tomatoes
1 green bell pepper, chopped
15 oz. can red kidney beans in chili sauce
salt and freshly ground black pepper
fresh, chopped Italian parsley, to garnish

Heat oil in a flameproof casserole and cook onion and garlic until soft. Add lentils, stock, chili powder, and tomatoes.

Cover and simmer gently 30 to 40 minutes until lentils are almost cooked.

Stir in green bell pepper and kidney beans and their sauce and simmer 10 to 15 minutes until lentils are cooked and liquid has been absorbed. Season with salt and pepper. Garnish with chopped parsley and serve.

Makes 4 servings.

MOROCCAN CASSEROLE

2 tablespoons olive oil
1 large onion, chopped
1 large eggplant, cut into chunks
2 cloves garlic, crushed
1 teaspoon ground cumin
1 teaspoon turmeric
1 teaspoon ground ginger
1 teaspoon paprika
1 teaspoon ground allspice
3 × 14½ oz. cans chopped tomatoes
15 oz. can chickpeas, drained
½ cup raisins
1 tablespoon chopped cilantro
3 tablespoons fresh, chopped parsley
salt and freshly ground black pepper

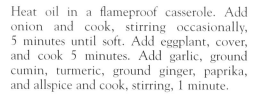

Heat oil in a flameproof casserole. Add onion and cook, stirring occasionally, 5 minutes until soft. Add eggplant, cover, and cook 5 minutes. Add garlic, ground cumin, turmeric, ground ginger, paprika, and allspice and cook, stirring, 1 minute.

Stir in tomatoes, chickpeas, raisins, and chopped cilantro and parsley. Season with salt and pepper. Bring to boil and simmer 45 minutes.

Makes 4 to 6 servings.

FENNEL & BEAN CASSEROLE

1½ cups dried kidney beans, soaked overnight
1 tablespoon olive oil
2 onions, chopped
2 cloves garlic, crushed
1 head celery, sliced
2 fennel bulbs, thinly sliced
2 tablespoons tomato paste
2 tablespoons fresh, chopped oregano
1 tablespoon fresh, chopped thyme
2 bay leaves
2 teaspoons each salt and sugar
2 × 14½ oz. cans chopped tomatoes
freshly ground black pepper
6 slices dried bread, made into crumbs
thyme sprigs, to garnish

Put kidney beans in a flameproof casserole. Cover with cold water. Bring to boil and boil rapidly 10 minutes. Cover and simmer 1 hour. Drain and set aside. Heat oil in the casserole. Add onions and garlic and cook, stirring occasionally, 5 minutes until soft. Add beans, celery, fennel, tomato paste, 1 tablespoon oregano, thyme, bay leaves, salt, sugar, and tomatoes. Season with black pepper. Cover and simmer 30 minutes.

Preheat oven to 425°F. Mix together bread crumbs and remaining oregano and sprinkle over the top of bean mixture. Cook 15 to 20 minutes until bread crumbs are golden brown. Garnish with thyme sprigs and serve.

Makes 4 to 6 servings.

LEEK & CHEESE BAKE

1 lb. leeks, chopped
1 teaspoon salt
½ stick butter
2 large onions, sliced
2 bunches scallions, sliced
1 cup crumbled feta cheese
2 eggs, beaten
freshly ground black pepper
2 tablespoons olive oil
8 sheets phyllo pastry
½ stick butter, melted

Put leeks into a colander, sprinkle with salt, and leave 30 minutes. Squeeze dry.

Heat butter in a flameproof dish. Add onions and scallions and cook, stirring occasionally, 3 to 5 minutes until soft but not colored. Remove from the heat and let cool 10 minutes. Preheat oven to 400°F. Add leeks, feta cheese, and eggs to onion mixture, season with black pepper, and mix well.

Crumple sheets of phyllo pastry and arrange on top of leek mixture. Brush with melted butter and bake 30 to 35 minutes until pastry is golden brown.

Makes 4 to 6 servings.

VEGETABLE BIRYANI

2 tablespoons sunflower oil
3 medium onions, sliced
3 or 4 carrots, diced
1 medium potato, diced
1 in. piece fresh ginger, peeled and grated
2 cloves garlic, crushed
1 tablespoon hot curry paste
1 teaspoon turmeric
½ teaspoon ground cinnamon
1¼ cups long-grain rice
4½ cups hot vegetable stock
½ cup cauliflower florets
salt and freshly ground black pepper
¾ cup frozen peas
⅓ cup cashews, toasted
2 tablespoons fresh, chopped cilantro

Heat half the oil in a large, flameproof casserole. Add half the onions and cook, stirring occasionally, 10 to 15 minutes until crisp and golden. Remove with a slotted spoon, drain on absorbent paper towels, and set aside. Heat remaining oil in the casserole and add carrots, potatoes, and remaining onions. Stir in ginger, garlic, curry paste, turmeric, and cinnamon and cook, stirring, 5 minutes.

Add rice and stir 1 minute. Pour in stock and bring to boil. Stir in cauliflower and salt and pepper. Cover and simmer gently 15 minutes. Stir in peas, cashews, and cilantro. Cover and cook 5 minutes until rice is tender and liquid has been absorbed. Sprinkle with reserved onions and serve.

Makes 4 servings.

ZUCCHINI GOUGÈRE

2 tablespoons olive oil
5 zucchini, thinly sliced
10 oz. button mushrooms
2 leeks, thinly sliced
2 teaspoons whole-grain mustard
1¼ cups sour cream
CHOUX PASTRY:
½ stick butter
2 cups all-purpose flour
2 eggs, beaten

To make choux pastry, gently melt butter in ⅔ cup water, then bring quickly to boil. Remove from the heat and immediately stir in flour.

Beat well until mixture is smooth and comes away from sides of the pan. Return to the heat and cook gently, stirring, 2 or 3 minutes. Remove from the heat and gradually add eggs, beating well. Set aside. Preheat oven to 425°F. Heat oil in a flameproof casserole. Add zucchini, button mushrooms, and leeks and cook, stirring occasionally, 6 to 8 minutes until tender.

Stir in mustard and sour cream and season with salt and pepper. Put choux pastry in a piping bag fitted with a plain, ½ in. nozzle. Pipe small balls of pastry around the edge of the zucchini mixture. Bake 20 to 30 minutes until pastry is risen and golden.

Makes 4 to 6 servings.

SAVORY BREAD PUDDING

MUSHROOM GRATIN

6 slices whole-wheat bread
2 zucchini, sliced
1 beefsteak tomato, chopped
6 oz. mushrooms, chopped
1¼ cups milk
5 eggs, beaten
1 tablespoon fresh, chopped chives
salt and freshly ground black pepper
1¼ cups shredded cheddar cheese
Italian parsley sprigs, to garnish

Preheat oven to 400°F. Cut bread into thin slices. Arrange half the slices in a shallow, ovenproof dish.

Spread zucchini, tomatoes, and mushrooms over bread and top with remaining bread slices. In a large bowl, mix together milk and eggs. Add chives and season with salt and pepper.

Pour milk mixture over bread. Sprinkle with cheese and bake 50 minutes until egg mixture has set and topping is golden brown. Garnish with Italian parsley and serve.

Makes 4 servings.

1 tablespoon butter
1 clove garlic, crushed
6 medium potatoes, thinly sliced
6 oz. chestnut mushrooms, sliced
4 oz. button mushrooms, sliced
salt and freshly ground black pepper
2 eggs, beaten
⅔ cup milk
⅔ cup sour cream
1½ cups shredded Gruyère cheese
fresh, chopped parsley, to garnish

Preheat oven to 400°F. Rub an ovenproof dish with butter and garlic. Add half the potatoes and all the mushrooms.

Top with remaining potatoes. Season generously with salt and pepper. Mix together eggs, milk, and sour cream and pour over vegetables. Bake 1 hour.

Sprinkle with cheese and bake an additional 25 minutes until cheese is melted and golden. Garnish with parsley and serve.

Makes 4 servings.

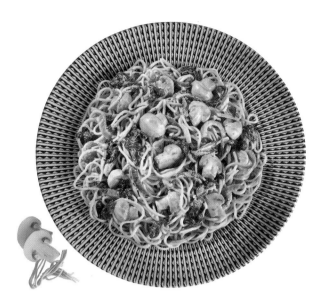

NOODLES WITH SPINACH

2 tablespoons olive oil
1 red onion, thinly sliced
10 oz. button mushrooms, halved
2½ cups roughly torn spinach
8 oz. thread egg noodles
1 cup cream cheese with garlic and herbs
salt and freshly ground black pepper

Heat oil in a flameproof casserole. Add onion and cook, stirring occasionally, 5 minutes until soft. Add mushrooms and spinach and cook, stirring occasionally, 10 to 15 minutes until spinach is wilted and mushrooms tender.

Meanwhile, put noodles in a large bowl and cover with boiling water. Leave 4 or 5 minutes until tender. Drain. Add garlic and cream cheese to spinach mixture and heat gently, stirring, until melted.

Add noodles to vegetable and cheese, season with salt and pepper, and mix well.

Makes 4 servings.

VEGETABLE COBBLER

1 tablespoon olive oil
1 clove garlic, crushed
2 leeks, thinly sliced
2 teaspoons mustard seeds
8 oz. mushrooms, sliced
1 cup broccoli florets
1¼ cups shelled fresh or frozen peas
1¼ cups light cream
large pinch freshly grated nutmeg
1 teaspoon prepared English mustard
1 tablespoon fresh, chopped parsley
7 oz. puff pastry, thawed if frozen
milk for brushing

Heat oil in a flameproof casserole. Add garlic and leeks and cook until soft.

Add mustard seeds and cook until they start to pop. Add mushrooms, broccoli, and peas. Cover and cook 8 to 10 minutes until tender. Remove from the heat. Stir in cream, nutmeg, mustard, and parsley. Preheat oven to 425°F.

Roll out pastry on a lightly floured surface. Using a pastry cutter, cut out twelve 2 in. rounds. Arrange on top of vegetable mixture. Brush with a little milk and bake 30 to 35 minutes until risen and golden.

Makes 4 to 6 servings.

BROCCOLI WITH CHILI DRESSING

10 medium ripe tomatoes
3 tablespoons olive oil
1 clove garlic, crushed
2 teaspoons lemon juice
1 teaspoon hot chili sauce
1 teaspoon balsamic vinegar
1 medium bunch broccoli
¼ cup pitted black olives, sliced
¼ cup pine nuts, toasted
1 tablespoon fresh, chopped parsley
¼ cup Parmesan shavings

Place tomatoes in a large, heatproof bowl and pour over boiling water to cover.

Leave 1 minute, then drain, rinse under cold water, and pat dry. Peel, discard skins and seeds, and finely chop flesh. Heat oil in a large saucepan, add tomatoes, garlic, lemon juice, chili sauce, and vinegar. Bring to boil, cover, and cook 10 minutes. Uncover, increase heat, and cook until slightly reduced and thickened.

Meanwhile, trim broccoli and steam 5 minutes. Add to sauce with olives, pine nuts, and parsley and stir well until combined. Transfer to a warmed serving dish, sprinkle with Parmesan shavings, and serve at once.

Makes 4 servings.

BROCCOLI CAPONATA

2 tablespoons olive oil
1 red onion, chopped
1 red bell pepper, seeded and chopped
1 clove garlic, chopped
1 teaspoon fresh, chopped thyme
⅓ cup red wine
5 medium tomatoes, peeled (see opposite), seeded, and chopped
⅔ cup vegetable stock
1 tablespoon red wine vinegar
1 tablespoon brown sugar
1 medium bunch broccoli, trimmed and chopped
2 tablespoons tomato paste
½ cup pitted green olives
¼ cup capers, drained
1 tablespoon shredded, fresh basil

In a large pan, heat oil and fry onion, bell pepper, garlic, and thyme 6 to 8 minutes until lightly browned. Add wine and boil rapidly 3 minutes. Add tomatoes, stock, vinegar, and sugar. Stir well, then cover and simmer gently 20 minutes.

Steam broccoli 5 minutes until almost cooked. Add to tomato mixture with tomato paste, olives, capers, and basil. Cook an additional 3 to 4 minutes, remove from heat, and let cool. Serve at room temperature.

Makes 4 servings.

VEGETABLE & FRUIT CURRY

1½ teaspoons each coriander and cumin seeds
¼ cup vegetable oil
1 large onion, chopped
2 carrots, chopped
2 potatoes, diced
3 cloves garlic, crushed, or 1 tablespoon garlic purée
2 teaspoons grated ginger
1 teaspoon each curry powder and turmeric
5 medium ripe tomatoes
2 cups vegetable stock
¾ cup frozen peas, thawed
1 apple, cored and chopped
1 mango, peeled, pitted, and chopped
⅔ cup cashews, toasted
1 oz. creamed coconut
1 tablespoon fresh, chopped cilantro

In a small pan, roast coriander and cumin seeds until browned and grind in a blender or spice grinder. Heat half the oil in a large pan and fry onion, carrots, and potatoes 10 minutes until browned. Heat remaining oil in a small pan and fry garlic, ginger, ground coriander and cumin seeds, curry powder, and turmeric 5 minutes. Peel, seed, and chop tomatoes and stir into spice mixture. Cover and cook 10 minutes. Stir into vegetable mixture with stock and simmer gently 20 minutes.

Add peas, apple, and mango and cook an additional 5 minutes. Grind half the cashews and mix with creamed coconut. Stir in enough pan juices to form a paste and carefully stir into curry until evenly combined. Heat through and serve at once, sprinkled with whole cashews and cilantro.

Makes 4 to 6 servings.

SAUCY BEANS

1 cup dried lima or pinto beans, soaked overnight in cold water to cover
1 bay leaf
¼ cup virgin olive oil
1 red onion, chopped
2 cloves garlic, chopped
1 tablespoon fresh, chopped sage
5 medium ripe tomatoes
1 teaspoon balsamic vinegar
salt and pepper
1 tablespoon fresh, chopped parsley

Drain beans. Place in a pan with bay leaf and fresh water to cover. Bring to boil, then simmer, covered, 40 to 45 minutes.

In a large pan, heat oil and fry onion, garlic, and sage 10 minutes until golden. Peel tomatoes, chop flesh, and add to the pan with vinegar. Cover and cook 5 minutes until softened.

Drain cooked beans, rinse well, and shake off excess water. Stir into onion mixture in pan, cover, and cook 4 or 5 minutes until heated through. Season to taste, sprinkle with chopped parsley, and drizzle with extra olive oil before serving.

Makes 4 servings.

Note: This dish is delicious served warm or cold. Serve with crusty bread to mop up juices.

MIXED VEGETABLE ROSTI

SPANAKOPITA

1 tablespoon olive oil
1 onion, sliced
8 oz. green beans, trimmed
1 cup cauliflower florets
4 tomatoes, peeled (see page 174) and quartered
1 tablespoon fresh, chopped parsley
salt and freshly ground black pepper
4 or 5 medium waxy potatoes, grated
1 cup shredded mozzarella cheese

Heat oil in a flameproof dish. Add sliced onion and cook, stirring occasionally, 5 minutes until soft. Preheat oven to 400°F.

Add beans, cauliflower, and tomatoes and cook, stirring occasionally, 10 minutes until tender. Stir in parsley and season with salt and pepper.

Spread potatoes over vegetables and top with cheese. Bake 30 minutes until potatoes are tender and cheese is melted and golden.

Makes 4 servings.

⅔ cup olive oil
1 onion, finely chopped
1 clove garlic, crushed
1 lb. frozen chopped spinach, thawed and well drained
2 tablespoons fresh, chopped cilantro
½ teaspoon freshly grated nutmeg
1 cup crumbled feta cheese
1 cup cottage cheese
salt and freshly ground black pepper
8 sheets phyllo pastry, each about 16 × 12 in.
cilantro, to garnish

Preheat the oven to 375°F. Brush a 12 × 9 in. baking pan with oil.

Heat 2 tablespoons oil in a skillet. Add onion and garlic and cook gently 5 minutes until soft. Add spinach and cook, stirring, 2 minutes. Remove from the heat and stir in cilantro, nutmeg, feta cheese, cottage cheese, and salt and pepper. Put one sheet of phyllo pastry in the baking pan. Brush pastry with oil and layer three more sheets on top, brushing each one with oil. Spread spinach mixture on top, then cover with remaining pastry sheets, brushing each one with oil.

Trim overhanging pastry, then tuck in edges to seal. Brush top with oil. With a sharp knife, cut through top layers to mark sixteen squares. Bake in the oven 30 minutes until golden brown and crisp. Leave in the pan 10 minutes, then cut into marked squares. Garnish with cilantro and serve hot or warm.

Makes 16 squares.

NUT BAKE WITH TOMATOES

2 tablespoons butter
1 onion, finely chopped
2 carrots, finely chopped
2 stalks celery, finely chopped
2½ cups finely chopped, mixed nuts
2 cups fresh whole-wheat bread crumbs
2 teaspoons yeast extract
1¼ cups hot vegetable stock
2 teaspoons dried thyme
salt and freshly ground black pepper
2 beefsteak tomatoes, sliced
1 cup shredded cheddar cheese

Preheat oven to 350°F. Heat butter in a flameproof casserole.

Add onion, carrot, and celery and cook gently, stirring occasionally, 10 minutes until soft. In a large bowl, mix together nuts and bread crumbs. Stir in cooked vegetables. Dissolve yeast extract in hot stock and stir into the bowl. Add thyme and season with salt and pepper. Mix well. Arrange half the tomato slices in the bottom of the casserole. Sprinkle with half the shredded cheese.

Spread half of the nut mixture on top. Add remaining tomato slices and cover with remaining nut mixture. Sprinkle with remaining shredded cheese and bake 50 to 60 minutes until cheese is melted and golden.

Makes 4 servings.

SUN-DRIED TOMATO RISOTTO

½ stick butter
1 tablespoon olive oil
2 red onions, chopped
12 sun-dried tomatoes, chopped
1 tablespoon pesto sauce
1¼ cups arborio (Italian risotto) rice
4½ cups vegetable stock
8 oz. mushrooms, sliced
salt and freshly ground black pepper
1 cup fresh Parmesan cheese shavings
fresh, chopped Italian parsley, to garnish

Heat butter and oil in a flameproof casserole. Add onions and cook, stirring occasionally, 5 minutes until soft.

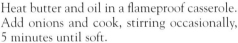
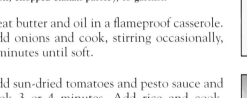

Add sun-dried tomatoes and pesto sauce and cook 3 or 4 minutes. Add rice and cook, stirring, 1 minute. Stir in about one third of the stock and simmer gently, stirring occasionally, until most of the liquid has been absorbed.

Stir in mushrooms and season with salt and pepper. Add half of the remaining stock and simmer, stirring occasionally. When most of the liquid has been absorbed, stir in remaining stock and simmer gently until all liquid has been absorbed and rice is tender and creamy. Top risotto with curls of Parmesan cheese, sprinkle with parsley, and serve.

Makes 2 to 4 servings.

MUSHROOM & NUT PILAF

3 tablespoons butter
½ cup pine nuts
½ cup sunflower seeds
1 onion, chopped
2 leeks, chopped
1 red bell pepper, chopped
1 carrot, diced
1¼ cups arborio (Italian risotto) rice
4½ cups vegetable stock
4 oz. button mushrooms, sliced
salt and freshly ground black pepper

Heat 1 tablespoon of butter in a flameproof casserole. Add pine nuts and sunflower seeds and cook until golden.

Remove from the casserole with a slotted spoon and set aside. Heat remaining butter in the casserole. Add onion, leeks, pepper, and carrot and cook, stirring occasionally, 3 minutes. Add rice and cook, stirring, 2 minutes. Add stock, cover, and bring to boil. Simmer 30 minutes until most of the liquid is absorbed and rice is just tender.

Add mushrooms, pine nuts, and sunflower seeds and cook gently, stirring frequently, 10 minutes. Season with salt and pepper and serve.

Makes 4 servings.

RATATOUILLE BEAN BAKE

1 red onion, thinly sliced
2 cloves garlic, crushed
1 small eggplant, weighing about 7 oz., diced
2 zucchini, sliced
1 yellow bell pepper, seeded and sliced
6 oz. chestnut mushrooms, sliced
14½ oz. can chopped tomatoes
2 tablespoons tomato paste
¼ cup olive oil
2 teaspoons dried herbes de Provence
salt and freshly ground black pepper
15 oz. can red kidney beans, rinsed and drained
15 oz. can flageolet beans, rinsed and drained
10 oz. dried orecchiette
finely grated Parmesan or shredded cheddar cheese,
  to serve

Preheat the oven to 350°F. Put onion, garlic, eggplant, zucchini, yellow bell pepper, mushrooms, tomatoes, tomato paste, olive oil, dried herbs, and salt and pepper in a large, ovenproof dish and stir to mix well. Cover and bake 30 minutes. Stir in beans, cover, and bake an additional 30 to 45 minutes, stirring once, until vegetables are cooked and tender.

Meanwhile, cook pasta in a large saucepan of lightly salted boiling water 12 to 15 minutes or until al dente. Drain thoroughly. Add pasta to ratatouille and toss well to mix. Serve on warmed plates and sprinkle generously with Parmesan or cheddar cheese.

Makes 4 to 6 servings.

ROAST BELL PEPPER & FENNEL

4 fennel bulbs
4 red bell peppers, seeded, and cut into thick slices
⅓ cup olive oil
juice 1 lemon
salt and freshly ground black pepper
1 lb. 2 oz. fresh strozzapretti
8 oz. mozzarella cheese, diced
2 tablespoons fresh, chopped Italian parsley
Italian parsley sprigs, to garnish

Preheat oven to 400°F. Trim fennel bulbs, cutting off fibrous tops. Cut each bulb into quarters and remove and discard core.

Cook fennel in a saucepan of boiling water 5 minutes. Drain thoroughly. Lightly butter a shallow, ovenproof dish or baking pan. Put fennel and bell peppers in the prepared dish. Whisk oil, lemon juice, salt, and pepper together and drizzle over fennel and bell peppers. Toss gently to mix. Bake in the oven about 30 minutes, stirring once or twice, until vegetables are tender and tinged brown around edges. Meanwhile, cook pasta in a large saucepan of lightly salted boiling water 3 minutes or until al dente.

Sprinkle vegetables with mozzarella and chopped parsley and stir gently to mix. Drain pasta thoroughly and serve on warmed plates. Spoon vegetable mixture and juices over pasta. Alternatively, lightly toss vegetables, cheese, and pasta together before serving. Garnish with parsley sprigs and serve.

Makes 4 servings.

TOMATO & BRIE PASTA BAKE

1 lb. cherry tomatoes, halved
3 tablespoons olive oil
4 shallots, thinly sliced
2 cloves garlic, crushed
8 oz. button mushrooms, sliced
1 lb. 2 oz. fresh radiatore
salt and freshly ground black pepper
1 cup mascarpone
¼ cup fresh, chopped basil
8 oz. Brie, rind removed and cheese diced (weight without rind)
½ cup finely grated Parmesan cheese
basil sprigs, to garnish

Preheat the oven to 350°F. Put tomatoes, cut-side up, in a single layer in a large, shallow, ovenproof dish and drizzle with 2 tablespoons oil. Bake 10 minutes. Meanwhile, heat remaining oil in a saucepan, add shallots, garlic, and mushrooms, and cook 5 minutes, stirring occasionally. Cook pasta in a large saucepan of lightly salted boiling water 4 minutes or until al dente. Drain thoroughly and return to the rinsed-out saucepan.

Add shallot mixture, mascarpone, chopped basil, and salt and pepper and toss well to mix. Add tomatoes and their juices and stir gently to mix, then gently fold in Brie. Transfer mixture to an ovenproof dish. Sprinkle with Parmesan cheese. Bake about 20 minutes or until top is golden. Garnish with basil sprigs and serve.

Makes 6 servings.

MIXED VEGETABLE CURRY

3 tablespoons vegetable oil
1 onion, sliced
1 teaspoon ground cumin
1 teaspoon chili powder
2 teaspoons ground coriander
1 teaspoon turmeric
1 large potato, diced
1 cup cauliflower florets
1 cup topped, tailed, and sliced green beans
2 medium carrots, diced
4 tomatoes, peeled (see page 174) and chopped
1¼ cups hot vegetable stock
onion rings, to garnish

Heat oil in a large saucepan, add onion, and fry 5 minutes until softened. Stir in cumin, chili powder, coriander, and turmeric and cook 2 minutes, stirring occasionally. Add potatoes, cauliflower, green beans, and carrots, tossing them in spices until coated.

Add tomatoes and stock and cover. Bring to boil, then reduce heat and simmer 10 to 12 minutes or until vegetables are just tender. Serve hot, garnished with onion rings.

Makes 4 servings.

Variation: Use any mixture of vegetables to make a total of 1½ lb.—turnips, rutabagas, zucchini, eggplant, parsnips, and leeks are all suitable for this curry.

CARIBBEAN RATATOUILLE

2 tablespoons oil
1 large onion, thinly sliced
2 cloves garlic, crushed
1 red chili, seeded and finely chopped
1 eggplant, peeled and cut into 1 in. cubes
1 red bell pepper, diced
1 green bell pepper, diced
4 oz. okra, sliced
1 chayote squash, peeled, seeded, and chopped
5 medium tomatoes, peeled (see page 174) and
  roughly chopped
1 teaspoon sugar
1 teaspoon dried thyme
2 teaspoons fresh, chopped basil
salt and freshly ground black pepper
fresh basil leaves, to garnish

Heat oil in a flameproof casserole. Add onion and cook 10 minutes until soft. Stir in garlic and chili and cook an additional 2 minutes. Stir in eggplant, red and green bell peppers, okra, chayote, tomatoes, sugar, thyme, basil, and seasoning.

Cover and cook gently 20 to 30 minutes, stirring occasionally, until vegetables are almost cooked. Remove lid and simmer a few minutes until vegetables are tender and most of the liquid has evaporated. Serve hot or cold, garnished with basil leaves.

Makes 6 servings.

Variation: Vegetables may be varied according to taste and what is available. Zucchini and celery may be used instead of chayote and okra, for example.

TAMIL NADU VEGETABLES

⅔ cup red split lentils
½ teaspoon turmeric
1 small eggplant
¼ cup vegetable oil
⅓ cup dried coconut
1 teaspoon cumin seeds
½ teaspoon mustard seeds
2 dried red chilies, crushed
1 red bell pepper, seeded and sliced
1 medium zucchini, thickly sliced
¾ cup topped, tailed, and sliced green beans
⅔ cup vegetable stock
salt
red bell pepper strips, to garnish

Wash lentils and put in a large saucepan with turmeric and 2½ cups water. Bring to boil, then reduce heat and simmer, covered, 15 to 20 minutes until lentils are soft. Meanwhile, dice eggplant. Heat oil in a large, shallow pan, add coconut, cumin and mustard seeds, and chilies.

Fry 1 minute, then add eggplant, red bell pepper, zucchini, green beans, stock, and salt. Bring to boil, then simmer, covered, 10 to 15 minutes until vegetables are just tender. Stir in lentils and any cooking liquid and cook an additional 5 minutes. Serve hot, garnished with red bell pepper strips.

Makes 4 servings.

VEGETABLE & COCONUT CURRY

1 butternut squash, peeled, seeded, and diced
2 sweet potatoes, diced
2 carrots, diced
3 tablespoons oil
3 cloves garlic, crushed
1 large onion, chopped
1 fresh red chili, seeded and finely chopped
1 teaspoon ground cumin
2 teaspoons curry powder
2 teaspoons molasses
2 tablespoons tomato paste
2 oz. creamed coconut
salt
⅔ cup vegetable stock
finely grated zest and juice 1 lime
1 tablespoon chopped cilantro

Place squash, sweet potatoes, and carrots in a pan of salted water. Bring to boil and simmer 5 to 8 minutes until barely tender. Drain and set aside. In a flameproof casserole, heat oil. Add garlic and onion and cook 10 minutes until soft. Stir in chili, cumin, and curry powder and cook an additional 1 minute.

Add molasses, tomato paste, and creamed coconut and cook 1 minute. Add salt, stock, lime zest and juice, and vegetables. Bring to boil, then reduce the heat, cover, and simmer gently, stirring occasionally, 10 to 15 minutes until vegetables are soft. Stir in cilantro. Serve with rice.

Makes 4 servings.

GRATIN OF VEGETABLES

⅔ cup long-grain rice
3 zucchini
1 red bell pepper
1 onion
6 ripe tomatoes
2 tablespoons olive oil
2 fresh thyme sprigs, chopped
2 fresh rosemary sprigs, chopped
2 bay leaves
1 teaspoon dried oregano
1 teaspoon fennel seeds, toasted
⅔ cup vegetable stock
¾ cup shredded Pecorino or cheddar

Preheat oven to 400°F. Put rice into a small pan and cover with cold water. Bring to boil and cook 3 minutes. Drain well and transfer to a gratin dish. Thickly slice zucchini, roughly chop pepper and onion, and peel, seed, and roughly chop tomatoes.

Place prepared vegetables in a large bowl, add oil, and stir well until vegetables are coated. Add thyme, rosemary, bay leaves, oregano, and fennel seeds. Stir and spoon over rice. Pour stock over vegetables, cover with aluminum foil, and bake 40 minutes. Remove foil, sprinkle with cheese, and bake an additional 10 to 15 minutes or until cheese is melted and all liquid is absorbed. Brown under a hot broiler, and serve hot.

Makes 6 servings.

TOMATO & BEAN TIAN

3 tablespoons olive oil
1 red onion, chopped
1 clove garlic, crushed
1 large red bell pepper, chopped
1 tablespoon fresh, chopped thyme
2 teaspoons fresh, chopped rosemary
14½ oz. can chopped tomatoes
15 oz. can cannellini beans, drained
½ cup fresh bread crumbs
¼ cup pine nuts, chopped
⅓ cup finely grated Parmesan cheese
2 large zucchini, thinly sliced
2 ripe beefsteak tomatoes, thinly sliced
rosemary sprigs, to garnish

Preheat oven to 375°F. In a saucepan, heat 2 tablespoons oil. Add onion, garlic, pepper, 2 teaspoons thyme, and 1 teaspoon rosemary and cook 5 minutes. Add tomatoes, cover, and cook 20 minutes. Stir in beans and transfer to a shallow baking dish.

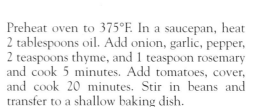

In a small bowl, mix bread crumbs, pine nuts, and cheese together. Sprinkle half the mixture over tomato layer. Arrange zucchini and tomatoes in rows over the top. Sprinkle with remaining crumb mixture. Drizzle with a little remaining oil and herbs. Cover with aluminum foil and bake 30 minutes. Remove foil and bake an additional 15 to 20 minutes or until golden. Garnish with rosemary sprigs and serve hot.

Makes 4 to 6 servings.

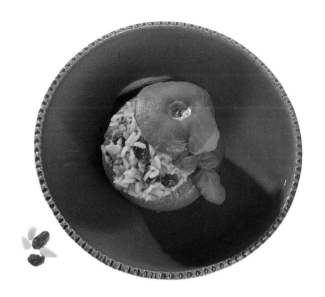

BUTTERNUT SQUASH CRUMBLE

1½ lb. butternut squash (about 2 small squash)
1 small fennel bulb, trimmed
1 clove garlic, crushed
1 tablespoon fresh, chopped sage
14½ oz. can chopped tomatoes
⅔ cup heavy cream
salt and pepper
1 cup whole-wheat flour
½ stick butter or margarine, diced
⅓ cup macadamia nuts, chopped
⅓ cup finely grated Parmesan cheese

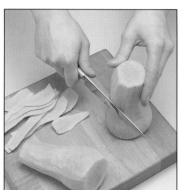

Preheat oven to 400°F. Peel squash, cut in half, and scrape out and discard seeds. Cut flesh into ½ in. pieces and place in a large ovenproof dish. Cut fennel crosswise into very thin slices. Sprinkle over squash with garlic and sage. Pour in tomatoes and cream and add a little salt and pepper.

Put flour in a bowl and cut in butter until mixture resembles fine bread crumbs. Stir in nuts and cheese. Sprinkle squash with topping. Cover with aluminum foil and bake 40 minutes. Remove foil and bake an additional 15 to 20 minutes until topping is golden and squash is tender.

Makes 6 servings.

RICE-FILLED TOMATOES

4 ripe beefsteak tomatoes
salt and freshly ground black pepper
2 cups cooked rice
1 tablespoon pine nuts
1 tablespoon raisins, soaked in hot water
1 stalk celery, finely chopped
2 tablespoons fresh, chopped basil
2 teaspoons balsamic vinegar
2 tablespoons olive oil

Preheat oven to 325°F. Slice a lid off tomatoes; reserve. Scoop out flesh and sprinkle insides of tomatoes with salt. Invert and drain on paper towels 15 minutes.

Strain tomato pulp and mix into cooked rice with pine nuts, raisins, celery, and half the basil. Season well and use this to fill tomatoes. Replace lids and place tomatoes in an oiled, shallow, ovenproof dish. Bake in the oven 45 minutes.

Whisk vinegar with oil. Remove tomatoes from the oven, take off lids, and drizzle each one with oil and vinegar. Replace lids and let cool. Serve at room temperature, garnished with remaining basil.

Makes 4 servings.

BEAN & LENTIL BOLOGNESE

1 teaspoon sunflower oil
1 onion, chopped
1 clove garlic, crushed
1¼ cup green or brown lentils, rinsed
4 carrots, sliced
8 oz. mushrooms, sliced
3 stalks celery, sliced
15 oz. can red kidney beans
15 oz. can cannellini beans
14½ oz. can chopped tomatoes
2 tablespoons tomato paste
2 cups vegetable stock
1¼ cups red wine
2 teaspoons dried herbes de Provence
salt and freshly ground black pepper
Italian parsley, to garnish

In a large saucepan, heat oil and cook onion and garlic 3 minutes. Add lentils, carrots, mushrooms, and celery and cook 5 minutes, stirring. Rinse and drain kidney and cannellini beans and add to saucepan with tomatoes, tomato paste, stock, wine, herbes de Provence, and salt and pepper. Mix well.

Bring to boil, cover, and simmer gently 15 minutes, stirring occasionally. Uncover and simmer 20 to 30 minutes, stirring occasionally, until lentils are tender. Garnish with Italian parsley and serve with freshly cooked spaghetti.

Makes 6 servings.

CHICKPEA & TOMATO PASTA

1 onion
2 cloves garlic
6 oz. button mushrooms
14½ oz. can chopped tomatoes
15 oz. can chickpeas, rinsed and drained
½ cup vegetable stock
2 tablespoons ruby port
1 tablespoon tomato paste
1 teaspoon dried rosemary
½ teaspoon cayenne pepper
rosemary sprigs, to garnish
freshly cooked pasta, to serve

Finely chop onion, crush garlic, and halve mushrooms.

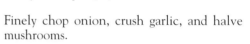

Place onion, garlic, and mushrooms in a large saucepan. Add tomatoes, chickpeas, stock, port, tomato paste, rosemary, cayenne pepper, and salt and pepper and mix well.

Bring to boil, cover, and simmer gently 30 minutes, stirring occasionally. Garnish with rosemary sprigs and serve with freshly cooked pasta.

Makes 4 servings.

VEGETABLE CHILI

8 oz. rutabaga, diced
4 carrots, sliced
1 onion, sliced
2 leeks, sliced
1 clove garlic, crushed
1 small red bell pepper, diced
8 oz. baby corn, halved
14½ oz. can chopped tomatoes
⅔ cup vegetable stock
¼ cup dry white wine
2 tablespoons tomato paste
2 teaspoons hot chili powder
salt and freshly ground black pepper
¾ cup broccoli florets
basil sprigs, to garnish

Place rutabaga, carrots, onion, leeks, garlic, red bell pepper, baby corn, and tomatoes in a saucepan and mix well. Add vegetable stock, wine, tomato paste, chili powder, and salt and pepper and mix well.

Bring slowly to boil, cover, and simmer 25 minutes, stirring occasionally. Uncover, add broccoli, and simmer 10 minutes, stirring occasionally, until sauce is thickened. Garnish with basil sprigs and serve with freshly cooked pasta or rice.

Makes 6 servings.

CHUNKY VEGETABLE KORMA

2 teaspoons sunflower oil
2 onions, sliced
2 cloves garlic, crushed
1 in. piece fresh ginger, peeled and finely chopped
1 tablespoon curry powder
1 teaspoon each ground cumin and turmeric
4 carrots, sliced
1½ cups cauliflower florets
6 oz. rutabaga, diced
1 small eggplant, diced
¼ cup golden raisins
1 tablespoon all-purpose flour
2 cups vegetable stock
salt and freshly ground black pepper
⅔ cup low-fat plain yogurt

In a large saucepan, heat oil and cook onions, garlic, and ginger 3 minutes. Add curry powder, cumin, and turmeric and cook 1 minute, stirring. Add carrots, cauliflower, rutabaga, eggplant, and golden raisins and cook 5 minutes, stirring. Stir in flour and cook 1 minute, stirring. Remove the pan from the heat and gradually stir in vegetable stock. Bring slowly to boil, stirring, and continue to cook, stirring, until mixture thickens. Add salt and pepper and mix well.

Cover and simmer gently 30 to 45 minutes until vegetables are tender, stirring occasionally. Remove pan from the heat and stir in half of the yogurt. Drizzle with remaining yogurt and serve with freshly cooked pasta or rice.

Makes 6 servings.

BELL PEPPER CHILI

2 onions
5 large, fresh red chilies, cored, seeded, and chopped
1 red bell pepper, chopped
1 large clove garlic, chopped
2 tablespoons dry white wine
1 tablespoon olive oil
1 green bell pepper, thinly sliced
1 tablespoon tomato paste
1 teaspoon ground cumin
1 cup canned red kidney beans, drained
basil sprigs, to garnish

Roughly chop one of the onions. Put in a food processor with chilies, red bell pepper, garlic, wine, and salt. Process 2 minutes.

Slice remaining onion. Heat oil in a flameproof casserole, add sliced onion, and cook, stirring occasionally, 5 minutes until soft. Add puréed mixture, 2 tablespoons water, and green bell pepper. Bring to boil, cover, and simmer gently 30 minutes.

Add tomato paste, cumin, and kidney beans. Simmer 10 to 15 minutes. Garnish with basil and serve.

Makes 2 to 4 servings.

MUSHROOM & BEAN CHILI

¼ cup olive oil
1 large eggplant, diced
6 oz. button mushrooms, wiped
1 large onion, chopped
1 clove garlic, chopped
1½ teaspoons paprika
½ to 1 teaspoon chili powder
1 teaspoon ground coriander
½ teaspoon ground cumin
10 medium tomatoes, peeled and chopped
⅔ cup vegetable stock
1 oz. tortilla chips
1 tablespoon tomato paste
15 oz. can red kidney beans
1 tablespoon chopped cilantro
salt and pepper

In a large pan, heat 2 tablespoons oil and stir-fry eggplant 10 minutes until golden, then remove from the pan with a slotted spoon and set aside. Add 1 tablespoon oil to the pan and stir-fry mushrooms until golden; remove with a slotted spoon and set aside. Add remaining oil to the pan and fry onion, garlic, paprika, ground coriander, and cumin 5 minutes. Add tomatoes and stock and cook, covered, 45 minutes.

Finely crush tortilla chips and blend with ¼ cup water and tomato paste. Whisk into chili sauce and add reserved mushrooms and eggplant. Drain beans and add to the pan with chopped cilantro. Cover and cook an additional 20 minutes. Season to taste and serve with plain rice and sour cream.

Makes 6 servings.

DESSERTS

CARAMEL RICE

CHERRY CLAFOUTI

⅓ cup white short-grain rice, washed and drained
2½ cups milk
1 vanilla bean
½ cup light cream
juice 1 orange
superfine sugar
orange peel strips, to decorate

Put rice, milk, and vanilla bean in a saucepan and simmer over very low heat 45 to 60 minutes until rice is soft and creamy.

Remove vanilla bean and stir in cream and orange juice. Spoon into a flameproof gratin or soufflé dish. Leave to cool, then refrigerate until ready to serve.

Cover top of pudding thickly and evenly with sugar. Place under a very hot broiler until sugar topping has caramelized. Serve at once, decorated with orange peel strips.

Makes 4 servings.

Note: Chill pudding again before serving, but serve within two hours.

1½ lb. pitted, dark, sweet cherries, thawed and drained if frozen
¾ cup all-purpose flour
pinch salt
3 eggs
⅓ cup superfine sugar
2 cups milk
1 tablespoon cherry brandy or kirsch
confectioners' sugar, to serve

Preheat oven to 400°F. Drain cherries if frozen and thawed. Butter a five-cup, oval baking dish and place cherries in it.

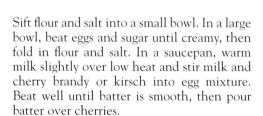

Sift flour and salt into a small bowl. In a large bowl, beat eggs and sugar until creamy, then fold in flour and salt. In a saucepan, warm milk slightly over low heat and stir milk and cherry brandy or kirsch into egg mixture. Beat well until batter is smooth, then pour batter over cherries.

Bake 30 minutes until set and golden. Serve warm, dusted with confectioners' sugar.

Makes 6 servings.

Note: Fresh cherries can taste a little bland when cooked. Add one or two drops almond extract to improve flavor.

BREAD & BUTTER PUDDING

¾ cup mixed golden raisins and currants
8 slices white bread, buttered
2 tablespoons candied fruit, chopped
superfine sugar for sprinkling
CUSTARD:
1 egg yolk
1¼ cups milk
⅔ cup light cream
1 vanilla bean
1 teaspoon superfine sugar

Put golden raisins and currants in a bowl, cover with water, and let swell. Preheat oven to 350°F. Butter a five-cup, oval baking dish.

Cut crusts from bread and sandwich four slices together. Cut in four squares and place in prepared dish. Drain fruit and sprinkle bread with fruit and chopped candied fruit. Top with remaining bread, buttered-side up.

To prepare custard, place egg yolk in a medium bowl. Put milk, cream, vanilla bean, and sugar into a saucepan and bring almost to boiling point. Pour over egg, stir, then strain into dish, pouring down sides so top slices of bread are not soaked. Leave to stand 30 minutes, then sprinkle with superfine sugar and place in a baking pan. Pour in enough boiling water to come halfway up sides of dish and bake 45 to 50 minutes until top is golden brown.

Makes 4 servings.

BAKED DEMELZA APPLES

3 tablespoons raisins
3 tablespoons golden raisins
⅓ cup ginger wine, Madeira, or sweet sherry
4 large cooking apples
¾ cup slivered almonds, toasted
1 or 2 tablespoons marmalade
chilled whipped cream, to serve

Preheat oven to 350°F. Put raisins and golden raisins into a small bowl and add ginger wine, Madeira, or sherry. Leave to soak for several hours.

Wash and dry apples, but do not peel. Remove core using an apple corer and score a line around the middle of each apple. Stand apples in an ovenproof dish. Drain dried fruit, reserving liquid. Mix fruit with almonds and marmalade in a bowl, then fill apple cavities with this mixture, pushing it down firmly. Pour strained liquid over apples.

Bake apples in the oven 45 to 60 minutes until soft. Spoon a dollop of whipped cream on top of each apple and serve immediately.

Makes 4 servings.

MOROCCAN RICE PUDDING

½ cup white short-grain rice
2½ cups milk
orange peel strip
¼ cup superfine sugar
½ cup ground almonds
2 teaspoons orange-flower water
ground cinnamon and toasted slivered almonds, to
    decorate
orange slices, to serve

Rinse rice and put in a bowl with ½ cup water. Put milk and orange peel in a saucepan and bring to boil.

Add sugar and stir until dissolved. Add rice and water. Cover and simmer gently 30 to 40 minutes until most of the liquid has been absorbed.

Add ground almonds and cook, stirring, 2 or 3 minutes. Stir in orange-flower water. Spoon into serving dishes and let cool. Decorate with ground cinnamon and slivered almonds and serve with orange slices.

Makes 4 servings.

AMARETTI-STUFFED PEACHES

4 large peaches
2 oz. amaretti cookies
1 egg yolk
4 teaspoons superfine sugar
2 tablespoons softened butter
1 cup sweet white wine
toasted slivered almonds, to serve
vine leaves, to decorate (optional)

Preheat the oven to 375°F. Butter an ovenproof dish. Cut peaches in half and remove pits.

Scoop out a little flesh from each peach half and place in a bowl. Crush amaretti cookies and add to the bowl. Stir in egg yolk, sugar, and butter and mix well. Put some filling in each peach half, forming it into a smooth mound.

Put peaches in the dish and pour in wine. Bake in the oven 30 to 40 minutes until peaches are tender and filling is firm. Transfer to serving plates, sprinkle with toasted almonds, and decorate with vine leaves. Spoon around baking juices and serve.

Makes 4 servings.

Note: Be careful not to bake peaches for too long—they should retain their shape.

ROAST FIGS

butter for greasing
12 figs
1 tablespoon orange juice
3 tablespoons superfine sugar
⅔ cup walnut halves
1 tablespoon honey
plain yogurt, to serve

SAFFRON NECTARINES

4 ripe nectarines
1 tablespoon butter
¼ cup blossom honey
pinch saffron threads
1 tablespoon rosewater
toasted slivered almonds, to decorate

Preheat the oven to 400°F. Butter a shallow, flameproof dish. Put figs side by side in the dish.

Cut nectarines in half and remove pits. Put nectarine halves in a saucepan with butter.

Sprinkle with orange juice and 2 tablespoons sugar. Bake 20 minutes, basting from time to time with cooking juices. Add walnuts and sprinkle with remaining sugar.

Spoon over honey and sprinkle with saffron. Add ½ cup water and rosewater. Bring slowly to boil and simmer gently 8 to 12 minutes until nectarines are tender.

Reduce the oven temperature to 300°F and bake an additional 10 minutes. Remove figs and walnuts with a slotted spoon and arrange on a serving dish. Add honey to cooking juices and warm through over low heat. Spoon syrup over figs and serve warm or cold with plain yogurt.

Makes 4 servings.

Remove with a slotted spoon and arrange on serving plates. Decorate with toasted slivered almonds and serve warm or cold.

Makes 4 servings.

BAKED PANNETONE PUDDING

3 eggs
½ cup superfine sugar
1¾ cups whole milk
few drops vanilla extract
butter for greasing
6 slices panettone with dried fruit
¼ cup marmalade
confectioners' sugar for dusting

In a large bowl, beat eggs and sugar until light and foamy. Add milk and vanilla extract and mix well.

Lightly butter a shallow, ovenproof dish. Spread panettone slices with marmalade. Sandwich together, two pieces at a time, and cut pieces in half. Arrange in the dish. Ladle custard mixture over panettone and let soak 15 minutes. Meanwhile, preheat the oven to 325°F.

Place the dish in a larger ovenproof dish or baking pan and pour in enough boiling water to come halfway up the sides of the dish. Bake 50 minutes until custard is set and top is golden with a slight crust. Sprinkle with confectioners' sugar and serve hot or cold.

Makes 4 to 6 servings.

FLAMBÉED FRUIT

½ stick butter
¼ cup superfine sugar
2 oranges, peeled and segmented
12 oz. canned pineapple pieces in natural juice
4 bananas, thickly sliced
1 tablespoon orange liqueur or brandy
mint sprigs, to decorate

Put butter and sugar in a flameproof dish and cook over gentle heat until butter has melted and turned a caramel color.

Add orange segments, pineapple pieces and juice, and bananas. Bring to boil and boil 5 minutes until sauce thickens.

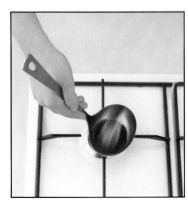

Put liqueur or brandy in a ladle and warm gently. Ignite and pour over fruit. Cook 1 minute, until flames die down. Decorate with mint sprigs and serve warm.

Makes 4 servings.

RHUBARB MERINGUE

1 lb. rhubarb, sliced
4 bananas, sliced
¼ cup brown sugar
½ teaspoon ground cinnamon
grated zest and juice 3 oranges
MERINGUE:
3 egg whites
¾ cup superfine sugar

Preheat the oven to 350°F. Put rhubarb and bananas in an ovenproof dish. Sprinkle with brown sugar, cinnamon, and orange zest. Pour over orange juice, making sure fruit is evenly coated.

Cover with a lid or piece of aluminum foil and bake 15 to 20 minutes until fruit is tender. Meanwhile, to make meringue, beat egg whites until they form stiff peaks. Fold in sugar.

Put meringue in a piping bag and pipe over fruit. Return to the oven and cook 20 minutes until meringue is crisp and golden. Serve warm or cold.

Makes 4 to 6 servings.

Note: If you prefer, you can simply spoon meringue over fruit.

BAKED APPLES IN BATTER

2 tablespoons light corn syrup
4 sweet dessert apples, cored
8 bay leaves
confectioners' sugar for dusting
BATTER:
½ cup all-purpose flour
2 eggs, beaten
few drops vanilla extract
1¼ cups milk
¼ cup superfine sugar
1 tablespoon butter, plus extra for greasing

Preheat oven to 375°F. Lightly butter an ovenproof dish and spread syrup over the bottom.

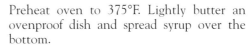

Place apples on top of syrup. Put a bay leaf in the cavity of each apple, reserving 4 remaining leaves for decoration. Bake 15 minutes. Meanwhile, make batter. Sift flour into a large bowl and make a well in the center. Add eggs, vanilla extract, and a little milk. Beat into flour, gradually adding more milk to form a smooth batter. Stir in sugar and melted butter.

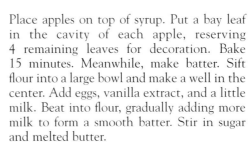

Pour batter over apples and bake 45 to 50 minutes until batter is risen and golden. Remove bay leaves from apples. Decorate with reserved bay leaves, dust with confectioners' sugar, and serve.

Makes 4 servings.

RICE PUDDING WITH PEACHES

3¾ cups whole milk
6 cardamom pods
⅔ cup white short-grain rice
½ cup pistachio nuts, chopped
½ cup brown sugar
½ stick butter, diced
2 egg yolks
16 oz. can peach halves, drained

Put milk in a flameproof casserole. Add cardamom pods, bring to boil, and simmer gently 5 minutes. Remove cardamom pods. Stir in rice.

Return to boil and simmer gently, stirring frequently, 15 to 20 minutes until rice is tender and most of the liquid has been absorbed. Remove from the heat and stir in pistachio nuts, half the brown sugar, butter, and egg yolks. Let cool slightly. Preheat oven to 325°F.

Remove half the mixture from the casserole and set aside. Arrange peaches on top of rice in the casserole and cover with remaining rice. Bake 25 minutes. Preheat broiler. Sprinkle pudding with remaining sugar and broil until sugar melts and turns a deep golden brown.

Makes 6 to 8 servings.

COFFEE BRULÉE

8 egg yolks
½ cup superfine sugar
1 cup whole milk
2 cups heavy cream
1 teaspoon coffee extract
summer berries, to decorate (optional)
TOPPING:
¼ cup superfine sugar

In a large bowl, beat together egg yolks and sugar until light and foamy.

Put milk, cream, and coffee extract in a flameproof casserole. Heat gently but do not boil. Remove from the heat and let cool. Preheat oven to 300°F. Pour milk mixture onto egg yolk mixture and stir well. Pour into a large jug and allow froth to rise to the surface. Skim off froth. Pour mixture back into the casserole.

Put a piece of waxed paper in a baking pan. Put the casserole on top of the paper. Pour enough boiling water into the pan to come halfway up the sides of the casserole. Bake 45 minutes until mixture has set. Let cool, then chill. To make topping, preheat the broiler. Sprinkle top of custard with sugar and broil until sugar melts and turns a deep golden brown. Decorate with summer berries and serve.

Makes 6 servings.

WINTER FRUIT SALAD

1 cup dried apricots
⅔ cup dried apple rings
⅔ cup prunes
⅓ cup golden raisins
⅓ cup raisins
1¾ cups unsweetened apple juice
2 × 2 in. cinnamon sticks
1 pear, peeled, cored, and quartered
thinly pared peel ½ lemon

Put dried apricots and apples, prunes, golden raisins, raisins, apple juice, and cinnamon sticks in a flameproof casserole. Cover and let soak 12 hours.

Add pear and lemon peel to the casserole. Bring to boil and simmer gently 15 minutes.

Remove cinnamon sticks and strips of lemon peel. Serve warm or cold.

Makes 4 to 6 servings.

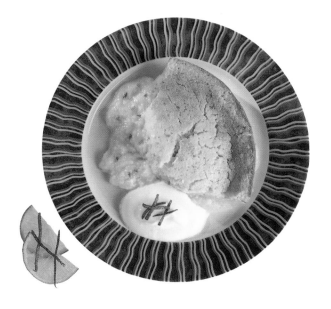

SAUCY LIME PUDDING

½ stick unsalted butter, plus extra for greasing
¼ cup superfine sugar
grated zest and juice 3 limes
2 eggs, separated
½ cup self-rising flour
1¼ cups milk

Preheat oven to 325°F. In a large bowl, beat together butter, sugar, and lime zest until light and fluffy. Stir in egg yolks and carefully fold in flour. Stir in milk and lime juice.

Whisk egg whites until they form stiff peaks. Fold into lime mixture. Lightly butter an ovenproof dish.

Pour lime mixture into the dish and bake 40 to 50 minutes until risen and golden. Serve warm.

Makes 4 to 6 servings.

CABINET PUDDING

⅓ cup raisins
2 tablespoons rum or brandy
10 oz. chocolate or plain sponge cake
1 cup chopped, mixed nuts
½ cup superfine sugar
4 eggs
2 cups milk
¼ cup slivered almonds
RASPBERRY SAUCE:
1½ cups fresh or frozen raspberries
2 tablespoons lemon juice
¼ to ⅓ cup superfine sugar
⅓ cup Framboise liqueur or water

Soak raisins in rum or brandy 1 hour.

Preheat oven to 350°F. Lightly butter an oval baking dish. Break up sponge cake coarsely and place in buttered dish. Add raisins and soaking liquid, then sprinkle with chopped, mixed nuts and 2 tablespoons sugar. In a bowl, beat eggs with remaining sugar and whisk in milk. Pour into dish. Sprinkle with slivered almonds.

Place dish in a roasting pan and add boiling water to come halfway up sides. Bake 1 to 1½ hours, until custard is lightly set. Meanwhile, make raspberry sauce. Put raspberries, lemon juice, sugar, and Framboise liqueur or water into a saucepan, bring slowly to boil, then simmer for a few minutes. Rub through a fine nylon strainer. Serve pudding hot with sauce.

Makes 6 servings.

FRUIT DUFF

12 oz. mixed fresh or frozen fruit, e.g., plums, black
  currants, and gooseberries, thawed if frozen
½ cup superfine sugar
1½ cups self-rising flour
2 teaspoons baking powder
pinch salt
1 tablespoon butter
⅓ cup milk
fresh mint, to decorate (optional)

Butter a medium-sized mixing bowl. Drain fruit and place in greased bowl.

Add ¼ cup sugar to fruit (add a little extra if using tart fruit such as gooseberries). Sift flour, baking powder, and salt into a large bowl and stir in remaining sugar. Cut in butter until incorporated into dry ingredients. Add milk and stir to form a soft dough. Turn out onto a lightly floured surface and pat to a circle to fit top of bowl; place on top of fruit.

Cover bowl with a piece of aluminum foil, pleated in the middle. Tie securely around the rim of the bowl. Set bowl in a saucepan of gently boiling water to come halfway up the sides and steam 1½ hours. Check water in pan occasionally and add more boiling water if necessary. Decorate with fresh mint. Serve hot.

Makes 4 servings.

SPOTTED DICK

1 cup self-rising flour
3 tablespoons cornstarch
1 teaspoon baking powder
½ cup superfine sugar
1 stick butter, softened
grated zest and juice 1 orange
2 eggs
⅔ cup golden raisins
⅓ cup chopped, mixed citrus peel
milk, if needed
BLACK CURRANT SAUCE:
2 cups black currants
¼ cup superfine sugar
2 tablespoons crème de cassis

Butter a mixing bowl or an 8 in. ring mold. Sift flour, cornstarch, and baking powder onto a plate. In a large bowl, cream sugar, butter, and grated orange zest until light and fluffy. In a separate bowl, beat eggs with orange juice. Beat gradually into butter mixture with 1 tablespoon of flour mixture. Fold in remaining flour with golden raisins and mixed citrus peel. Mixture should be a soft dropping consistency; if too stiff, add a small amount of milk.

Spoon mixture into prepared bowl or mold and cover with a piece of buttered aluminum foil pleated in the middle. Tie securely around rim of bowl or mold and set in a saucepan of gently boiling water to come halfway up sides. Steam 1½ to 2 hours. To make sauce, put black currants, sugar, and ½ cup water into a pan and cook until tender. Drain fruit and push through a strainer. Stir in crème de cassis. Turn out pudding and serve with sauce.

Makes 6 servings.

LEMON BELVOIR PUDDING

1 stick butter, softened
½ cup superfine sugar
2 large egg yolks
2½ cups fresh bread crumbs
grated zest and juice 2 lemons
1 teaspoon baking powder
confectioners' sugar and lemon peel, to decorate
HOT LEMON SAUCE:
grated zest and juice 3 lemons
¾ stick butter
⅓ cup superfine sugar
1 rounded teaspoon cornstarch

Generously butter a 4½ cup charlotte mold.

In a large bowl, cream butter and sugar until light and fluffy. Beat in egg yolks and bread crumbs. When well mixed, stir in lemon zest and juice and baking powder. Spoon into buttered mold and cover top with a piece of aluminum foil pleated in the middle. Tie securely around mold, then set mold in a saucepan of enough gently boiling water to come halfway up the sides. Steam 45 to 60 minutes.

Check water in pan occasionally and add more boiling water as necessary. Meanwhile, make sauce. Put lemon zest and juice, butter, and sugar in a saucepan and stir over gentle heat until butter has melted and sugar dissolved. Mix cornstarch to a smooth paste with a little water and stir into pan. Bring sauce to boil, stirring constantly. Simmer 1 or 2 minutes, stirring occasionally. Turn out pudding, decorate with confectioners' sugar and lemon peel, and serve with sauce.

Makes 4 servings.

SPICE ISLAND CRUMBLE

1 stick butter
4 firm bananas, cut into 1 in. pieces
1 large ripe mango, peeled and cut into chunks
1 ripe papaya, peeled, seeded, and cut into chunks
4 ripe passion fruit
⅔ cup light brown sugar
juice 1 orange
juice 1 lime
1¼ cups all-purpose flour
1 teaspoon ground cinnamon
¼ teaspoon ground allspice
¼ teaspoon ground cloves
¼ teaspoon freshly grated nutmeg
1⅓ cups dried coconut
whipped heavy cream and rum, to serve

QUEEN OF PUDDINGS

2¼ cups milk
½ stick butter
2 cups cake crumbs
grated zest 1 lemon
grated zest 1 orange
¼ cup superfine sugar
4 egg yolks, beaten
2 egg whites, whisked
¼ cup strawberry jelly
½ cup sliced strawberries
confectioners' sugar for dusting
MERINGUE:
2 egg whites
¼ cup superfine sugar

Preheat oven to 375°F. Use 1 tablespoon butter to grease a large, shallow, ovenproof gratin dish. Arrange banana, mango, and papaya pieces in dish. Cut passion fruits in half, scoop out pulp and seeds, and spread over fruit. Sprinkle with 3 tablespoons sugar, pour over orange and lime juices, and gently mix fruit together.

Preheat oven to 325°F. Put milk and butter in an ovenproof casserole dish and heat gently until butter melts. Stir in cake crumbs and lemon and orange zest. Add sugar and egg yolks. Fold in egg whites. Put the casserole in a deep baking pan and pour in enough boiling water to come halfway up the sides of the casserole. Bake 45 to 50 minutes until set. Remove from oven. Mix together jelly and strawberries and spread over the top of the pudding.

Sift flour, cinnamon, allspice, cloves, and nutmeg into a bowl. Stir in remaining sugar and coconut. Cut in remaining butter until mixture resembles bread crumbs. Sprinkle over fruit. Bake 35 to 40 minutes until fruit is tender and top is brown and crisp. If topping browns too quickly, reduce heat. Stir a little rum into whipped cream and serve with crumble.

Makes 6 servings.

To make meringue, beat egg whites until they form stiff peaks. Fold in sugar. Put mixture in a piping bag and pipe in a trellis pattern on top of the pudding. Dust with confectioners' sugar and bake in the oven, out of the baking pan, an additional 30 minutes. Serve pudding warm.

Makes 4 to 6 servings.

SAFFRON RICE PUDDING

1 cup basmati rice
⅓ cup milk
pinch saffron threads
3 tablespoons butter
2 green cardamom pods, bruised
1 in. cinnamon stick
2 cloves
½ cup golden raisins
¼ cup superfine sugar
⅓ cup slivered almonds, toasted

Wash rice under cold running water and put into a large saucepan with 2½ cups cold water.

Bring to boil, then reduce heat and simmer, covered, 5 minutes. Drain. Measure 2 tablespoons milk into a small bowl, add saffron, and let soak 5 minutes. Melt butter in a heavy-bottomed saucepan, add rice, cardamom pods, cinnamon stick, and cloves and fry 2 or 3 minutes or until rice becomes opaque.

Stir in remaining milk, saffron-infused milk, golden raisins, and sugar and bring to boil, then simmer, covered, 6 to 8 minutes until rice is tender and liquid has been absorbed. Remove whole spices and serve hot, sprinkled with slivered almonds.

Makes 4 servings.

GOLDEN SEMOLINA PUDDING

½ cup superfine sugar
3 tablespoons butter or ghee (clarified butter)
¾ cup semolina
seeds from 3 cardamom pods
3 tablespoons raisins
½ cup slivered almonds, toasted
plain yogurt, to serve (optional)

Put sugar in a heavy-bottomed saucepan with ⅔ cup water. Cook over low heat, stirring occasionally, until sugar has dissolved. Bring to boil and boil 1 minute, then remove from heat and set aside.

Melt butter or ghee in a large, heavy-bottomed skillet, add semolina, and cook 8 to 10 minutes over medium heat, stirring constantly, until semolina turns golden brown.

Remove from heat and let cool slightly, then stir in sugar syrup and cardamom seeds. Cook over low heat 3 to 5 minutes, stirring frequently, until thick. Stir in half the raisins and almonds. Decorate with remaining raisins and almonds and serve warm, with plain yogurt.

Makes 4 to 6 servings.

BAKED MANGO CUSTARDS

2 large ripe mangoes
juice 1 lime
4 egg yolks
⅓ cup superfine sugar
1 teaspoon ground ginger
¼ teaspoon ground allspice
2½ cups heavy cream
toasted slivered almonds, to decorate

Preheat oven to 325°F. Peel mangoes. Cut away and discard pits and coarsely chop flesh. Place mango flesh into a blender or food processor, add lime juice, and purée until smooth.

In a bowl, beat egg yolks, sugar, ginger, and allspice together until pale and thick. Stir in mango purée. Put 2 cups cream into a pan and heat until gently simmering. Beat into mango mixture until evenly blended and pour into 8 ramekin dishes. Place in a roasting pan and pour in enough boiling water to come two thirds of the way up the sides of the ramekins. Bake 30 minutes or until set, remove from the oven, and let cool. Refrigerate for several hours.

In a bowl, beat remaining cream until stiff. Spoon or pipe a swirl onto each custard and decorate with toasted slivered almonds.

Makes 8 servings.

COCONUT CUSTARDS

3 eggs
2 egg yolks
2 cups coconut milk
⅓ cup superfine sugar
few drops rosewater or jasmine extract
toasted coconut, to decorate

Preheat the oven to 350°F. Place four individual heatproof dishes in a baking pan.

In a bowl, stir together eggs, egg yolks, coconut milk, sugar, and rosewater or jasmine extract until sugar dissolves. Pass through a strainer into dishes. Pour boiling water into baking pan to surround dishes.

Cook in oven about 20 minutes until custards are lightly set in the center. Remove from baking pan and allow to cool slightly before unmolding. Serve warm or cold, decorated with toasted coconut.

Makes 4 servings.

SLOW COOKING

INTRODUCTION

Slow cooking is the perfect way to prepare a wide variety of delicious food, from soups to fruit compotes, and it's hard to beat the aroma of a delicious dinner, perfectly cooked and ready to eat, when you arrive home at the end of a tiring day! Slow cookers are simple and economical to use and require little or no attention once the ingredients for your recipe have been prepared. Foods are usually cooked for long periods of time, so meat—even the toughest cuts—and vegetables become deliciously tender. Slow cooking also retains all the goodness and develops the flavor of foods. There is little evaporation, so food doesn't dry out.

CHOOSING A SLOW COOKER

A good selection of slow cookers is widely available, many at a modest price, in a range of shapes and colors and varying in capacity from approximately two to six quarts. All slow cookers operate at a low wattage and consume a similar amount of electricity and the efficient insulation built into the appliance ensures that only the food inside the cooker heats up and not the whole kitchen.

There are two main types of slow cooker. The most common ones have a removable inner earthenware or ceramic cooking pot. The outer casing of these models is usually made of metal or heat-resistant plastic and is fitted with an inner metal casing. The removable cooking pot sits in the inner casing and the heating elements are situated between the inner and outer casings. Lids are made of heat-resistant glass or ceramic. Other, less common types comprise an earthenware or ceramic pot that is permanently fixed into an outer casing. The heating elements are housed between the outer casing and the cooking pot.

USING A SLOW COOKER

Always read through the manufacturer's instructions before using your slow cooker for the first time. Models vary slightly and even on the same setting, some will cook faster than others. Use your slow cooker several times before

trying the recipes in this book; the timings given are intended to be an accurate guide, but you may find that your model cooks more quickly or more slowly and that you need to adjust the cooking times accordingly.

Most slow cookers have three basic settings—OFF, LOW, and HIGH; others also include an AUTO setting. Most models have a power indicator light. On the LOW setting, the slow cooker will cook foods very gently with hardly any simmering. On the HIGH setting, the cooker may actually boil some foods and liquids. With the AUTO setting, cooking starts at a high temperature, then automatically switches to a LOW cook and the temperature is thermostatically controlled. Most of the recipes in this book use the HIGH or LOW settings.

The slow cooker may need to be preheated on HIGH about twenty minutes (refer to the manufacturer's instructions for your specific model). You can often use this time to prepare the ingredients for cooking. To preheat your slow cooker (if applicable), simply place the empty cooking pot in the slow cooker bottom, place the lid in position, plug in, and switch on with the control set on HIGH. Once the cooker is preheated, add the prepared ingredients to the cooking pot, replace the lid, and continue cooking as directed in the recipe.

ADAPTING YOUR OWN RECIPES

Once you are accustomed to using your slow cooker, you will easily be able to adapt your own recipes to cook in the slow cooker. Simply refer to similar recipes in this book, or in the manufacturer's handbook, and change cooking times accordingly. It is also worth remembering, however, that because there is less evaporation in a slow cooker, you will almost always need to reduce the quantity of liquid used. In a slow cooker, steam condenses on the lid and returns to the pot and, in doing so, forms a seal around the lid that retains heat and flavor. As a guide, use about half the quantity of liquid given in a conventional recipe—you can always add a little more liquid at the end of the cooking time if the cooked result is too thick. If you wish to reduce the quantity of liquid at the end of the cooking time, remove the lid after cooking, turn the setting to HIGH, and reduce by simmering for an additional thirty to forty-five minutes.

PREPARING FOOD FOR SLOW COOKING

Trim excess fat from meat and cut meat into small, even, bite-sized pieces. Cut vegetables, especially root vegetables, into small dice or thin slices. (Surprisingly, vegetables often take longer to cook than meat in a slow cooker.) Place the diced vegetables in the bottom or toward the bottom half of the cooking pot and ensure that they are covered completely with liquid.

You can speed up the cooking a little by precooking vegetables in oil or butter in a pan to soften before adding them to the slow cooker. Browning or sealing meat in oil or melted butter in a pan before adding it to the slow cooker also improves the appearance, texture, and flavor of the cooked food. It is often a good idea to bring the cooking liquid to boil before adding it to the slow cooker. If you don't have time to precook vegetables or meat, preheat the slow cooker on HIGH while preparing the ingredients. Place the chopped vegetables in the bottom of the cooking pot, add the meat or poultry, then add herbs or seasonings and pour over enough boiling stock or liquid to just cover the food. Switch the setting to LOW and cook as instructed—you will need to add about two to three hours to the minimum recommended cooking time.

Food to be slow cooked should be seasoned lightly with salt and pepper, especially salt. Add the minimum amount of salt and then check and adjust the seasoning before serving.

Always defrost frozen ingredients thoroughly before placing them in a slow cooker. Defrosted frozen vegetables are usually added toward the end of the cooking time.

Soak dried beans in plenty of cold water for at least ten hours or overnight, then drain, place in a large pan, cover with fresh, cold water, and boil ten minutes. Drain them and use as required. Lentils do not need precooking. Use easy/quick-cooking varieties of rice and pasta.

To avoid separation or curdling, dairy products, such as cream and milk, are best added toward the end of the cooking time—or at the end of cooking, if possible. You should use whole milk, rather than low-fat or nonfat milk.

Use dried herbs rather than fresh. Dried herbs tend to create a better flavor during the long, slow cooking process. (To further enhance the flavor and appearance of a dish, you can stir fresh, chopped herbs into the finished dish or sprinkle them on top.)

TIPS FOR SLOW COOKING

Unless the recipe specifies otherwise, do not lift the lid during the cooking process, as this will break the water seal around the rim and will interfere with the cooking time. (With most recipes, there is no need to turn or stir the food, as it will not stick, burn, or boil over, and slow cooking provides a very even method of cooking.) If you do need to lift the lid while cooking, remember to increase the cooking time by about twenty to thirty minutes in order to allow the slow cooker to regain lost heat. If you need to speed up the cooking process, simply switch the control to the HIGH setting. As an approximate guide, the cooking time on HIGH is just over half that on LOW.

When cooking joints of meat or foods that are cooked in dishes such as pudding basins, ensure that the food or dish fits comfortably in the cooking pot and that the lid fits securely before you begin to prepare the recipe. Ideally slow cookers should be filled to a maximum of ½ to 1 in. from the top of the cooking pot. Make sure that the cooking pot is at least half full and no more than three quarters full. Dishes to be cooked in a slow cooker should always contain some liquid.

Once cooking time is complete, you can keep food hot by switching the setting to LOW. If at the end of cooking time the food is not ready, replace the lid, switch the setting to HIGH, and continue cooking for an additional thirty to sixty minutes or until the food is thoroughly cooked. With dishes such as soups and casseroles, once the cooking time is complete, always stir the dish well before serving.

Cold cooked food should not be reheated in the slow cooker, as it will not reach a high enough temperature to be safe.

CARING FOR AND CLEANING A SLOW COOKER

Refer to the manufacturer's guidelines about caring for and cleaning your slow cooker. Do not subject the cooking pot to sudden changes in temperature and never plunge it into cold or boiling water. Do not leave the pot immersed in water, as this may adversely affect the porous bottom.

Remove any stubborn stains with a soft brush or nylon cleaning pad. Do not use abrasive cleaners or scourers on the cooking pot or outer casing of your slow cooker. The latter should never be immersed in water, filled with liquid or food, or used for cooking without the inner cooking pot. To clean, wipe with a cloth soaked in warm, soapy water.

Most cooking pots and lids are not suitable for washing in a dishwasher and many cannot be placed in an oven, freezer, or microwave or on a conventional burner—check the manufacturer's instructions for your model.

Rice pudding with orange (page 222)

BACON & CORN CHOWDER

2 tablespoons butter
8 slices lean smoked bacon, diced
1 large onion, chopped
3 stalks celery, finely chopped
2 or 3 medium potatoes, peeled and finely diced
6 oz. button mushrooms, sliced
4 cups vegetable stock
salt and freshly ground black pepper
15¼ oz. can corn kernels, drained
¼ to ⅓ cup light cream
3 or ¼ cup fresh, chopped parsley

Preheat the slow cooker on HIGH while preparing ingredients.

Melt butter in a pan, add bacon, and cook 3 minutes, stirring. Add onion, celery, and potatoes and sauté 5 minutes. Add mushrooms, stock, and seasoning and stir to mix. Bring to boil, then transfer to the cooking pot. Cover, reduce the temperature to LOW, and cook 6 hours.

Stir in corn, cover, and cook on LOW an additional 1 to 2 hours. Stir in cream and chopped parsley and adjust seasoning to taste. Ladle into warmed soup bowls.

Makes 4 to 6 servings.

Note: Thicken soup with a little cornstarch. Blend 1 or 2 tablespoons cornstarch with a little water and stir into soup. Cook on HIGH 20 to 30 minutes.

MEXICAN BEAN SOUP

1¼ cups dried red kidney beans
2 tablespoons olive oil
2 red onions, finely chopped
2 cloves garlic, crushed
1 red bell pepper, seeded and diced
1 fresh red chili, seeded and finely chopped
2 teaspoons ground coriander
1 teaspoon ground cumin
14½ oz. can chopped tomatoes
3¾ cups vegetable stock
1 tablespoon chili sauce, plus extra to taste
salt and freshly ground black pepper
2 or 3 tablespoons fresh, chopped cilantro
¼ cup sour cream (optional)

Place kidney beans in a large bowl and cover with plenty of cold water. Soak for at least 10 hours or overnight. Preheat the slow cooker on HIGH while preparing ingredients. Drain beans, place in a large pan, cover with cold water, and bring to boil. Boil rapidly 10 minutes, then rinse, drain, and set aside. Meanwhile, heat oil in a large pan, add onions, garlic, bell pepper, and chili and sauté 5 minutes. Add ground spices and cook gently 1 minute, stirring. Add kidney beans, tomatoes, stock, chili sauce, and seasoning and bring to boil.

Transfer to the cooking pot, cover, reduce the temperature to LOW, and cook 8 to 12 hours. Stir in chopped cilantro and extra chili sauce. Stir in sour cream (if using) and ladle into warmed soup bowls.

Makes 4 to 6 servings.

THAI-SPICED CHICKEN SOUP

2 tablespoons sunflower oil
6 shallots, finely chopped
5 or 6 medium carrots, thinly sliced
4 stalks celery, thinly sliced
1 clove garlic, crushed
1 red chili, seeded and finely chopped
1 in. piece fresh ginger, peeled and finely chopped
1 lb. 2 oz. skinless boneless chicken thighs, diced
1 tablespoon Thai seasoning
1 cup topped, tailed, and sliced green beans
4 cups chicken stock
salt and freshly ground black pepper
3 oz. spaghetti, broken into small lengths
2 or 3 tablespoons fresh, chopped cilantro

Preheat the slow cooker on HIGH while preparing ingredients. Heat oil in a pan, add shallots, carrots, celery, garlic, chili, and ginger, and sauté 3 minutes. Add chicken and cook until sealed all over, stirring frequently. Add Thai spice and green beans and cook 1 minute, stirring. Add stock and seasoning and bring to boil.

Transfer to the cooking pot, cover, then reduce the heat to LOW and cook 5 hours. Stir in spaghetti, cover, and cook on LOW an additional 1 to 2 hours or until spaghetti is cooked and tender. Stir in chopped cilantro and serve.

Makes 4 to 6 servings.

PEA & HAM SOUP

1 onion
2 leeks, washed
3 cups fresh, shelled peas
1 clove garlic, crushed (optional)
4½ cups vegetable stock
salt and freshly ground black pepper
1 cup cooked lean smoked ham, diced
fresh, chopped parsley, to garnish

Preheat the slow cooker on HIGH while preparing ingredients. Finely chop onion and thinly slice leeks.

Place in the cooking pot with peas, garlic, stock, and seasoning and stir to mix. Cover, reduce the temperature to LOW, and cook 7 to 8 hours. Cool slightly, then purée mixture in a blender or food processor until smooth.

Return soup to the rinsed-out cooking pot and stir in ham. Cover and cook on LOW 1 to 2 hours. Ladle into warmed soup bowls, garnish with chopped parsley, and serve.

Makes 4 to 6 servings.

TUNA & TOMATO CASSEROLE

2 tablespoons olive oil
1 red onion, thinly sliced
1 yellow bell pepper, seeded and thinly sliced
2 cloves garlic, crushed
2 tablespoons all-purpose flour
1 cup fish or vegetable stock
⅔ cup red or dry white wine
7 plum tomatoes, peeled (see page 174) and chopped
8 oz. button mushrooms, halved
2 zucchini, sliced
salt and freshly ground black pepper
12 oz. can tuna in water
15¼ oz. corn kernels, drained
¾ cup pitted black olives
2 tablespoons fresh, chopped, mixed herbs
cooked pasta, such as fusilli or penne, to serve

Preheat the slow cooker on HIGH while preparing ingredients. Heat oil in a pan, add onion, bell pepper, and garlic, and sauté 5 minutes. Stir in flour and cook 1 minute, stirring. Gradually stir in stock and wine, then add tomatoes, mushrooms, zucchini, and seasoning and bring to boil, stirring.

Transfer to the cooking pot, cover, and cook on HIGH 3 to 4 hours. Drain and flake tuna. Stir tuna, corn, and olives into vegetable sauce, cover, and cook on HIGH an additional 1 to 2 hours or until casserole is piping hot. Stir in chopped, mixed herbs and serve with cooked pasta such as fusilli or penne.

Makes 6 servings.

SALMON & BROCCOLI RISOTTO

2 tablespoons butter
6 shallots, thinly sliced
2 cloves garlic, crushed
1 red bell pepper, seeded and diced
8 oz. chestnut mushrooms, sliced
1¼ cups arborio rice (Italian risotto) or
  long-grain rice
1¼ fl. oz. dry white wine
2 to 2¾ cups fish or vegetable stock
salt and freshly ground black pepper
1 cup small broccoli florets, cut in half
14 oz. skinless, boneless cooked salmon, flaked
2 tablespoons fresh, chopped Italian parsley
fresh Parmesan cheese shavings, to serve

Preheat the slow cooker on HIGH while preparing ingredients. Melt butter in a pan. Add shallots, garlic, bell pepper, and mushrooms and sauté 5 minutes. Add rice and cook 1 minute, stirring. Stir in wine, 2 cups stock, and seasoning and bring to boil. Transfer to the cooking pot, cover, and cook on HIGH 1 to 2 hours or until rice is just cooked and tender and most of the liquid has been absorbed.

Meanwhile, cook broccoli in a pan of boiling water about 5 minutes or until just tender. Drain well. Stir broccoli and salmon into risotto, adding a little extra hot stock if required. Cover and cook on HIGH about 30 minutes or until salmon is hot and rice is tender. Stir in chopped parsley and sprinkle with Parmesan shavings. Serve with ciabatta or other fresh crusty bread.

Makes 4 servings.

CHICKEN TAGINE WITH FIGS

8 chicken thighs, skinless
1 quantity spice mix (see Note)
2 tablespoons olive oil
2 onions, chopped
2 carrots, thinly sliced
2 cloves garlic, crushed
2 teaspoons grated, fresh, peeled ginger
6 oz. button mushrooms, halved
8 large dried figs, roughly chopped
2 tablespoons all-purpose flour
1¾ cups chicken stock
2 tablespoons tomato paste
1 tablespoon lemon juice
¾ cup black olives
⅓ cup pistachio nuts or pine nuts
fresh, chopped parsley, to garnish

Preheat slow cooker on HIGH while preparing ingredients. Toss chicken in spice mix until coated. Heat oil in a pan, add chicken, and cook until lightly browned all over, turning occasionally. Transfer to cooking pot with a slotted spoon. Set aside. Add onions, carrots, garlic, and ginger to the pan and sauté about 5 minutes or until slightly softened. Add mushrooms and figs, stir in flour, and cook 1 minute, stirring. Gradually stir in stock, tomato paste, and lemon juice. Bring slowly to boil, stirring, then pour over chicken. Stir gently to mix.

Cover and cook on HIGH 3 to 5 hours (or on MEDIUM 4 to 6 hours) or until chicken is tender. About 1 hour before serving, stir in olives and nuts. Garnish with parsley. Serve with couscous.

Makes 4 servings.

Note: To make spice mix, combine 2 tablespoons olive oil, 2 teaspoons each ground coriander and ground cumin, 1½ teaspoons each ground cinnamon and turmeric, finely grated zest and juice ½ lemon, and 1½ teaspoons harissa paste.

CHICKEN & CHICKPEA CASSEROLE

3 tablespoons olive oil
1½ lb. skinless, boneless chicken thighs, diced
8 shallots, thinly sliced
2 leeks, washed and thinly sliced
1 green or red bell pepper, seeded and thinly sliced
1 yellow bell pepper, seeded and thinly sliced
8 oz. chestnut mushrooms, sliced
2 tablespoons all-purpose flour
1 cup dry white wine
⅔ cup chicken stock
14½ oz. can chopped tomatoes
2 tablespoons sun-dried tomato paste
15 oz. can chickpeas, rinsed and drained
2 teaspoons dried Italian herb seasoning
salt and freshly ground black pepper

Preheat the slow cooker on HIGH while preparing ingredients. Heat 2 tablespoons oil in a pan, add chicken, and cook until lightly browned all over. Transfer to the cooking pot with a slotted spoon and set aside. Heat remaining oil in the pan, add shallots, leeks, bell peppers, and mushrooms, and sauté 5 minutes. Stir in flour and cook 1 minute, stirring. Gradually stir in wine and stock, then add tomatoes, tomato paste, chickpeas, dried herbs, and seasoning.

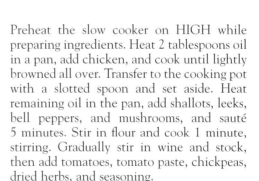

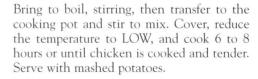

Bring to boil, stirring, then transfer to the cooking pot and stir to mix. Cover, reduce the temperature to LOW, and cook 6 to 8 hours or until chicken is cooked and tender. Serve with mashed potatoes.

Makes 6 servings.

Variation: Use canned black-eyed peas or red kidney beans instead of chickpeas.

FRAGRANT CHICKEN CURRY

3 tablespoons sunflower oil
2 onions, chopped
4 carrots, thinly sliced
2 cloves garlic, crushed
1 fresh green chili, seeded and finely chopped
1 in. piece fresh ginger, finely chopped
1½ lb. skinless, boneless chicken thighs, diced
2 tablespoons all-purpose flour
2 teaspoons each turmeric, ground coriander, and
    ground cumin
salt and freshly ground black pepper
1¼ cups chicken stock
⅔ cup passata or tomato sauce
⅔ cup golden raisins
⅓ cup cashews, toasted
2 or 3 tablespoons fresh, chopped cilantro

Preheat the slow cooker on HIGH while preparing ingredients. Heat 1 tablespoon oil in a pan, add onions, carrots, garlic, chili, and ginger, and sauté 5 minutes. Transfer to the cooking pot and set aside. Toss chicken in flour, ground spices, and seasoning until coated all over. Heat remaining oil in the pan, add chicken in batches, and cook quickly until sealed all over. Transfer to the cooking pot.

Add stock and passata to the pan and bring to boil, stirring, scraping up any brown bits in the pan. Add to the cooking pot and stir to mix well. Cover, reduce the temperature to LOW, and cook 6 hours. Stir in golden raisins, cover, and cook on LOW an additional 1 to 2 hours or until chicken is cooked and tender. Stir in cashews and chopped cilantro. Serve with rice.

Makes 4 servings.

COUNTRY CHICKEN CASSEROLE

2 tablespoons butter
4 chicken fillets, each cut into 3 pieces
12 baby onions or shallots
2 leeks, washed and thinly sliced
2 stalks celery, thinly sliced
8 oz. baby carrots
8 oz. button mushrooms
½ cup pearl barley
14½ oz. can chopped tomatoes
2 tablespoons tomato paste
1 cup chicken stock
1 cup dry white wine
salt and freshly ground black pepper
1 bouquet garni
herb sprigs, to garnish

Preheat the slow cooker on HIGH while preparing ingredients. Melt butter in a pan, add chicken, and cook until lightly browned all over, stirring occasionally. Transfer to the cooking pot with a slotted spoon and set aside. Add onions or shallots, leeks, celery, carrots, and mushrooms and sauté 5 minutes. Stir in pearl barley, tomatoes, tomato paste, stock, wine, and seasoning, then bring to boil.

Pour over chicken in the cooking pot and add bouquet garni. Cover, reduce the temperature to LOW, and cook 8 to 10 hours or until chicken is cooked and tender. Garnish with herb sprigs and serve with mashed potatoes and green beans.

Makes 4 to 6 servings.

ITALIAN CHICKEN CASSOULET

1 cup dried black-eyed peas or cranberry beans
2 tablespoons olive oil
4 chicken portions, skinless
2 large red onions, thinly sliced
2 cloves garlic, crushed
2 red bell peppers, seeded and diced
2 tablespoons all-purpose flour
1 cup chicken stock
⅔ cup red wine
14½ oz. can chopped tomatoes
8 oz. mushrooms, sliced
1 tablespoon fresh, chopped thyme
1 tablespoon fresh, chopped oregano
salt and freshly ground black pepper
herb sprigs, to garnish

Place beans in a large bowl. Cover with cold water and let soak for at least 10 hours or overnight. Preheat the slow cooker on HIGH while preparing ingredients. Drain beans, place in a large pan, cover with fresh, cold water, and bring to boil. Boil 10 minutes, then rinse, drain, and set aside. Meanwhile, heat oil in a large pan, add chicken portions, and cook until lightly browned all over, turning occasionally. Transfer to the cooking pot and set aside. Add onions, garlic, and bell peppers to the pan and sauté 5 minutes.

Stir in flour and cook 1 minute, stirring. Gradually stir in stock and wine, then add tomatoes, mushrooms, chopped thyme and oregano, and seasoning. Bring to boil, stirring, then spoon over chicken in the cooking pot. Cover and cook on HIGH 2 hours, then reduce the temperature to LOW and cook an additional 4 to 6 hours or until chicken is cooked and tender. Garnish with herb sprigs and serve with warm ciabatta bread.

Makes 6 servings.

CURRIED TURKEY WITH COCONUT

2 tablespoons olive oil
1 onion, chopped
2 cloves garlic, crushed
1 green bell pepper, seeded and thinly sliced
1 lb. 2 oz. skinless, boneless turkey meat, diced
1 teaspoon ground coriander
1 teaspoon ground cumin
4 teaspoons green Thai curry paste
4 oz. green beans, halved
6 oz. baby corn, halved
1¼ cups chicken stock
⅔ cup coconut milk
2 tablespoons cornstarch
2 or 3 tablespoons fresh, chopped cilantro
toasted flaked coconut, to garnish

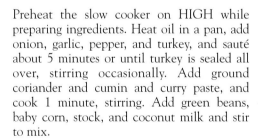

Preheat the slow cooker on HIGH while preparing ingredients. Heat oil in a pan, add onion, garlic, pepper, and turkey, and sauté about 5 minutes or until turkey is sealed all over, stirring occasionally. Add ground coriander and cumin and curry paste, and cook 1 minute, stirring. Add green beans, baby corn, stock, and coconut milk and stir to mix.

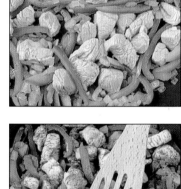

In a small bowl, blend cornstarch with a little water, add to curry, and stir well to mix. Bring to boil, stirring, then transfer to the cooking pot. Cover, reduce the temperature to LOW, and cook 6 to 8 hours or until turkey is cooked and tender. Stir in chopped cilantro and garnish with toasted flaked coconut. Serve with plain rice.

Makes 4 servings.

TURKEY & MUSHROOM RISOTTO

¼ cup dried porcini mushrooms
2 tablespoons sunflower oil
6 shallots, thinly sliced
1 clove garlic, crushed
3 stalks celery, finely chopped
8 oz. skinless turkey fillet, cut into small pieces
1¼ cups risotto rice or long-grain rice
8 oz. mixed fresh wild mushrooms, sliced
1¼ cups dry white wine
2 to 2¾ cups chicken stock
salt and freshly ground black pepper
15¼ oz. can corn kernels
2 tablespoons fresh, chopped, mixed herbs
finely grated Parmesan cheese, to serve

Preheat the slow cooker on HIGH while preparing ingredients. Place dried porcini mushrooms in a small bowl, pour over ½ cup boiling water, and let soak 20 minutes. Drain mushrooms, reserving soaking liquid, then snip into small pieces using scissors. Set aside. Heat oil in a pan, add shallots, garlic, and celery, and sauté 5 minutes. Add turkey and cook until lightly browned all over, stirring frequently. Add rice and fresh and soaked mushrooms and cook 1 minute, stirring.

Add wine, 2 cups stock, reserved mushroom liquid, and seasoning and bring to boil. Transfer to the cooking pot. Cover and cook on HIGH 1 hour. Stir in corn and add a little extra hot stock, if needed. Cover and cook on HIGH an additional 30 to 60 minutes or until turkey and rice are cooked and tender and all liquid has been absorbed. Stir in chopped herbs and sprinkle with Parmesan. Serve with crusty bread.

Makes 4 to 6 servings.

VENISON CASSEROLE

2 tablespoons sunflower oil
1½ lb. lean stewing venison, diced
2 red onions, thinly sliced
4 carrots, thinly sliced
3 stalks celery, thinly sliced
3 tablespoons all-purpose flour
1 cup game or chicken stock
1 cup red wine
7 oz. button mushrooms
⅔ cup dried cranberries
2 tablespoons cranberry sauce
1 tablespoon fresh, chopped thyme
salt and freshly ground black pepper
herb sprigs, to garnish

Preheat the slow cooker on HIGH while preparing ingredients. Heat oil in a large pan, add venison, and cook until sealed all over, stirring occasionally. Transfer to the cooking pot with a slotted spoon and set aside. Add onions, carrots, and celery to the pan and sauté 5 minutes. Stir in flour and cook 1 minute, stirring. Gradually stir in stock and wine, then add mushrooms, dried cranberries, cranberry sauce, chopped thyme, and seasoning and bring to boil, stirring.

Transfer to the cooking pot and stir to mix well. Cover, reduce the temperature to LOW, and cook 8 to 10 hours or until venison is cooked and tender. Garnish with herb sprigs and serve with mustard-flavored mashed potatoes and broccoli florets.

Makes 4 to 6 servings.

Variation: Use lean braising or stewing beef instead of venison.

STEWED LAMB WITH ROSEMARY

2 tablespoons sunflower oil
2¼ lb. lean boneless leg or shoulder of lamb, diced
12 baby onions or shallots
3 cloves garlic, crushed
8 oz. button mushrooms
2 tablespoons all-purpose flour
1 cup lamb or vegetable stock
1 cup red wine
8 oz. can chopped tomatoes
1 tablespoon tomato paste
2 tablespoons fresh, finely chopped rosemary
salt and freshly ground black pepper
rosemary sprigs, to garnish

Preheat the slow cooker on HIGH while preparing ingredients. Heat oil in a pan, add lamb, and cook until sealed all over. Transfer to the cooking pot with a slotted spoon and set aside. Add onions or shallots, garlic, and mushrooms to the pan and sauté 5 minutes. Stir in flour and cook 1 minute, stirring.

Gradually add stock and wine, then stir in tomatoes, tomato paste, chopped rosemary, and seasoning. Bring to boil, stirring, then transfer to the cooking pot and stir to mix. Cover, reduce the temperature to LOW, and cook 6 to 8 hours or until meat is cooked and tender. Garnish with rosemary sprigs and serve with boiled new potatoes and baby carrots.

Makes 4 servings.

LAMB & PEPPER STEW

2 tablespoons sunflower oil
8 lean lamb loin chops
2 onions, thinly sliced
2 red bell peppers, seeded and sliced
3 stalks celery, thinly sliced
4 carrots, thinly sliced
3 baking potatoes, peeled and thinly sliced
1½ cups lamb or vegetable stock
2 tablespoons tomato paste
2 teaspoons dried, mixed herbs
1 tablespoon butter, melted (optional)
herb sprigs, to garnish

Preheat slow cooker on HIGH while preparing ingredients.

Heat oil in a pan. Add lamb chops and cook in batches until sealed all over. Transfer to a plate and set aside. Add onions, bell peppers, celery, and carrots to the pan and sauté 5 minutes. Place four lamb chops in the bottom of the cooking pot. Arrange one third of potato slices over lamb and top potatoes with half the vegetable mixture. Repeat these layers once again, then finish with a final layer of potato slices on top.

Mix stock, tomato paste, dried, mixed herbs, and seasoning and pour into cooking pot. Cover, reduce the temperature to LOW, and cook 8 to 10 hours or until lamb and vegetables are cooked and tender. Brush top of potatoes with melted butter and place under a preheated broiler until golden. Garnish with herb sprigs.

Makes 4 servings.

Note: Use a slow cooker with a capacity of five quarts for best results.

BRAISED PORK WITH CABBAGE

1 tablespoon olive oil
2 tablespoons butter
4 lean pork loin chops
1 large onion, thinly sliced
3 stalks celery, finely chopped
2 tablespoons all-purpose flour
1 cup chicken or vegetable stock
1 cup dry or medium cider
12 oz. white cabbage, shredded
1 large cooking apple, peeled, cored, and sliced
1 teaspoon dried sage
salt and freshly ground black pepper
herb sprigs, to garnish

Preheat the slow cooker on HIGH while preparing ingredients. Heat oil and butter in a pan. Add chops and cook until sealed all over, turning once. Transfer to the cooking pot with a slotted spoon and set aside. Add onion and celery to the pan and sauté 5 minutes. Stir in flour and cook 1 minute, stirring. Gradually stir in stock and cider, then bring to boil, stirring. Add cabbage, apple, sage, and seasoning and stir to mix.

Spoon mixture over chops. Cover, reduce temperature to LOW, and cook 6 to 8 hours or until pork is cooked and tender. Garnish with herb sprigs. Serve with mashed potatoes and vegetables.

Makes 4 servings.

Variation: Use fresh or dried thyme instead of sage.

PORK & BEAN CASSOULET

1¼ cups dried kidney beans
3 tablespoons butter
1½ lb. lean pork tenderloin, diced
1 onion, chopped
1 clove garlic, crushed
2 leeks, washed and thinly sliced
2 stalks celery, sliced
3 carrots, thinly sliced
¼ cup all-purpose flour
1 tablespoon paprika
1¼ cups chicken or vegetable stock
1 cup dry or medium cider
8 oz. can chopped tomatoes
1 tablespoon tomato paste
salt and freshly ground black pepper
1 bouquet garni

Place beans in a large bowl. Cover with cold water and let soak for at least 10 hours or overnight. Preheat the slow cooker on HIGH while preparing ingredients. Drain beans, place in a large pan, cover with fresh, cold water, and bring to boil. Boil 10 minutes, then rinse, drain, and set aside. Meanwhile, melt butter in a pan, add meat, and cook until sealed all over. Transfer to the cooking pot with a slotted spoon and set aside. Add onion, garlic, leeks, celery, and carrots to the pan and sauté 5 minutes.

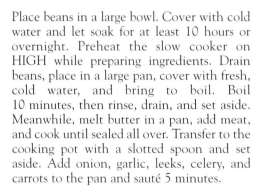

Stir in flour and paprika and cook 1 minute, stirring. Gradually stir in stock and cider, then add tomatoes, tomato paste, beans, and seasoning. Bring to boil, stirring, then add bouquet garni. Transfer to the cooking pot and stir to mix. Cover, reduce the temperature to LOW, and cook 8 to 10 hours or until pork is cooked. Remove and discard bouquet garni. Serve with sautéed potatoes and broccoli.

Makes 4 to 6 servings.

SAUSAGE & LEEK CASSEROLE

12 thin, herby pork sausages
3 tablespoons butter
1 onion, thinly sliced
3 leeks, washed and thinly sliced
1 clove garlic, crushed
1 butternut squash, peeled, seeded, and diced
3 tablespoons all-purpose flour
1¾ cups vegetable stock
8 oz. can chopped tomatoes
1 tablespoon whole-grain mustard
2 teaspoons fresh, chopped thyme
salt and freshly ground black pepper
herb sprigs, to garnish

Preheat the slow cooker on HIGH while preparing ingredients. Preheat the broiler to medium. Broil sausages until lightly browned all over, then transfer to the cooking pot and set aside. Meanwhile, melt butter in a pan, add onion, leeks, garlic, and squash, and sauté 5 minutes. Stir in flour and cook 1 minute, stirring. Gradually stir in stock, then add tomatoes, mustard, chopped thyme, and seasoning.

Bring to boil, stirring, then spoon mixture over sausages. Cover, switch the setting to AUTO, and cook 6 to 10 hours (or on LOW 8 to 10 hours). Garnish with herb sprigs and serve with mashed potatoes.

Makes 4 servings.

Variations: Use 1 teaspoon dried thyme instead of fresh thyme. Use dry white wine instead of half the stock.

SAUSAGE & MUSHROOM STEW

8 thick, spicy pork sausages
2 tablespoons sunflower oil
1 red onion, thinly sliced
1 clove garlic, crushed
1 fresh red chili, seeded and finely chopped
2 parsnips, diced
2 carrots, thinly sliced
2 stalks celery, thinly sliced
12 oz. chestnut mushrooms, sliced
2 tablespoons all-purpose flour
1 cup vegetable stock
1 cup passata or tomato sauce
2 teaspoons chili sauce
salt and freshly ground black pepper
4 or 5 medium potatoes, peeled and thinly sliced
1 tablespoon butter, melted (optional)

Preheat the slow cooker on HIGH while preparing ingredients. Preheat the broiler to medium. Broil sausages until lightly browned all over. Cut each sausage into three pieces and set aside. Meanwhile, heat oil in a pan, add onion, garlic, chili, parsnips, carrots, celery, and mushrooms, and sauté 5 minutes. Stir in flour and cook 1 minute, stirring. Gradually add stock and passata, then add chili sauce and seasoning. Bring to boil, stirring.

Put one third of vegetable mixture in the cooking pot, then arrange one third of potato slices on top and then half the sausages. Repeat these layers once again. Top with remaining vegetable mixture and finish with a final layer of potato slices on top. Cover, reduce the temperature to LOW, and cook 8 to 10 hours or until cooked. Brush tops of potatoes with melted butter and place under a preheated broiler until golden.

Makes 4 to 6 servings.

CHILI CON CARNE

1 tablespoon sunflower oil
2 red onions, chopped
1 clove garlic, crushed
1 red bell pepper, seeded and chopped
2 fresh red chilies, seeded and finely chopped
1 lb. 2 oz. (2¼ cups) lean ground beef
1 tablespoon all-purpose flour
1 teaspoon ground coriander
1 teaspoon ground cumin
½ teaspoon hot chili powder
⅔ cup beef stock
14½ oz. can chopped tomatoes
15 oz. can red kidney beans, rinsed and drained
2 tablespoons tomato paste
salt and freshly ground black pepper
shredded cheddar cheese, to serve (optional)

SPICY BEEF & BEAN STEW

1¼ cups dried kidney beans
3 tablespoons sunflower oil
1 large red onion, chopped
2 cloves garlic, crushed
2 red bell peppers, seeded and chopped
2 fresh red chilies, seeded and finely chopped
2 lb. lean stewing or braising steak, diced
3 tablespoons all-purpose flour
1 tablespoon ground coriander
1 tablespoon ground cumin
salt and freshly ground black pepper
2 cups beef stock
⅔ cup red wine

Preheat the slow cooker on HIGH while preparing ingredients. Heat oil in a pan, add onions, garlic, pepper, and chilies, and sauté 5 minutes. Add ground beef and cook until sealed all over, stirring occasionally. Stir in flour, ground coriander and cumin, and chili powder. Cook 1 minute, stirring. Add stock, tomatoes, kidney beans, tomato paste, and seasoning, then bring to boil, stirring.

Place beans in a large bowl. Cover with plenty of cold water and let soak for at least 10 hours or overnight. Preheat the slow cooker on HIGH while preparing ingredients. Drain beans, place in a large pan, cover with cold water, and bring to boil. Boil 10 minutes, then rinse, drain, and set aside. Meanwhile, heat 1 tablespoon oil in a large pan, add onion, garlic, bell peppers, and chilies, and sauté 5 minutes. Transfer to the cooking pot and set aside.

Transfer to the cooking pot. Cover, switch the setting to AUTO, and cook 8 to 12 hours or until cooked. Serve on a bed of rice and sprinkle with shredded cheese.

Makes 4 to 6 servings.

Toss meat in flour, coriander, cumin, and seasoning until coated. Heat remaining oil in the pan, add meat in batches, and cook quickly until brown. Transfer to the cooking pot. Add beans, stock, and wine to the pan and bring to boil, stirring and scraping up any brown bits in the pan. Add to the cooking pot and stir to mix well. Cover, reduce temperature to LOW, and cook 7 to 9 hours or until beef is cooked and tender. Serve with rice and green beans.

Makes 4 to 6 servings.

BEEF IN WINE WITH DUMPLINGS

3 tablespoons butter
8 slices lean smoked bacon, diced
2¼ lb. lean stewing or braising steak, diced
¼ cup all-purpose flour
1¼ cups red wine
⅔ cup beef stock
2 tablespoons brandy
16 baby onions or shallots
8 oz. button mushrooms
2 thyme sprigs
salt and freshly ground black pepper
1 cup self-rising flour
1 teaspoon baking powder
½ cup shredded beef or vegetable suet
1 teaspoon dry mustard
2 tablespoons fresh, chopped, mixed herbs

Preheat the slow cooker on HIGH while preparing ingredients. Melt butter in a large pan, add bacon, and cook 3 minutes, stirring. Add beef and cook until sealed all over, stirring occasionally. Stir in flour and cook 2 minutes, stirring. Gradually stir in wine, stock, and brandy. Add onions or shallots, mushrooms, thyme sprigs, and seasoning and bring to boil, stirring. Transfer to the cooking pot. Cover, reduce temperature to LOW, and cook 8 to 10 hours, until beef is cooked and tender. Remove and discard thyme sprigs.

Sift flour and baking powder into a bowl and stir in suet, mustard, chopped herbs, and seasoning. Add enough cold water to make a firm dough. Divide dough into sixteen pieces and, with floured hands, roll each piece into a small ball. Put dough balls all around edge of pot on top of casserole. Cover, increase temperature to HIGH, and cook 40 to 60 minutes or until dumplings are cooked. Serve with vegetables.

Makes 4 servings.

CURRIED POT ROAST

2 teaspoons turmeric
2 teaspoons ground coriander
2 teaspoons ground cumin
1 teaspoon hot chili powder
1 teaspoon garam masala
salt and freshly ground black pepper
3 lb. lean beef joint, e.g., round
3 tablespoons sunflower oil
8 shallots, sliced
4 carrots, thinly sliced
4 stalks celery, thinly sliced
1 rutabaga, diced
2¼ to 2¾ cups beef stock
2 tablespoons cornstarch

Preheat the slow cooker on HIGH while preparing ingredients. In a large bowl, mix together turmeric, coriander, cumin, chili powder, garam masala, and seasoning. Add beef and toss in spice mixture to coat. Heat 2 tablespoons oil in a nonstick skillet, add beef, and brown quickly, turning until sealed all over. Transfer to the cooking pot. Heat remaining oil in the pan, add shallots, carrots, celery, and rutabaga, and sauté 5 minutes; spoon around beef. Add stock to the pan, gently scraping up brown bits in pan with a wooden spoon, and bring to boil.

Pour enough stock into cooking pot to just cover vegetables. Cover, reduce temperature to LOW, and cook 6 to 8 hours until beef is tender. Remove beef, place on a plate, cover, and keep hot. Transfer vegetable mixture to a pan. In a small bowl, blend cornstarch with a little water until smooth. Stir into vegetable mixture, then bring to boil, stirring, until thickened. Simmer gently 3 minutes, stirring. Slice beef and spoon vegetable sauce over. Serve with rice.

Makes 6 servings.

MEDITERRANEAN VEGETABLES

2 tablespoons olive oil
2 red onions, thinly sliced
2 cloves garlic, crushed
2 yellow bell peppers, seeded and thinly sliced
3 zucchini, sliced
8 oz. button mushrooms, halved
5 plum tomatoes, peeled (see page 174) and sliced
¼ cup red wine
2 tablespoons sun-dried tomato paste
salt and freshly ground black pepper
2 tablespoons fresh, chopped basil
2 tablespoons fresh, chopped Italian parsley
fresh Parmesan cheese shavings, to serve

Preheat the slow cooker on HIGH while preparing ingredients. Heat oil in a large pan, add onions, garlic, and bell peppers, and sauté 5 minutes. Add zucchini, mushrooms, tomatoes, wine, tomato paste, and seasoning, then bring to boil, stirring.

Transfer to the cooking pot, cover, reduce the temperature to LOW, and cook 6 to 8 hours or until vegetables are cooked and tender. Stir in chopped basil and parsley and sprinkle with Parmesan shavings. Serve with warm ciabatta bread.

Makes 4 servings.

RATATOUILLE BEAN STEW

3 tablespoons olive oil
1 large onion, thinly sliced
2 cloves garlic, crushed
1 eggplant, diced
1 green, 1 red, and 1 yellow bell pepper, seeded and thinly sliced
15 oz. can red kidney beans
15 oz. can black-eyed peas
2 zucchini, sliced
14½ oz. can chopped tomatoes
⅓ cup dry white wine or vegetable stock
1 tablespoon tomato paste
2 teaspoons dried herbes de Provence
salt and freshly ground black pepper
herb sprigs, to garnish (optional)
shredded cheddar or Gruyère cheese, to serve

Preheat the slow cooker on HIGH while preparing ingredients. Heat oil in a large pan, add onion, garlic, eggplant, and bell peppers, and sauté 5 minutes. Rinse and drain kidney beans and black-eyed peas and add to pan with zucchini, tomatoes, wine or stock, tomato paste, dried herbs, and seasoning. Stir to mix well.

Bring to boil, stirring occasionally, then transfer to the cooking pot. Cover, reduce the temperature to LOW, and cook 6 to 8 hours or until vegetables are tender. Garnish with herb sprigs, sprinkle with a little grated cheddar or Gruyère cheese, and serve with fresh crusty bread.

Makes 4 to 6 servings.

MACARONI & BROCCOLI BAKE

2 cups dried macaroni
1 cup small broccoli florets
¾ stick butter
8 oz. leeks, washed and thinly sliced
½ cup all-purpose flour
4 cups milk
1½ cups shredded cheddar cheese
1 teaspoon prepared English mustard
15¼ oz. can corn kernels, drained
salt and freshly ground black pepper
½ cup fresh bread crumbs (optional)
⅓ cup finely grated Parmesan cheese (optional)
2 tablespoons fresh, chopped chives (optional)

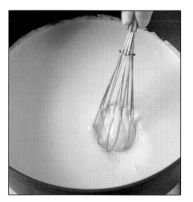

Preheat the slow cooker on HIGH while preparing ingredients. Cook macaroni in a pan of boiling water 8 minutes or until just tender. Add broccoli for final 3 minutes of cooking time. Drain well and set aside. Melt 2 tablespoons butter in a pan, add leeks, and sauté 8 to 10 minutes or until softened. Remove leeks to a plate and set aside. Add remaining butter to the pan with flour and milk and heat gently, whisking, until sauce comes to boil and thickens. Simmer gently 3 minutes, stirring.

Remove the pan from the heat and stir in broccoli, leeks, mustard, corn, and seasoning, and mix well. Butter cooking pot of slow cooker. Transfer macaroni mixture to the cooking pot. Cover, reduce temperature to LOW, and cook 3 to 4 hours. Preheat broiler to high, combine bread crumbs, Parmesan, and chives, sprinkle over the top, and broil until golden. Serve with broiled tomatoes.

Makes 6 servings.

SPICED ROOT VEGETABLES

2 tablespoons olive oil
1 onion, thinly sliced
1 clove garlic, crushed
3 stalks celery, thinly sliced
3 carrots, thinly sliced
8 oz. peeled rutabaga, diced
2 small peeled parsnips, diced
2 potatoes, peeled and diced
2 teaspoons each ground coriander, ground cumin, and hot chili powder
1 cup green lentils, rinsed and drained
14½ oz. can chopped tomatoes
3 cups vegetable stock
salt and freshly ground black pepper
2 tablespoons fresh, chopped cilantro

Preheat the slow cooker on HIGH while preparing ingredients. Heat oil in a large pan, add onion, garlic, and celery, and sauté 3 minutes. Add carrots, rutabaga, parsnips, and potatoes and sauté 5 minutes. Add ground coriander, cumin, and chili powder and cook 1 minute, stirring. Add lentils, tomatoes, stock, and seasoning and stir to mix. Bring to boil, stirring, then transfer to the cooking pot.

Cover and cook on HIGH 3 to 4 hours or until vegetables and lentils are cooked and tender. Stir in chopped cilantro and serve with fresh crusty bread.

Makes 4 to 6 servings.

Variation: Use sweet potatoes instead of standard potatoes.

VEGETARIAN CHILI BAKE

2 tablespoons sunflower oil
6 shallots, sliced
2 cloves garlic, crushed
3 stalks celery, finely chopped
1 green bell pepper, seeded and diced
1 large, fresh green chili, seeded and finely chopped
3 carrots, thinly sliced
6 oz. peeled turnip or rutabaga, diced
2 teaspoons ground cumin
1 teaspoon hot chili powder
14½ oz. can chopped tomatoes
2 tablespoons tomato paste
1 cup vegetable stock
8 oz. chestnut mushrooms, sliced
15 oz. can red kidney beans, rinsed and drained
salt and freshly ground black pepper
1 tablespoon cornstarch

Preheat the slow cooker on HIGH while preparing ingredients. Heat oil in a pan, add shallots, garlic, celery, pepper, and chili and sauté 3 minutes. Add carrots and turnip or rutabaga and sauté 5 minutes. Add ground cumin and chili powder and cook 1 minute, stirring. Add tomatoes, tomato paste, stock, mushrooms, kidney beans, and seasoning and stir to mix. In a small bowl, blend cornstarch with a little water, then stir into vegetable mixture.

Bring to boil, stirring, then transfer to the cooking pot. Cover, reduce the temperature to LOW, and cook 6 to 8 hours or until vegetables are cooked and tender. Garnish with herb sprigs and serve on a bed of plain rice.

Makes 4 servings.

CHEESY ZUCCHINI STRATA

2 tablespoons butter, plus extra for greasing
1 onion, finely chopped
1 small leek, washed and thinly sliced
2 zucchini, sliced
7 oz. can corn kernels, drained
salt and freshly ground black pepper
9 slices bread, crusts removed and slices cut
  into strips
3 eggs
2½ cups hot milk
2 tablespoons fresh, chopped chives
2 tablespoons fresh, chopped parsley
1 cup shredded cheddar cheese

Preheat the slow cooker on HIGH while preparing ingredients. Butter a 7½ to 9 cup ovenproof soufflé or similar dish and set aside. Melt butter in a pan, add onion, leek, and zucchini, and sauté 8 to 10 minutes or until softened. Remove the pan from the heat and stir in corn and seasoning. Set aside. Place one third of the bread strips in the bottom of the prepared dish. Top with half the zucchini mixture. Repeat layers, ending with a layer of bread.

Whisk together eggs, hot milk, chopped herbs, and seasoning, then pour into the dish over the bread and vegetables. Sprinkle with cheese. Cover dish loosely with buttered aluminum foil. Place in the cooking pot of the slow cooker. Add sufficient boiling water to the cooking pot to come halfway up the sides of the dish. Cover and cook on HIGH 3 to 4 hours (or on LOW 4 to 6 hours) or until lightly set. Serve with broccoli and cauliflower or a mixed salad.

Makes 4 to 6 servings.

VEGETABLE RAGOUT

2 tablespoons olive oil
1 onion, chopped
1 clove garlic, finely chopped
2 carrots, thinly sliced
2 stalks celery, finely chopped
1 green bell pepper, seeded and diced
1 yellow bell pepper, seeded and diced
6 oz. baby corn, halved
8 oz. button mushrooms
2 tablespoons butter
¼ cup all-purpose flour
1¼ cups passata or tomato sauce
⅔ cup medium or dry cider
2 teaspoons dried, mixed herbs
salt and freshly ground black pepper
herb sprigs, to garnish

Preheat the slow cooker on HIGH while preparing ingredients. Heat oil in a pan, add onion, garlic, carrots, celery, bell peppers, and corn, and sauté 5 minutes. Transfer to the cooking pot with mushrooms and set aside. Add butter to the pan and heat until melted. Stir in flour and cook 1 minute, stirring. Gradually stir in passata and cider, then heat gently, stirring continuously, until sauce comes to boil and thickens. Simmer gently 2 minutes, stirring.

Stir in dried herbs and seasoning, then spoon over vegetables in the cooking pot and stir to mix well. Cover, reduce the temperature to LOW, and cook 6 to 8 hours or until vegetables are cooked and tender. Garnish with herb sprigs.

Makes 4 servings.

Note: You can use vegetable stock or wine instead of cider.

HARVEST VEGETABLE STEW

2 tablespoons sunflower oil
6 shallots, sliced
2 leeks, washed and sliced
2 stalks celery, finely chopped
1 red bell pepper, seeded and sliced
about 3 cups diced root vegetables, e.g., carrots,
    parsnips, and rutabaga or turnip
1 cup small cauliflower florets, halved
14½ oz. can chopped tomatoes
⅔ cup vegetable stock
⅔ cup dry white wine or cider
2 teaspoons dried herbes de Provence
salt and freshly ground black pepper
2 tablespoons cornstarch
3 or 4 medium potatoes, peeled and thinly sliced
1 tablespoon butter, melted

Preheat the slow cooker on HIGH while preparing ingredients. Heat oil in a large pan, add shallots, leeks, and celery, and sauté 5 minutes. Add bell pepper, root vegetables, and cauliflower and sauté an additional 5 minutes. Add tomatoes, stock, wine or cider, dried herbs, and seasoning and mix well. In a small bowl, blend cornstarch with a little water, then stir into vegetable mixture. Bring to boil, stirring continuously, until mixture thickens. Simmer gently 2 minutes, stirring.

Spoon one third of the vegetable mixture into the cooking pot, then arrange one third of the potato slices on top. Repeat these layers twice more, finishing with a neat layer of potatoes on top. Cover, reduce the temperature to LOW, and cook 6 to 8 hours or until vegetables are cooked and tender. Brush top layer of potatoes with melted butter and place under a preheated broiler until golden. Garnish with herb sprigs and serve with green beans.

Makes 4 to 6 servings.

ROOT VEGETABLE CURRY

2 tablespoons olive oil
1 red onion, chopped
2 cloves garlic, crushed
1 fresh red chili, seeded and finely chopped
1 in. piece fresh ginger, peeled and finely chopped
1½ lb. mixed root vegetables, e.g., sweet potato, potato, carrots, celery, and rutabaga, diced
2 tablespoons all-purpose flour
2 teaspoons each of ground turmeric, ground coriander, and ground cumin
1½ cups vegetable stock
⅔ cup passata or tomato sauce
⅔ cup golden raisins
salt and freshly ground black pepper
2 or 3 tablespoons fresh, chopped cilantro

Preheat the slow cooker on HIGH while preparing ingredients. Heat oil in a large pan, add onion, garlic, chili, and ginger, and sauté 3 minutes. Add root vegetables and sauté gently 10 minutes. Stir in flour and ground turmeric, coriander, and cumin and cook 1 minute, stirring. Gradually stir in stock and passata, then add golden raisins and seasoning.

Bring to boil, stirring, then transfer to the cooking pot. Cover, reduce the temperature to LOW, and cook 8 to 10 hours or until vegetables are cooked and tender. Stir in chopped cilantro and serve with plain rice.

Makes 4 servings.

FRUIT & NUT PILAF

1 tablespoon olive oil
1 onion, finely chopped
2 cloves garlic, crushed
1 fresh red chili, seeded and finely chopped
1 red bell pepper, seeded and diced
1½ teaspoons ground coriander
1½ teaspoons ground cumin
1¼ cups long-grain rice
⅔ cup golden raisins
1 cup dried apricots, chopped
3¼ cups vegetable stock
3 tablespoons dry sherry
salt and freshly ground black pepper
¾ cup unsalted cashews, toasted
2 tablespoons fresh, chopped cilantro
cilantro sprigs, to garnish

Preheat the slow cooker on HIGH while preparing ingredients. Heat oil in a pan, add onion, garlic, chili, and pepper, and sauté 5 minutes. Add ground coriander and cumin and rice. Cook 1 minute, stirring. Add golden raisins, apricots, stock, sherry, and seasoning and mix well.

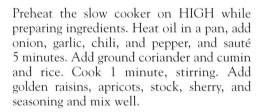

Bring to boil, stirring, then transfer to the cooking pot. Cover and cook on HIGH 1 to 2 hours or until rice is cooked and tender and all liquid has been absorbed. Stir once halfway through cooking time and add a little extra hot stock, if needed. Stir in cashews and chopped cilantro. Garnish with cilantro sprigs and serve with a mixed green salad and cherry tomatoes.

Makes 4 servings.

APRICOT BREAD PUDDING

3 tablespoons butter, softened
6 slices bread, crusts removed
1½ cups dried apricots, finely chopped
3 tablespoons light brown sugar
2 teaspoons ground allspice
3 large eggs
2 cups light cream

Preheat the slow cooker on HIGH while preparing ingredients. Lightly butter a 7½ to 9 cup ovenproof soufflé or similar dish that will sit in your cooking pot and set aside.

Spread butter over bread slices, then cut bread into small triangles or fingers. Arrange half the bread in the bottom of the prepared dish, butter-side up. Mix together apricots, sugar, and allspice and sprinkle over bread. Top with remaining bread, butter-side up. Beat eggs and cream together and pour over bread. Set aside 30 minutes to allow bread to absorb some of the liquid.

Cover with buttered aluminum foil, then place in the cooking pot of the slow cooker. Add sufficient boiling water to the cooking pot to come halfway up the sides of the dish. Cover, reduce temperature to LOW, and cook 3 to 5 hours or until set. Serve with fresh peaches, nectarines, or apricots.

Makes 4 to 6 servings.

Variation: Use golden raisins or dried pears instead of apricots. Use ground cinnamon or ginger instead of allspice.

RHUBARB WITH ORANGE & GINGER

1½ lb. rhubarb, trimmed
⅓ cup light brown sugar
finely grated zest and juice 1 orange
½ cup freshly squeezed orange juice
3 tablespoons preserved ginger syrup
1 teaspoon ground allspice
2 or 3 pieces preserved ginger, finely chopped

Preheat the slow cooker on HIGH while preparing ingredients. Cut rhubarb into 1 in. lengths and place in the cooking pot.

Add sugar and orange zest and stir to mix. Mix orange juice, syrup, and allspice together, pour over rhubarb, and stir to mix. Cover, reduce the temperature to LOW, and cook 4 to 6 hours or until rhubarb is tender.

Stir in chopped preserved ginger and extra sugar, if required. Serve warm or cold with sour cream, custard, or ice cream.

Makes 4 servings.

Variations: Use plums, pitted and halved, instead of rhubarb. Use ground ginger or cinnamon instead of allspice.

WINTER FRUIT COMPOTE

1½ cups dried apricots
⅓ cup dried apple rings
⅔ cup prunes
⅓ cup golden raisins
⅓ cup raisins
1 pear, peeled, cored, and cut into 8 slices
2 cinnamon sticks
thinly pared peel 1 lemon
2½ cups unsweetened apple juice
mint sprigs, to decorate

Preheat the slow cooker on HIGH 15 to 20 minutes. Put dried apricots and apple rings, prunes, golden raisins, raisins, and pear in the cooking pot.

Add cinnamon sticks, lemon peel, and apple juice and stir gently to mix. Cover, reduce the temperature to LOW, and cook 8 to 10 hours or until fruit is plumped up and tender.

Remove and discard cinnamon sticks and lemon peel. Decorate with mint sprigs. Serve compote warm or cold, with sour cream, mascarpone cheese, or plain yogurt.

Makes 6 servings.

Variation: Use your own choice of mixed dried fruits in similar proportions to above, if preferred.

RICE PUDDING WITH ORANGE

2 tablespoons butter
½ cup short-grain rice, rinsed and drained
⅓ cup superfine sugar
3 cups milk
1 cup evaporated milk
finely grated zest 1 large orange
seeds from 3 cardamom pods, crushed
orange peel strips, to decorate

Butter the inside of the cooking pot of the slow cooker with a little of the butter.

Place rice, sugar, milk, evaporated milk, orange zest, and crushed cardamom seeds in the cooking pot and stir to mix.

Dot with any remaining butter. Cover and cook on HIGH 3 to 4 hours (or on LOW 4 to 6 hours) or until the rice is cooked and most of the liquid has been absorbed, stirring once or twice during the final 2 hours of cooking, if possible. Decorate with pared orange zest. Serve rice pudding on its own or with stewed fresh fruit such as plums or warm fruit compote.

Makes 4 to 6 servings.

CLAY POT COOKING

INTRODUCTION

Using terra-cotta pots for cooking is one of the oldest traditions and dates back to Roman times, when the first great gourmets appreciated the fine results that could be obtained by soaking clay pots before cooking in them. The soaked pots absorb water, which generates moisture during cooking to create a unique baking environment that calls for the minimum use of fat and results in maximum flavor. The pot keeps food superbly moist, at the same time encouraging flavors to mingle and preventing rapid overcooking. Basting is largely unnecessary and the covered pot prevents roasts from drying out. While the pot ensures succulent results, the oven is kept free from the usual splashing and spitting associated with most roasting.

Clay pot cooking is, in essence, a means of creating full-flavored dishes with a minimum of effort. It does not involve complicated preparation or specialty techniques, but there are a few basic rules that should be followed. It is important to follow the manufacturer's instructions to prevent damage to the clay pot and to ensure successful recipes.

PREPARING THE CLAY POT FOR COOKING

Wash a new pot in warm water, adding a little dishwashing liquid, and rinse it thoroughly. The first step in preparing a clay pot recipe is to soak the pot in cold water 15 minutes or until you are ready to put the food in the pot. If the pot has never been used before, it should be soaked 30 minutes. Place the pot and lid in the sink. Invert the lid on top of the pot to save space and fill the sink or bowl with cold water to completely submerge the pot and lid.

The unglazed porous pot absorbs water during soaking. As the pot heats in the oven, the water creates a moist cooking atmosphere. Not only does this prevent foods from drying out, but it also encourages some ingredients to create a flavorful cooking liquid. The moist atmosphere promotes tender results when roasting meat and preserves the natural flavor of seafood and vegetables. The material and moisture that is retained in the pot makes it unnecessary to add fat for basic cooking. For example, meat and poultry may be roasted without any additional fat and fish or smaller cuts of meat and poultry may be baked without adding oil or butter.

Above: Tortilla Topper (page 245)

If you intend to use the same clay pot for all types of cooking, do not cook fish as the first food in the pot. Once the pot has been used for other dishes, then it can be used for fish and seafood. Ideally, it is best to keep a separate clay pot for desserts.

COOKING TEMPERATURE AND TEMPERATURE CHANGES

Never expose a clay pot to sudden changes of temperature or to direct heat. Do not place it on the burner or under the broiler. Never place it in a preheated oven. If you are using a gas oven, do not turn the oven to the maximum required setting immediately: Do this in two stages, selecting an intermediate oven temperature for the first 5 minutes. Do not place the clay pot in the freezer. You should also avoid pouring boiling liquid into a cold clay pot or very cold liquid into a hot one.

The clay pot must be placed in a cold oven and heated gradually. Set an electric oven to the required temperature as soon as the pot is placed in it. If using a gas oven, heat the oven in two stages by selecting a low setting for the first 5 minutes, then increase the setting to the required temperature.

A very hot oven—above 400°F—is generally used when cooking in a clay pot. The clay, combined with the moisture from soaking, acts as a barrier to keep food from burning and overcooking. The high temperature rapidly evaporates the moisture retained in the clay to produce the moist baking environment within the pot.

All settings given in the following recipes are for a standard oven. If you have a convection oven, cooking times may be slightly less, depending on the food. Even standard ovens vary slightly and this can be particularly noticeable when cooking food at high temperatures. When you first cook in a clay pot, check on cooking progress about 10 minutes before the suggested cooking time, or 15 minutes if using a convection oven. Once you have used the pot in your oven a few times, you will quickly learn if you need to make any adjustments. The nature of the pot is such that food does not overcook rapidly when the lid is on. Check closely, however, when you remove the lid to brown and crisp any food in the oven.

Below: Stuffed Squash (page 247)

DURING AND AFTER COOKING

Once the clay pot is in the oven and the required temperature setting is reached in a gas oven, the food needs little or no attention for perfect results. The moisture from the pot and the lid ensure that the food does not dry out on the surface, acting, in some ways, as a self-basting cooking method for fish, joints of meat, or whole birds. This enclosed, moist environment also promotes the maximum flavor permeation. By arranging the food in the pot as explained in the recipes, ingredients such as herbs and spices will impart all their flavors to the main food.

Depending on the type of food and cooking time, there may be a certain amount of browning even with the lid on the pot. However, many recipes suggest removing the lid for a short period before the end of cooking, so that roasts, baked dishes, and gratin-style toppings brown and develop a crisp texture. This final stage is very quick because of the heat of the oven.

Before removing the pot from the oven, prepare a dry wooden board or trivet on which to place the hot clay pot. Alternatively, lay a thick, folded dish towel or pot holder on the work surface. Never place the pot on a cold or wet surface. Remember that the same also applies to the lid, so have another suitable stand or cloth ready to hold this when it is removed.

The clay pot makes an attractive serving dish for a variety of foods, particularly soups, gratins, and casseroles. Simply add a garnish and stand the pot on a suitable heatproof mat on the table. (It is a good idea to wrap a decorative cloth around the bottom of the pot for holding the pot when serving the food). Any leftovers should be removed from the pot promptly and transferred to a suitable container for chilling. Cover the container and cool the food quickly, then place it in the refrigerator.

ADAPTING RECIPES FOR CLAY POT COOKING

The clay pot may be used for a wide variety of dishes and you will find it ideal for many of your favorite recipes. For the majority of dishes, the oven temperatures are significantly greater than those used for cooking containers made of other materials. In some cases, the cooking times are also slightly longer. However, when roasting, the higher temperature compensates to a

Below: Buckwheat Pilaf (page 248)

Above: Peach and Blackberry Cobbler (page 251)

large extent for the insulation protection provided by the clay pot. Follow the recipes in this book when adapting your favorite dishes. For example, select one of the roast meat or poultry recipes as a guide when adding your particular choice of seasonings. There are also many basic seafood recipes, casseroles, and vegetable dishes with which to compare other recipes.

CLEANING AND STORING THE CLAY POT

In time the clay pot naturally changes color slightly to develop a not-unattractive "used" appearance—rather like a well-seasoned pan. Never use detergents or abrasive cleaning agents on the clay pot, as these will impair its cooking qualities. Wash the pot promptly after use in hot water with a little dishwashing liquid. Use a brush to scrub the inside of the pot lightly. Rinse well in clean hot water and allow to drain. Leave to dry completely before putting it away. Check your manufacturer's instructions to find out if your clay pot is dishwasher-proof. Remove any food residue first by rinsing the hot pot under very hot water.

If the pot is stained or has any baked-on residue, it should be soaked for several hours or overnight in very hot water with washing soda added. If the pot is still stained, pour off the soaking water, add cold water and washing soda with a little dishwashing liquid, then put the pot in the cold oven. Set the oven at 350°F and leave 30 minutes. Increase the oven temperature to 450°F and leave an additional 40 to 60 minutes. Allow to stand 15 minutes. Scrub the inside of the pot gently with boiling water, then rinse in plenty of clean, boiling water and allow to dry.

After use, allow the washed clay pot to dry completely. Then invert the lid in the pot and place it in a cool, dry cupboard. Do not put the lid on the pot as for cooking, and do not store the pot while it is still damp or keep it in damp conditions. Do not seal the pot in a plastic bag. If the pot is damp when stored, not thoroughly cleaned, or left in a damp place, mold can grow on the clay. This will need to be removed by soaking and baking with washing soda, as described above. If the pot has been out of use for some time, then wash it thoroughly, particularly if it has been accidentally stored in damp or dusty conditions.

PEA SOUP

BEAN & SAUSAGE SOUP

1 cup dried peas, soaked overnight
2 tablespoons oil
1 onion, chopped
2 potatoes, diced
1 bay leaf
1 rosemary sprig
1 teaspoon dried marjoram
5 cups ham or chicken stock
1½ cups diced, cooked ham
salt and pepper
pinch grated nutmeg
croutons, to serve

1¼ cups black beans or pinto beans, soaked
   overnight
2 tablespoons oil
1 large onion, chopped
1 clove garlic, crushed
1 green chili, seeded and chopped
4 stalks celery, diced
1 carrot, diced
1 tablespoon ground coriander
½ teaspoon ground mace
pinch ground cloves
3¾ cups chicken stock (unsalted)
1 lb. smoked pork sausage
2 tablespoons all-purpose flour
2 tablespoons tomato paste
sour cream and paprika, to serve

Drain peas and place in the soaked clay pot.
Heat oil in a saucepan. Add onion, potatoes,
bay leaf, and rosemary. Cook, stirring often,
10 minutes until onion is softened. Stir
in marjoram.

Drain beans and place in a saucepan with
cold water to cover. Bring to boil and boil
rapidly 10 minutes. Drain beans and place in
the soaked clay pot. Heat oil in a saucepan.
Add onion, garlic, chili, celery, and carrot,
and cook 10 minutes until onion is softened.
Stir in coriander, mace, and cloves and cook
2 minutes. Add onion mixture to beans in
the clay pot, then pour in stock. Cover the
pot and place in a cold oven. Set the oven at
400°F and cook 2 hours.

Tip onion mixture into the pot, then pour in
stock and stir well. Add ham. Sprinkle in a
little pepper and nutmeg but do not add salt
at this stage. Cover the pot and place in a
cold oven. Set the oven at 400°F. Cook 2 to
2½ hours or until peas are thoroughly tender.
Taste for seasoning and sprinkle with
croutons before serving.

Makes 6 servings.

Meanwhile, cut sausages into chunks. Stir
flour to a paste with 3 tablespoons cold water,
add a little of the hot soup, then pour mixture
into the pot. Add sausage and tomato paste,
and cook, covered, an additional 1 hour. Stir
in seasoning to taste and mash some of the
beans slightly. Serve topped with sour cream
and paprika.

Makes 4 servings.

SPICY MULLIGATAWNY

3 tablespoons oil
2 onions, chopped
1 clove garlic, crushed
1 potato, diced
2 carrots, diced
2 tablespoons ground coriander
1 tablespoon cumin seeds
6 cardamom pods
1 bay leaf
1¼ cups red lentils
salt and pepper
6¼ cups chicken stock
¼ cup plain yogurt
chopped cilantro, to garnish

Heat oil in a saucepan. Add onions, garlic, potato, and carrots and cook 10 minutes, stirring all the time, until onion is slightly softened. Stir in ground coriander and cumin seeds and cook 2 minutes, then turn mixture into the soaked clay pot. Add cardamom pods, bay leaf, and lentils. Sprinkle in seasoning, mix well, then stir in stock.

Cover pot and place in a cold oven. Set the oven at 400°F. Cook 1½ to 2 hours, stirring once. The lentils should be cooked until mushy, so that they thicken the soup, and vegetables should be very tender. Taste for seasoning, then serve each portion topped with a little yogurt and sprinkled with cilantro.

Makes 4 servings.

LEEK & POTATO SOUP

1 tablespoon butter
1 tablespoon oil
1 lb. leeks, sliced
4 or 5 medium potatoes, diced
1 tablespoon all-purpose flour
2 cups chicken stock
salt and pepper
1 bay leaf
2 tarragon sprigs or 1 teaspoon dried tarragon
2 cups milk

Heat butter and oil in a large saucepan. Reserve a few pieces of leek for garnish. Add remaining leeks and potatoes, then cook, stirring, about 5 minutes until leeks are slightly softened. Stir in flour, then pour in stock, stirring all the time.

Transfer leek and potato mixture to the soaked clay pot. Stir in seasoning, bay leaf, and tarragon. Cover the pot and place in a cold oven. Set the oven at 400°F. Cook 50 minutes. Gradually stir milk into soup. Cook, covered, an additional 40 minutes until vegetables are tender. Serve soup either chunky or blended until smooth in a blender. Taste for seasoning before serving, garnished with reserved leeks.

Makes 4 servings.

HALIBUT ON VEGETABLES

2¼ lb. small new potatoes
1½ cups shelled fresh peas
4 small carrots, thinly sliced
4 small zucchini, trimmed and thinly sliced
6 scallions, chopped
salt and pepper
grated zest and juice 1 lime
1½ lb. halibut fillet, cut into 4 portions
1 tablespoon chopped tarragon
½ stick butter, melted

TUNA BAKE

1¼ cups long-grain rice
1 onion, chopped
1 green bell pepper, seeded and diced
2½ cups vegetable or chicken stock
salt and pepper
15¼ oz. can corn kernels
9 oz. can tuna, drained and flaked
1 cup light cream or plain yogurt
1 cup shredded cheese
parsley sprigs, to garnish

Cook potatoes in boiling water 8 to 10 minutes until almost tender. Drain and place in the soaked clay pot. Blanch peas in boiling water 5 minutes, drain, and set aside. Blanch carrots 2 minutes, then add to potatoes. Add zucchini, scallions, seasoning, and lime zest to vegetables in the pot and mix well. Arrange halibut on top of vegetables, add a little seasoning, then sprinkle with tarragon, lime juice, and melted butter.

Mix rice, onion, and bell pepper in the soaked clay pot. Pour in stock and add seasoning to taste. Cover the pot and place in a cold oven. Set the oven at 425°F. Cook 40 minutes or until rice is almost tender and most of the stock is absorbed.

Cover the pot and place in a cold oven. Set the oven at 425°F. Cook 30 minutes. Add peas, carefully arranging them between halibut portions, then cook an additional 5 to 10 minutes or until halibut is cooked and vegetables are tender.

Makes 4 servings.

Fork corn, tuna, cream or yogurt, and two thirds of the shredded cheese into rice mixture. Sprinkle with remaining cheese and cook, uncovered, an additional 10 minutes or until lightly browned. Garnish with parsley and serve.

Makes 4 servings.

SPICED FISH WITH SPINACH

1 lb. spinach, trimmed
½ stick butter or margarine
2 cloves garlic
3 tablespoons grated ginger
1 tablespoon cumin seeds
4 cardamom pods
1 tablespoon ground coriander
1 teaspoon ground turmeric
2 tablespoons plain yogurt
salt and pepper
8 oz. cooked, peeled shrimp
8 flounder fillets, skinned
4 tomatoes, peeled (see page 174) and chopped
1 tablespoon chopped cilantro
lemon wedges, to garnish

Wash spinach, then put wet leaves in a large saucepan. Cover and cook over high heat, shaking the pan often, about 5 minutes or until leaves have wilted. Drain well, then place spinach in the soaked clay pot. Melt butter or margarine in pan. Add garlic and ginger and cook 3 minutes, stirring. Add cumin seeds, cardamom pods, ground coriander, and turmeric and cook an additional 2 minutes. Remove from heat and stir in yogurt and plenty of seasoning.

Spread shrimp out over spinach. Arrange fish fillets over the top, then spoon spice mixture over. Cover the pot and place in a cold oven. Set the oven at 425°F. Cook 40 minutes or until fish is just firm. Top with tomatoes and sprinkle with chopped cilantro, then serve garnished with lemon wedges.

Makes 4 servings.

Note: Basmati rice and naan bread are ideal accompaniments to this dish.

FISHERMAN'S FAVORITE

1½ lb. white fish fillet, skinned and cut into chunks
grated zest and juice 1 lemon
salt and pepper
8 oz. mushrooms, sliced
¼ cup chopped parsley
4 scallions, chopped
1½ cups shredded cheese
¼ cup dry cider or white wine
½ cup cream cheese
6 medium potatoes, cooked and sliced
pat butter

Lay half the fish in the soaked clay pot. Top with half the lemon zest and juice and season well. Add half the mushrooms, parsley, and scallions, then sprinkle with about one third of the shredded cheese. Repeat layers once more. Pour cider or wine over ingredients and dot evenly with cream cheese. Finally, cover with a layer of potato, overlapping slices neatly. Sprinkle with remaining shredded cheese and dot with butter.

Cover pot and place in a cold oven. Set the oven at 425°F. Cook 35 minutes. Uncover the pot and cook an additional 15 minutes or until potato topping is golden brown and layers of fish are cooked through.

Makes 4 servings.

SEAFOOD WITH FENNEL

½ stick butter
2 tablespoons olive oil
1 onion, sliced
2 bulbs fennel, sliced
salt and pepper
2 × 14½ oz. cans chopped tomatoes
8 oz. cooked, peeled shrimp
8 oz. cooked, shelled mussels
8 raw, shelled scallops
1 lb. white fish fillet, skinned and cut in chunks
10 black olives, pitted and sliced
4 large sprigs basil, shredded
freshly grated Parmesan cheese, to serve

OYSTERS ROCKEFELLER

2 tablespoons butter
2 tablespoons finely chopped onion
2 tablespoons chopped celery leaves
3 cups shredded fresh spinach leaves
salt and pepper
24 oysters, opened and liquid reserved
2 tablespoons chopped parsley
1 cup fresh bread crumbs
3 tablespoons light cream
1 tablespoon Pastis, Pernod, or other aniseed liqueur
dash Tabasco

Melt butter with oil in a saucepan. Add onion and fennel. Sprinkle in plenty of seasoning and cook, stirring often, 20 minutes or until onion and fennel are softened. Stir in tomatoes and bring to boil. Simmer 3 minutes, then turn mixture into the soaked clay pot.

Melt butter in a large saucepan. Add onion, celery leaves, and spinach. Cook, stirring, until spinach wilts, then continue to cook over fairly high heat about 10 minutes or until excess moisture has evaporated. Reduce heat. Stir in seasoning and liquid from oysters. Add parsley and half the bread crumbs. Spoon mixture into the soaked clay pot and spread it out evenly.

Mix shrimp, mussels, and scallops into tomato and fennel mixture in the pot. Add white fish, distributing chunks on the surface of the tomato mixture. Cover the pot and place in a cold oven. Set the oven at 425°F. Cook 35 minutes or until fish is cooked. Taste for seasoning, then combine fish gently with fennel and sauce, adding olives and basil. Serve at once, with Parmesan cheese, accompanied by rice, pasta, or chunks of crusty bread.

Makes 4 servings.

Arrange oysters on spinach. Mix cream, aniseed liqueur, and a small dash of Tabasco, then trickle this mixture over oysters. Sprinkle with remaining bread crumbs. Cover the pot and place in a cold oven. Set the oven at 425°F. Cook 30 minutes. Uncover the pot and cook an additional 5 minutes to brown crumbs slightly.

Makes 4 to 6 servings.

CHICKEN WITH BROCCOLI

8 chicken thighs
2 tablespoons all-purpose flour
salt and pepper
2 tablespoons oil
1 teaspoon fresh (chopped) or dried thyme
1 tablespoon fresh, chopped or 1½ teaspoons dried sage
1 cup dry white wine
2 cups broccoli florets
½ cup sour cream

CHICKEN BOULANGÈRE

1 lemon, sliced
2 bay leaves
6 medium potatoes, sliced
1 large onion, thinly sliced
¼ cup chopped tarragon
salt and pepper
2 tablespoons butter, melted
4 chicken quarters

Dust chicken thighs all over with flour and plenty of seasoning. Heat oil in a skillet. Brown chicken portions all over, then transfer to the soaked clay pot. Add any remaining flour to pan juices, stir in thyme and sage, then pour in wine. Pour this sauce over chicken. Cover the pot and place in a cold oven. Set the oven at 425°F. Cook 30 minutes.

Lay half the lemon slices in the bottom of the soaked clay pot. Add bay leaves, then layer potatoes and onion on top. Sprinkle with half the tarragon and plenty of seasoning. Drizzle with half the melted butter. Arrange chicken quarters on top of vegetables. Season well and sprinkle with remaining tarragon. Drizzle rest of melted butter over chicken, then tuck remaining lemon slices around portions.

Meanwhile, blanch broccoli spears in boiling salted water 3 minutes and drain well. Add spears to the pot, tucking them between chicken, and baste with sauce. Cook, covered, an additional 15 minutes or until chicken is thoroughly cooked. Transfer chicken and broccoli to warmed serving plates. Stir sour cream into sauce, check seasoning, then spoon it over chicken.

Makes 4 servings.

Cover the pot and place in a cold oven. Set the oven at 425°F. Cook 40 minutes. Uncover the pot and cook an additional 15 to 20 minutes or until chicken quarters are cooked through, crisp, and golden. The vegetables should be tender. Serve chicken with vegetables, discarding lemon slices or using them as a garnish.

Makes 4 servings.

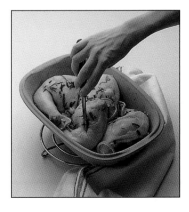

CHICKEN WITH EGGPLANT

2 large eggplants, sliced
salt and pepper
½ stick butter
1 onion, sliced
1 tablespoon ground coriander
8 thyme sprigs
5 oranges
grated nutmeg
4 chicken quarters

FESTIVE CHICKEN

4 chicken fillets
salt and pepper
½ teaspoon ground mace
2 tablespoons butter
4 pearl onions, halved
1 tablespoon all-purpose flour
¼ cup brandy
1 cup dry white wine
2 cups dried apricots, halved
⅔ cup prunes, halved
4 bay leaves
4 oz. small button mushrooms

Place eggplant slices in a colander, sprinkling each layer with salt. Set aside over a bowl 30 minutes. Rinse and pat dry, then place in the soaked clay pot. Melt half the butter in a skillet, add onion, and cook 3 minutes. Sprinkle eggplant with coriander, then spread onion slices on top and pour cooking juices over. Place chicken portions in the pot, tucking a thyme sprig under each one.

Make two or three small cuts across each chicken portion, then season well and sprinkle with mace. Melt butter in a skillet and brown chicken, then put in the soaked clay pot. Brown onions in butter in the pan, then transfer to the pot.

Grate zest and squeeze juice from 1 orange and sprinkle over chicken portions with some grated nutmeg and seasoning. Cover the pot and place in a cold oven. Set the oven at 425°F. Cook 40 minutes. Cut all peel and pith from remaining oranges, then slice, discarding seeds. Arrange around chicken and dot with remaining butter. Cook, uncovered, an additional 15 to 20 minutes. Serve garnished with remaining thyme sprigs.

Makes 4 servings.

Stir flour into remaining fat. Pour in brandy and wine, then bring to boil, stirring. Add apricots, prunes, bay leaves, and mushrooms. Stir well, then pour mixture over chicken. Cover the pot and place in a cold oven. Set the oven at 425°F. Cook 50 minutes or until chicken is cooked through. Taste sauce for seasoning and serve.

Makes 4 servings.

CHICKEN CHEERIO

8 chicken thighs
1 tablespoon cornstarch
salt and pepper
1 teaspoon ground ginger
2 × 15 oz. cans chickpeas
15 oz. can artichoke hearts, drained
grated zest and juice 1 lemon
6 cardamom pods
4 bay leaves
½ cup chicken stock
1 tablespoon pistachio or walnut oil
2 tablespoons sunflower oil

Dust chicken thighs with cornstarch, seasoning, and ginger. Tip chickpeas and can liquid into the soaked clay pot. Mix in artichoke hearts. Arrange chicken portions on top, then sprinkle with lemon zest and juice.

Add cardamom pods and bay leaves. Pour in stock. Drizzle pistachio or walnut oil over chicken first, then top with sunflower oil. Cover the pot and place in a cold oven. Set the oven at 450°F. Cook 35 minutes. Baste chicken with cooking juices and cook, uncovered, an additional 10 to 15 minutes to brown chicken.

Makes 4 servings.

TURKEY WITH BELL PEPPERS

1 lb. boneless turkey breast, cut into chunks
2 tablespoons all-purpose flour
salt and pepper
3 tablespoons olive oil
1 clove garlic, crushed
1 onion, halved and sliced
1 green bell pepper, seeded and thinly sliced
1 red bell pepper, seeded and thinly sliced
1 teaspoon dried marjoram
8 plum tomatoes, chopped
1 cup red wine
12 black olives, pitted and sliced
handful of basil leaves
8 taco shells, to serve (optional)
½ cup sour cream

Coat turkey with flour and plenty of seasoning and place in the soaked clay pot. Heat oil in a skillet. Add garlic, onion, and bell peppers and cook 5 minutes, then pour mixture over turkey. Top with marjoram and tomatoes, then pour in wine. Cover the pot and place in a cold oven. Set the oven at 450°F. Cook 50 minutes, stirring the mixture once or until turkey is well cooked.

Stir in olives. Reserve some basil for garnish, then use scissors to shred remaining leaves and soft stems. Mix shredded basil into turkey mixture and taste for seasoning. The mixture may be served in taco shells. Heat shells on a baking sheet in the oven 2 or 3 minutes before turkey is cooked. Spoon mixture into shells. Spoon a little sour cream over turkey and garnish with basil. Serve at once.

Makes 4 servings.

DUCK WITH BABY CORN

4 boneless duck breasts
2 tablespoons oil
2 teaspoons walnut or pistachio oil
salt and pepper
1 teaspoon paprika
2 tablespoons chopped, mixed herbs
8 oz. baby corn
4 oz. mange-tout
1 small leek, white part only, sliced
¼ cup dry sherry
¼ cup shelled pistachio nuts
herb sprigs, to garnish

GARLIC DUCK WITH LENTILS

2 garlic heads
4 duck quarters
grated zest and juice 1 lime
⅓ cup chopped parsley
4 savory or thyme sprigs
2 blades of mace
1 cinnamon stick
salt and pepper
1¾ cups green lentils
1 large onion, chopped
2 tablespoons all-purpose flour
1 cup chicken stock

Prick skin on duck portions, then place in the soaked clay pot. Sprinkle with both oils, salt and pepper, paprika, and herbs. Cover the pot and place in a cold oven. Set at 450°F. Cook 40 minutes. Meanwhile, add baby corn to a small saucepan of boiling water and boil 3 minutes. Add leeks and cook 1 minute, then add mange-tout, shake the pan, and drain at once. Set aside.

Peel garlic cloves. Place in a small saucepan and pour in water to cover. Bring to boil, reduce the heat, and cover the pan. Simmer 20 minutes, then drain. Prick duck portions, place in the soaked clay pot, and add garlic cloves around them. Sprinkle with lime zest and juice and parsley. Add thyme, mace, and cinnamon, tucking them under duck. Season well. Cover the pot and place in a cold oven. Set at 425°F. Cook 40 minutes.

Remove duck from the pot. Put in all vegetables, toss in cooking juices, then replace duck on top. Sprinkle sherry over, then pistachio nuts. Return the pot, uncovered, to the oven and cook an additional 15 minutes. Garnish with herb sprigs and serve at once with fresh noodles, couscous, or a mixture of wild rice and basmati rice.

Makes 4 servings.

Meanwhile, place lentils in a saucepan with water to cover. Add onion and bring to boil. Reduce the heat, cover, and simmer 30 minutes. Drain. Drain cooking juices from duck into a saucepan. Stir in flour and heat, then add stock and bring to boil, stirring. Add seasoning. Set duck joints aside, pour lentils into the pot, then replace duck on top. Pour in sauce. Return the pot, uncovered, to the oven and cook an additional 15 minutes.

Makes 4 servings.

IRISH STEW

8 middle neck lamb chops or cutlets
salt and pepper
2 bay leaves
6 parsley sprigs
6 thyme sprigs
4 small rosemary sprigs
2 large onions, thinly sliced
4 to 6 carrots, sliced
4 large potatoes, sliced
1 tablespoon butter, melted

NOISETTES WITH CALVADOS

2 tablespoons oil
1 onion, finely chopped
2 dessert apples, peeled, cored, and sliced
3 cups shelled fresh peas
1 bay leaf
salt and pepper
1 cup medium-dry cider
4 mint sprigs
8 thick lamb noisettes
¼ cup Calvados or brandy
1 small head romaine, coarsely shredded
mint sprigs, to garnish

Trim any excess fat from chops, then place four of them in the soaked clay pot. Add plenty of seasoning and top with a bay leaf and three parsley, three thyme, and two rosemary sprigs. Add layers of onion, carrot, and potato, seasoning each lightly. Then place remaining lamb in the pot, season well, and add remaining herbs and vegetables as before, ending with a neat layer of potatoes.

Heat half the oil in a skillet. Add onion and cook 5 minutes, then mix in apples, peas, bay leaf, and seasoning. Turn mixture into the soaked clay pot and pour in cider. Top with mint sprigs.

Pour in 2½ cups water. Cover the pot and place in a cold oven. Set the oven at 425°F. Cook 2½ hours. Brush top of potatoes with butter and cook, uncovered, an additional 20 minutes until browned. Serve with cabbage.

Makes 4 servings.

Note: Neck of lamb may be used instead of chops or cutlets.

Heat remaining oil in the skillet. Quickly brown noisettes on all sides. Pour Calvados or brandy over lamb, ignite, and allow to burn out. Then arrange noisettes on top of vegetables in the pot. Season well. Cover the pot and place in a cold oven. Set at 425°F. Cook 40 minutes. Uncover the pot, add romaine, and cook an additional 10 minutes. Serve garnished with mint.

Makes 4 servings.

SULTAN'S PILAF

2 tablespoons butter
1 lb. lean boneless lamb, diced
2 onions, sliced
1 clove garlic
1 cinnamon stick
4 cloves
1 bay leaf
pared peel 1 lemon
salt and pepper
2½ cups chicken stock
1 cup dry white wine
1¼ cups long-grain rice
2 tablespoons chopped dates
1½ cups frozen peas
4 hard-boiled eggs, quartered
1 lemon, cut into wedges

Melt butter in a large skillet. Brown lamb all over, then use a slotted spoon to transfer meat to the soaked clay pot. Add onions to fat in the pan and cook 2 minutes, then transfer two thirds to the pot and continue cooking remainder until golden brown. Drain and set aside. Add a little of the stock to the pan, stir well, then pour it into the pot. Add remaining stock, garlic, spices, bay leaf, and lemon zest. Season well.

Cover the pot and place in a cold oven. Set the oven at 425°F. Cook 1 hour or until meat is extremely tender. Add wine, rice, and dates and cook, covered, an additional 15 minutes. Stir in peas. Cook, covered, for a final 20 minutes, then let stand, without removing the lid, 15 minutes. Serve pilaf garnished with eggs, lemon wedges, and reserved onions.

Makes 4 to 6 servings.

LAMB WITH CAULIFLOWER

1½ lb. lean boneless lamb, diced
3 tablespoons all-purpose flour
salt and pepper
2 tablespoons oil
1 onion, halved and sliced
1 cup lamb or chicken stock
1 cup dry white wine or cider
1 tablespoon chopped mint
2 tablespoons chopped fennel
½ teaspoon ground mace
1 cauliflower, broken into small florets
½ cup sour cream (optional)
mint and fennel sprigs, to garnish

Toss lamb with flour and plenty of seasoning. Heat oil in a skillet and brown meat. Add onion with any remaining flour. Stir 2 minutes, then pour in stock and wine. Add half the mint and fennel and stir well. Transfer to the soaked clay pot. Add mace. Cover the pot and place in a cold oven. Set the oven at 425°F. Cook 50 minutes.

Add cauliflower to the pot, stirring florets into meat mixture. Cook, covered, an additional 40 minutes until lamb is tender and cauliflower cooked. Taste for seasoning, then lightly mix in remaining mint and fennel. Serve topped with sour cream, and garnished with mint and/or fennel.

Makes 4 servings.

Note: New potatoes and peas are excellent accompaniments to this dish.

PORK WITH SAUERKRAUT

1 clove garlic, crushed
1 teaspoon paprika
salt and pepper
1 pork tenderloin
8 slices smoked bacon
2 tablespoons butter
1 large onion, chopped
1 teaspoon caraway seeds
2 cups sauerkraut
1 cup dry white wine
parsley sprigs, to garnish

Mix together garlic, paprika, and a little salt and pepper. Rub this mixture all over pork. Stretch bacon slices out thinly with the back of a knife. Wrap slices around tenderloin to enclose it completely, tying them neatly in place.

Melt butter in a small saucepan and cook onion with caraway seeds 5 minutes. Squeeze liquid from sauerkraut, then slice it. Place sauerkraut in the soaked clay pot, then mix in onion and pour wine over. Lay pork on top. Cover the pot and place in a cold oven. Set the oven at 425°F. Cook 50 minutes. Uncover the pot and cook an additional 15 minutes. Untie and slice pork, serve on sauerkraut, and garnish.

Makes 4 servings.

PORK WITH RED CABBAGE

3 lb. rolled loin of pork
2 teaspoons fresh or ¾ teaspoon dried thyme
¼ teaspoon ground allspice
salt and pepper
2 cloves garlic, crushed
1 tablespoon oil
1 onion, thinly sliced
1 carrot, coarsely shredded
1½ lb. red cabbage, shredded
2 cooking apples, peeled, cored, and sliced
2 bay leaves
2 tablespoons brown sugar
2 tablespoons wine vinegar
1 cup red wine
2 teaspoons cornstarch

Rub pork all over with thyme, allspice, salt and pepper, and garlic. Heat oil in a large skillet, then roll pork in it over high heat to sear rind. Mix onion, carrot, cabbage, and apples together in the soaked clay pot. Tuck bay leaves into vegetables. Sprinkle with salt and pepper, add sugar, vinegar, and wine. Place pork, with oil from searing, on top of cabbage mixture. Cover the pot and place in a cold oven. Set the oven at 425°F. Cook 1½ hours.

Mix cornstarch with a little water, then add a little of the cooking liquid before stirring mixture into vegetables and juices around pork. Cook, covered, 15 minutes, then uncover pot and cook for a final 15 minutes. Transfer meat to a serving platter and serve cut in thick slices. Turn cabbage into a serving dish.

Makes 6 servings.

Note: Creamy mashed potatoes are an excellent accompaniment to this dish.

PORK STEW WITH SALSA

1 lb. lean boneless pork, diced
3 tablespoons all-purpose flour
salt and pepper
¼ cup olive oil
4 sage sprigs
2 onions, finely chopped
1 cup medium-dry cider
4 large potatoes, diced
2 or 3 medium tomatoes, peeled and chopped
1 green chili, seeded and chopped
1 clove garlic, crushed
1 tablespoon superfine sugar
1 tablespoon lime or lemon juice
1 tablespoon sesame seeds
¼ cup chopped parsley
½ cup light cream

Toss pork with flour and plenty of seasoning. Heat half the oil in a skillet and brown pork, then transfer to the soaked clay pot. Fry sage and half the chopped onion in oil remaining in the pan, then stir in any leftover flour and the cider. Pour this sauce over pork. Mix in potatoes. Cover the pot and place in a cold oven. Set the oven at 425°F. Cook 1½ hours.

Mix remaining onion and oil with tomato, chili, garlic, sugar, lime or lemon juice, and seasoning. Dry-fry sesame seeds in a small saucepan until they are lightly browned, shaking often. Add sesame seeds to tomato salsa and stir well. Set aside for at least 1 hour. Taste pork for seasoning and add parsley. Stir in cream and serve at once, with salsa to top individual portions.

Makes 4 servings.

PORK CHOPS WITH SQUASH

1 tablespoon oil
1 large onion, chopped
about 6 cups diced squash flesh
1 teaspoon ground cinnamon
grated nutmeg
salt and pepper
4 pork chops
4 rosemary sprigs
grated zest and juice 1 orange
halved orange slices, to garnish

Heat oil in a large skillet. Add onion and cook 2 minutes, stir in squash, then turn mixture into the soaked clay pot. Sprinkle with cinnamon, a little grated nutmeg, and seasoning. Lay pork chops on top and tuck rosemary in between. Season chops, then sprinkle with orange zest and juice.

Cover pot and place in a cold oven. Set the oven at 450°F. Cook 1 hour. Baste chops with cooking juices and cook, uncovered, an additional 5 to 10 minutes. Garnish with orange slices and rosemary sprigs used in cooking. Serve with baked potatoes topped with sour cream.

Makes 4 servings.

SPICY PORK WITH BANANA

SWEET & SPICY RIBS

1½ lb. lean boneless pork, diced
1 tablespoon ground coriander
1 teaspoon paprika
¼ teaspoon ground cloves
1 teaspoon ground mace
salt and pepper
2 cloves garlic, crushed
1 teaspoon sesame oil
2 tablespoons sunflower oil
grated zest and juice 1 lime
1 cup coconut milk
2 plantains or unripe bananas, halved lengthwise
  and sliced
2 tablespoons chopped cilantro
1 lime, cut into wedges

4 lb. meaty pork spareribs
8 carrots
1 onion, finely chopped
2 tablespoons honey
juice 1 lemon
1 tablespoon curry powder
salt and pepper

Place spareribs in the soaked clay pot. Cut carrots in half, then quarter pieces lengthwise.

Place pork in a bowl. Add coriander, paprika, ground cloves, mace, seasoning, garlic, sesame and sunflower oils, and lime zest and juice. Mix well, cover, and let marinate 24 hours. Tip mixture into the soaked clay pot. Pour in coconut milk and stir well. Cover the pot and place in a cold oven. Set the oven at 450°F. Cook 45 minutes. Then add plantains (if using) and mix lightly.

Add carrots to spareribs in the clay pot and sprinkle with chopped onion. Mix together honey, lemon juice, curry powder, and plenty of seasoning, then trickle mixture evenly over spareribs. Cover the pot and place in a cold oven. Set the oven at 475°F and cook 1 hour.

Cook, covered, an additional 20 minutes. If using bananas (which require less cooking than plantains), stir them in at this stage. Finally, cook, uncovered, 10 minutes or until pork is tender and well flavored. Sprinkle with chopped cilantro and serve at once, with lime wedges for their juice.

Makes 4 servings.

Transfer carrots to a serving dish and keep hot. Rearrange spareribs and baste with juices, then cook, uncovered, turning ribs once more, an additional 20 minutes or until well browned.

Makes 4 servings.

CABBAGE, POTATO & HAM BAKE

1½ lb. cabbage (white or green), shredded
2 onions, thinly sliced
4 large potatoes, thinly sliced
8 slices bacon, diced (optional)
2 bay leaves
salt and pepper
1 cup milk
1 tablespoon butter

PORK CHILI

1 lb. lean boneless pork, diced
2 tablespoons all-purpose flour
2 teaspoons ground cumin
1 teaspoon oregano
salt and pepper
2 tablespoons oil
2 cloves garlic, crushed
2 onions, halved and sliced
2 to 4 canned jalapeño chilies, chopped
2 × 15 oz. cans red kidney beans, drained
1 cup vegetable stock
2 avocados
2 tablespoons chopped cilantro
1 tablespoon chopped mint
1 lime, cut into wedges

Layer cabbage, onions, potatoes, and bacon (if using) in the soaked clay pot, ending with a layer of potato on top. Add bay leaves somewhere around the middle of the pot and season the layers well, especially if not using bacon. Pour milk over. Cover the pot and place in a cold oven. Set the oven at 425°F. Cook 1 hour.

Mix pork with flour, cumin, oregano, and plenty of seasoning. Heat oil in a skillet and quickly brown meat. Add garlic and onions and cook 2 minutes, then turn mixture into the soaked clay pot. Add chilies (see Note), kidney beans, and stock. Cover the pot and place in a cold oven. Set the oven at 450°F. Cook 1¼ hours or until meat is very tender.

Dot potatoes with butter and cook, uncovered, an additional 15 minutes or until golden brown.

Makes 4 servings.

Variation: Thinly sliced smoked sausage is also delicious layered with potatoes.

When chili is cooked, halve, pit, and peel avocados, then slice. Top each portion of chili with cilantro, mint, and avocado. Serve lime wedges for their juice.

Makes 4 servings.

Note: Make chili as hot as you like by adding more jalapeño chilies. Canned jalapeños are quite mild and a whole small can will not make the dish too fiery. Fresh chilies, particularly small ones, are very hot.

STUFFED BELL PEPPERS

4 green bell peppers
8 oz. pork sausage meat
8 oz. (1 cup) ground beef
1 tablespoon dried basil
3 tablespoons fresh, chopped or 1 tablespoon
  dried sage
1 cup fresh bread crumbs
1 onion, chopped
1 egg
salt and pepper
sage sprigs and tomato wedges, to garnish

SQUASH WITH CHORIZO

1 large onion, finely chopped
about 6 cups diced squash flesh
8 oz. small button mushrooms
12 oz. chorizo, sliced
salt and pepper
2 bay leaves
4 thyme sprigs
2 avocados
juice 1 lime
1 teaspoon sugar
1 cup sour cream (optional)
lime slices and thyme sprigs, to garnish

Slice tops off bell peppers and set aside, then scoop out all seeds and pith. Rinse and drain upside down. Mix together sausage meat, ground beef, basil, sage, bread crumbs, onion, and egg. Add plenty of seasoning and make sure all ingredients are thoroughly combined. Divide mixture into four and pack one portion into each of the bell peppers. Replace tops on peppers and stand them in the soaked clay pot.

Place onion, squash, mushrooms, and chorizo in the soaked clay pot. Mix in seasoning, then add bay leaf and thyme. Sprinkle squash mixture with ½ cup water. Cover the pot and place in a cold oven. Set the oven at 425°F. Cook 1 hour or until squash is tender. Stir once during cooking.

Cover the pot and place in a cold oven. Set the oven at 475°F. Cook 50 minutes or until peppers are thoroughly tender and meat filling is cooked through. Serve piping hot, with rice or pasta tossed with Parmesan cheese. Garnish with sage and tomato.

Makes 4 servings.

Just before squash is cooked, halve avocados and remove pits. Peel and dice flesh, then mix it with lime juice and sugar. Serve squash mixture topped with sour cream (if using) and diced avocado mixture.

Makes 4 to 6 servings.

CORNED BEEF SPECIAL

1 large onion, sliced
4 lb. rolled joint of corned beef or beef brisket
salt and pepper
1 tablespoon pickling spice
1 cup red wine
4 bay leaves
4 sprigs parsley
1 small green cabbage, cut into wedges
6 carrots, sliced
6 large potatoes, halved

Separate onion slices into rings and spread over the bottom of the soaked clay pot. Place beef on top. If using brisket, sprinkle with salt. Add pepper and pickling spice, then pour in wine and ½ cup water. Add bay leaves and parsley sprigs, tucking them around joint.

Cover the pot and place in a cold oven. Set the oven at 450°F. Cook 1½ hours. Arrange cabbage, carrots, and potatoes in the pot. Pour in ½ cup hot water. Cook, covered, an additional 1 hour, until meat is cooked through and vegetables are tender. Transfer meat and vegetables to a serving platter. Carve joint into thick slices to serve. Serve cooking juices separately.

Makes 6 servings.

POT ROAST

3 lb. piece chuck steak
salt and pepper
2 large onions, thickly sliced
4 carrots, thickly sliced
2 parsnips, thickly sliced
½ teaspoon ground mace
1 bouquet garni
4 slices bacon
2 cups stout
6 large potatoes, quartered

Tie meat into a neat shape, then season it well all over. Sprinkle onions over the bottom of the soaked clay pot. Top with a layer of carrots and another of parsnips. Add mace and bouquet garni, then place meat on top of herbs. Cover meat with bacon slices and pour in stout. Add 1 cup water. Cover the pot and place in a cold oven. Set the oven at 450°F. Cook 1½ hours.

Baste meat well and add potatoes to the pot, arranging them around meat. Cook, uncovered, an additional 45 minutes until potatoes are tender and meat is cooked through. Transfer meat to a serving plate with vegetables. Strain cooking liquid and serve separately.

Makes 6 servings.

BRISKET WITH JUNIPER

3 lb. boned and rolled beef brisket
2 tablespoons all-purpose flour
10 juniper berries, crushed
1 teaspoon chopped rosemary
1 teaspoon chopped thyme
1 teaspoon grated nutmeg
salt and pepper
2 teaspoons cider vinegar
1 tablespoon brown sugar
2¼ lb. pearl onions
1 lb. button mushrooms
1 cup red wine

Make sure meat is trimmed of excess fat and neatly tied, then place it in the soaked clay pot. Mix together flour, juniper berries, rosemary, thyme, nutmeg, and plenty of seasoning. Add cider vinegar and brown sugar. Rub this seasoning mixture all over meat. Pour red wine into the bottom of the pot and add 1 cup water. Add onions. Cover the pot and place in a cold oven. Set the oven at 450°F. Cook 2 hours.

Baste meat and add mushrooms. Cook, covered, an additional 1 hour, basting 2 or 3 times, until meat is succulent and tender. Uncover the pot and cook an additional 15 minutes to brown meat on top. Serve with boiled or mashed potatoes, rice, or pasta.

Makes 6 servings.

BEEF CHUKA-CHUKA

1 lb. braising steak, finely diced
1 green chili, seeded and chopped
2 cloves garlic, crushed
¼ teaspoon ground allspice
½ teaspoon ground ginger
¼ cup raisins
2 large onions, finely chopped
juice ½ lemon
2 tablespoons mango chutney, chopped
salt and pepper
4 or 5 medium sweet potatoes, diced
1 firm mango, peeled and diced
1 tablespoon chopped mint
1 head iceberg lettuce or romaine

Place beef in a bowl. Add chili, garlic, allspice, ginger, raisins, onions, lemon juice, and mango chutney. Sprinkle in seasoning, mix thoroughly, and let marinate for at least 1 hour. The mixture may be chilled overnight. Turn it into the soaked clay pot and add 1 cup water. Cover the pot and place in a cold oven. Set the oven at 425°F. Cook 30 minutes.

Stir in sweet potato and cook, covered, an additional 30 minutes. Finally, add mango and cook, covered, an additional 30 minutes until meat is really succulent. The mixture should be juicy, neither watery nor too dry, so add a little extra hot water if necessary. Mix in mint lightly and serve with lettuce leaves to wrap.

Makes 4 to 6 servings.

243

BEEF DOPIAZA

2¼ lb. lean stewing beef, diced
2 tablespoons ground coriander
1 teaspoon ground cumin
½ teaspoon chili powder (optional)
salt and pepper
¼ cup oil
4 medium onions, thinly sliced
1 cup plain yogurt
4 cloves garlic
¼ cup grated ginger
1 cinnamon stick
4 cloves
6 cardamom pods
2 tablespoons chopped cilantro
lemon wedges, to serve

Place beef in a bowl. Add coriander, cumin, chili (if using), and plenty of seasoning. Toss beef to coat in spices and set aside. Heat half the oil in a skillet. Add two thirds of the onions and fry until golden brown. Meanwhile, purée remaining oil and onions with yogurt, garlic, and ginger. Pour this paste over meat, add cinnamon, cloves, and cardamom pods, and mix well.

Reserve some of the browned onion for garnish. Layer the rest of the onions and the meat mixture in the soaked clay pot. Cover the pot and place in a cold oven. Set the oven at 400°F. Cook 2½ hours, until meat is tender. Taste for seasoning, then sprinkle with reserved onions and cook, uncovered, 10 minutes. Serve garnished with chopped cilantro and with lemon wedges for their juice.

Makes 4 to 6 servings.

SHEPHERD'S PIE

1 tablespoon oil
1 large onion, chopped
1 lb. (2 cups) ground beef
1 carrot, diced
4 oz. mushrooms, sliced
1 teaspoon dried, mixed herbs
salt and pepper
2 tablespoons all-purpose flour
1½ cups beef stock
4 or 5 medium potatoes, boiled and mashed
1 tablespoon butter
parsley sprigs, to garnish (optional)

Heat oil in a large skillet. Add onion and cook 5 minutes, then stir in ground beef and cook until lightly browned. Add carrot, mushrooms, herbs, and seasoning. Stir in flour, then pour in stock, stirring. Turn meat mixture into the soaked clay pot.

Cover meat mixture with mashed potatoes and mark the top with a fork. Dot with butter. Cover the pot and place in a cold oven. Set the oven at 450°F. Cook 30 minutes. Uncover the pot and cook an additional 15 minutes or until top of pie is golden. Serve piping hot, garnished with parsley.

Makes 4 servings.

TORTILLA TOPPER

2 tablespoons oil
2 onions, halved and sliced
1 green bell pepper, seeded and chopped
1 clove garlic, crushed
2 stalks celery, sliced
1 lb. (2 cups) ground beef
½ to 1 teaspoon chili powder
1 tablespoon ground cumin
2 × 14½ oz. cans chopped tomatoes
2 × 15 oz. cans red kidney beans
4 oz. mushrooms, sliced
salt and pepper
1 large package tortilla chips
2 tomatoes, peeled (see page 174) and diced
10 green olives, pitted and sliced
4 oz. Monterey Jack cheese, diced

Heat oil in a skillet. Cook half the sliced onion with bell pepper, garlic, and celery 10 minutes. Stir in ground beef, chili powder, and cumin and cook 5 minutes, stirring. Turn mixture into the soaked clay pot. Add tomatoes, kidney beans, and mushrooms with plenty of seasoning. Mix well. Cover the pot and place in a cold oven. Set the oven at 425°F. Cook 50 minutes.

Stir meat mixture and taste it for seasoning. Sprinkle with reserved onion slices, tortilla chips, tomatoes, olives, and cheese. Cook, uncovered, an additional 10 minutes or until topping is bubbling and golden. Serve at once with warm crusty bread.

Makes 4 to 6 servings.

ONE-POT PASTA

1 tablespoon oil
1 onion, chopped
1 clove garlic, crushed
1 red bell pepper, seeded and diced
1 green bell pepper, seeded and diced
2 carrots, diced
2 stalks celery, diced
8 slices bacon, diced
8 oz. (1 cup) ground beef
2½ cups beef stock
1 bay leaf
1 teaspoon dried oregano
salt and pepper
2 × 14½ oz. cans chopped tomatoes
12 oz. pasta bows
finely grated Parmesan cheese, to serve

Heat oil in a skillet. Add onion, garlic, bell peppers, carrots, and celery. Cook 5 minutes, then stir in bacon and ground beef and cook an additional 5 minutes. Turn mixture into the soaked clay pot. Stir in stock, bay leaf, oregano, seasoning, and tomatoes. Cover the pot and place in a cold oven. Set the oven at 475°F. Cook 50 minutes.

Reduce the oven temperature to 400°F. Stir meat mixture well, then stir in pasta. Cook, covered, an additional 30 minutes or until pasta is tender. The mixture should be juicy, neither too wet nor too dry. Taste for seasoning before serving with Parmesan.

Makes 4 to 6 servings.

BROCCOLI CREAM

2 cups young broccoli florets
3 tablespoons snipped chives
1 cup shredded cheese
3 eggs
salt and pepper
1½ cups light cream
¼ cup fresh bread crumbs
2 tablespoons butter, melted
chives, to garnish (optional)

Blanch broccoli in boiling water 2 minutes, then drain well. Place in the soaked clay pot. Sprinkle with chives and two thirds of the cheese. Beat eggs with plenty of seasoning. Add cream, then pour mixture over broccoli. Cover the pot and place in a cold oven. Set the oven at 425°F. Cook 30 minutes or until custard is set.

Mix remaining cheese with bread crumbs. Sprinkle this over top of broccoli mixture, then trickle butter over. Cook, uncovered, an additional 10 to 15 minutes or until crisp and golden brown. Serve at once, garnished with chives.

Makes 4 servings.

RICH VEGETABLE RAGOUT

2 tablespoons butter
4 leeks, sliced
2 stalks celery, sliced
2 large potatoes, diced
2 carrots, halved and sliced
2 parsnips, halved and sliced
½ cauliflower, broken into florets
15 oz. can chickpeas, drained
2 tablespoons tomato paste
1 cup dry cider
1 tablespoon sugar
salt and pepper
1 bay leaf
1 cup shredded cheese
¼ cup fresh bread crumbs
2 tablespoons sesame seeds

Melt butter in a large saucepan. Add leeks and celery and cook 5 minutes until leeks are softened and reduced in volume. Turn leek mixture into the soaked clay pot. Add potatoes, carrots, parsnips, cauliflower florets, and chickpeas and mix together well. In a bowl or pitcher, stir together tomato paste, cider, and sugar, add a generous sprinkling of seasoning, and pour mixture over vegetables. Tuck bay leaf into ingredients.

Cover the pot and place in a cold oven. Set the oven at 425°F. Cook 1 hour. Stir well and taste for seasoning. Mix together shredded cheese, bread crumbs, and sesame seeds. Sprinkle this topping over ragout and cook, uncovered, an additional 15 minutes or until topping is golden and vegetables are tender.

Makes 4 to 6 servings.

BAKED BUTTERNUT SQUASH

2 small butternut squash
½ stick butter, melted
1 tablespoon lemon juice
salt and pepper
¼ cup walnut oil
¼ cup dry sherry
¼ cup chopped parsley
2 tablespoons snipped chives
2 tablespoons chopped walnuts
2 tablespoons fresh bread crumbs
2 tablespoons finely grated Parmesan cheese
parsley sprigs, to garnish

STUFFED SQUASH

2 tablespoons oil
1 large onion, chopped
½ teaspoon dried oregano
salt and pepper
⅓ cup rice
½ cup chicken or vegetable stock
1 small marrow squash, peeled
14½ oz. can chopped tomatoes
2 tablespoons currants
¼ cup pine nuts
1 clove garlic, crushed
¼ cup finely grated Parmesan cheese
¼ cup chopped parsley

Cut squash in half lengthwise. Scoop any small amount of fiber from central hole, then place squash halves in the soaked clay pot. Trickle butter and lemon juice over cut surface of each half, then season lightly. Cover the pot and place in a cold oven. Set the oven at 425°F. Cook 45 minutes.

Heat oil in a small saucepan, add onion, and cook 2 minutes. Stir in oregano, seasoning, rice, and stock. Bring just to boil, reduce heat, and cover the pan. Simmer 20 minutes. Meanwhile, halve squash and discard seeds. Place squash halves side by side in the soaked clay pot.

Mix walnut oil and sherry with parsley and chives. Spoon this over squash halves. Sprinkle with walnuts, bread crumbs, and Parmesan and cook, uncovered, an additional 15 minutes or until topping is crisp and golden and squash is tender. Serve garnished with parsley.

Makes 4 servings.

Mix tomatoes, currants, pine nuts, garlic, Parmesan cheese, and most of the parsley with the rice mixture, then spoon this into hollows in squash halves. Cover the pot and place in a cold oven. Set the oven at 450°F. Cook 50 to 60 minutes or until squash is tender. Sprinkle with remaining parsley to serve.

Makes 4 to 6 servings.

STUFFED VINE LEAVES

8 oz. package vine leaves in brine, drained
⅔ cup long-grain rice
1 bay leaf
1 lemon
¼ cup olive oil
1 onion, chopped
2 cloves garlic, crushed
2 tablespoons currants
2 tablespoons pine nuts
2 teaspoons oregano
salt and pepper
1½ cups dry white wine

Blanch vine leaves in boiling water 3 minutes, drain and rinse under cold water, then let drain. Place rice in a saucepan with bay leaf. Pare lemon peel and add it to rice with plenty of cold water. Bring to boil and cook 10 minutes, then drain. Remove bay leaf and lemon peel from rice. Discard lemon peel and reserve bay leaf. Cut lemon into wedges and set aside. Heat half the oil in a skillet. Add onion, garlic, currants, and pine nuts, and cook 5 minutes. Stir in plenty of seasoning and rice.

Place a heaping teaspoonful of rice in the center of each vine leaf. Fold sides over, then roll up and place each in the soaked clay pot. Pour in wine and drizzle with oil. Add reserved bay leaf and lemon wedges. Cover the pot and place in a cold oven. Set the oven at 425°F. Cook 1 hour or until leaves are tender and most of the liquid is absorbed. Serve hot or cold.

Makes about 35.

BUCKWHEAT PILAF

2 tablespoons butter
1 onion, chopped
1 clove garlic, crushed
1 cup dried apricots, roughly chopped
2 tablespoons golden raisins
1¼ cups roasted buckwheat
2½ cups chicken stock
salt and pepper
8 oz. smoked pork, diced
⅔ cup cooked chicken, diced
⅔ cup lean cooked ham, diced
2 tablespoons chopped parsley
¼ to ⅓ cup plain yogurt (optional)
parsley sprigs, to garnish (optional)

Melt butter in a small saucepan. Add onion and garlic, cook 2 minutes, then stir in apricots and golden raisins. Cook an additional 2 minutes. Place buckwheat in soaked clay pot, add onion mixture, and pour in stock. Add seasoning and stir well.

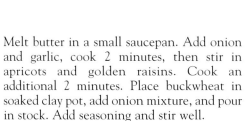

Cover the pot and place in a cold oven. Set the oven at 425°F. Cook 20 minutes. Sprinkle with pork, chicken, and ham and cook, covered, an additional 10 minutes. Let stand, without removing the lid, 10 minutes, then fork meat and parsley into buckwheat. Serve topped with yogurt and garnished with parsley.

Makes 4 servings.

BANANAS WITH BRANDY

4 large, firm bananas
juice 1 lemon
¼ cup brown sugar
½ stick butter
¼ cup brandy
¼ cup chopped, mixed, candied fruit (see Note)
whipped cream or ice cream, to serve

Halve bananas lengthwise, place in the soaked clay pot, and sprinkle with lemon juice. Top with sugar and dot with butter. Cover the pot and place in a cold oven. Set the oven at 425°F. Cook 30 to 35 minutes or until sugar has melted and bananas are hot and juicy.

Pour brandy over and ignite. When flames have subsided, transfer bananas to serving plates and top with candied fruit. Add whipped cream or ice cream and serve at once.

Makes 4 servings.

Note: Angelica, cherries, pineapple, candied peel, and ginger are all suitable. Look for cartons of mixed candied fruit with ginger.

STEWED APPLES WITH APRICOTS

2 cooking apples, peeled, cored, and sliced
¼ cup sugar
2 cups apricots, roughly chopped
2 tablespoons slivered almonds
cream or custard, to serve

Layer apples, sugar, and apricots in the soaked clay pot. Cover the pot and place in a cold oven. Set the oven at 425°F. Cook 40 minutes or until apples are soft.

Sprinkle with almonds and cook, uncovered, an additional 5 to 10 minutes to brown nuts. Serve with cream or custard.

Makes 4 servings.

Variations: Without apricots, plain stewed apples may be beaten until smooth to make apple sauce. Apples may be sprinkled with chopped walnuts or crumbled chocolate graham crackers instead of slivered almonds.

RHUBARB & FIG COMPOTE

2¼ lb. tender rhubarb, trimmed
½ cup sugar
3 tablespoons chopped crystallized ginger
15 oz. can green figs in syrup
6 small mint sprigs

FESTIVE WINTER FRUIT

1 lb. mixed dried fruit
1 bottle red wine
2 cardamom pods
1 cinnamon stick
pared peel and juice 1 orange
¼ cup brandy
2 to 4 tablespoons honey

Cover the pot and place in a cold oven. Set the oven at 425°F. Cook 40 minutes or until rhubarb is tender but not mushy. The cooking time will vary—older, thick rhubarb takes longer than tender, young fruit.

Place fruit in a bowl. Pour in wine and, if necessary, add just enough water to cover fruit. Cover and leave overnight.

Gently mix figs and two of the mint sprigs with rhubarb and cook, covered, 5 minutes to heat figs and give the compote a refreshing mint taste. Decorate individual portions with a mint sprig to serve.

Makes 4 servings.

Turn fruit into the soaked clay pot, with all the soaking liquid. Add cardamom pods and cinnamon, then stir in orange juice. Shred half the peel finely and add it to fruit. Cover the pot and place in a cold oven. Set the oven at 375°F. Cook 1 hour or until fruit and peel are tender. Stir in brandy and honey to taste before serving. The compote is also good cold.

Makes 8 servings.

PEACH & BLACKBERRY COBBLER

3½ cups blackberries
⅔ cup superfine sugar, plus extra for sprinkling
5 fresh peaches
1 cinnamon stick
1½ cups self-rising flour
3 tablespoons butter or margarine
½ cup milk
dash lemon juice

Place blackberries and ½ cup sugar in the soaked clay pot. Peel, pit, and slice 4 peaches and add to the pot with cinnamon stick. Mix fruit together. Cover the pot and place in a cold oven. Set the oven at 425°F. Cook 40 minutes or until blackberries are cooked.

Place flour in a bowl and cut in butter or margarine. Mix in remaining sugar and enough milk to make a soft dough. Roll out thickly and cut out 1½ in. round scones. Overlap these on top of fruit. Brush with milk and sprinkle with sugar, then cook, uncovered, an additional 15 to 20 minutes or until scones are cooked. Pit and slice remaining peach, toss with lemon juice, then use to decorate cooked cobbler.

Makes 6 servings.

PINEAPPLE & PEAR CRUNCH

8 firm pears, peeled, cored, and sliced
8 oz. can pineapple chunks in syrup
¾ cup all-purpose flour
½ stick butter
4 oz. coconut cookies
plain yogurt, to serve

Place pears in the soaked clay pot, then add pineapple and syrup from the can. Place flour in a bowl and cut in butter. Place cookies in a plastic bag and crush with a rolling pin. Add to flour and butter mixture.

Sprinkle this mixture over fruit in the pot. Cover the pot and place in a cold oven. Set the oven at 425°F. Cook 30 minutes. Uncover the pot and cook an additional 10 minutes or until golden brown and crisp on top. The pears should be tender. Serve with plain yogurt.

Makes 4 to 6 servings.

RECIPE INDEX